The Walter Lynwood Fleming
Lectures in Southern History
Louisiana State University

A
Southern
Odyssey

A Southern Odyssey

Travelers in the Antebellum North

John Hope Franklin

Louisiana State
University Press
Baton Rouge

ISBN 0-8071-0161-3
Library of Congress Catalog Card Number 74-27190
Copyright © 1976 by Louisiana State University Press
All rights reserved
Manufactured in the United States of America
Designed by Albert Crochet

Winner of the
Jules F. Landry Award
for 1975

To
Paul Herman Buck
Pioneer Historian
of the
North-South Connection

Contents

Preface

Whenever one reads any of the works that the great northern traveler Frederick Law Olmsted wrote about the South, he is tempted to ask, "Who was Olmsted's southern counterpart who wrote about the North?" The answer is a simple one: "There was no southerner who wrote so comprehensively about the North." That deficiency was not altogether unfortunate, however, for the report of one outstanding observer such as Olmsted would have been so singular in its character and influence as to diminish all other comments about the section. Few persons bother—if, indeed, they know—about the reports of the travels in the South of such luminaries as Ralph Waldo Emerson, William C. Bryant, Bronson Alcott, Walt Whitman, and Thomas Wentworth Higginson. They need not have gone at all for all the influence they wielded in shaping opinions about the South in their section; and in any case their comments reflected their quite limited experiences in only a few places for short periods of time. Olmsted's reports were simply too unique and, indeed, too overpowering for his day and ours to share the spotlight with someone else.

Even if there had been one outstanding southern observer of the North, his report could hardly have been representative of southern views. This would especially have been the case if his travels had been motivated—as were Olmsted's—by the kind of curiosity that sought to satisfy the interests of an inquisitive reading public. Since there were relatively few northerners traveling in the South and writing about it, one did not need to search for a representative or typical view. What Olmsted said, in the newspapers and in the three books that he wrote about the South, had the ring of authority and was widely accepted as such. But it was not possible for any one traveler to represent the views of southerners, for there were so very many southerners traveling in the North and they went there for such a variety of reasons. Their reactions and experiences were almost as numerous as they were themselves. In addition to those who traveled north out of curiosity, there were those who went for recreation, for reasons of health, to secure an education, to engage in a variety of business transactions, to make purchases for store and home, to attend religious and political conventions, to instruct northerners about the superior qualities of the southern way of life, and to warn them of the consequences of unbridled abolitionist attacks. Many more southerners went north than northerners came south. Many had quite definite reactions to their experiences; and some of them recorded their reactions for the benefit of posterity as well as their contemporaries.

The records of those southerners who traveled in the North— letters, diaries, a few published books, articles in newspapers, essays in magazines, and speeches in Congress and the legislatures—provide a remarkable collection of the experiences and reactions of persons making excursions into that strange and distant land. Some were understandably confused and unable to sort out what they saw. Others were rather inarticulate and experienced difficulty conveying their impressions to their readers. Still others had no intellectual or social equipment with which to analyze and understand what they saw. Happily, some could very well compete with Olmsted in keenness of perception and clarity of expression. In their respective ways, all of them made some contribution to the South's view of the North in the years before the Civil War.

Because of the large numbers of well-to-do and influential

southerners who made the annual trek northward, some argued that they knew infinitely more about the North than northerners knew about the South. Where the impression was favorable, regarding, for example, the admirable diversity of the North's economy, they considered it a valuable learning experience. When it was unfavorable, as in the case of abolitionist activity, they regarded it as a portent of worse things to come. Regardless of what they saw and did in the North, the experience provided southerners with a sense of authority regarding the northern way of life. And most of them seemed persuaded that the North was an alien land and culture. In a time of crisis, such as the decade of the 1850s, those who had traveled North would succeed in persuading those who had not been there that northern intentions toward the South were sinister and that when one dealt with the North at any level, he did so at his own peril. This was the message that many travelers conveyed to their fellow southerners during that final prewar decade.

But southerners never spoke in one voice about the North. Their attitudes ranged from the fawning pronorthernism of S. H. Dickson of South Carolina to the seething hatred of everything northern on the part of C. K. Marshall of Mississippi. If they came to know the North better, through frequent visits, it did not follow, as one southerner hoped, that they would love it more. If the majority was suspicious of the North, many of them could not, under any circumstances, give up the idea of making just one more trip. If they were fully aware of the South's subordinate position in economic matters, they were unwilling to accept any responsibility for this, merely because they had spent lavishly while in the North. One responsibility was theirs, however, even if they did not accept it. They were responsible, to a considerable degree, for shaping the attitude of the South toward the North before the Union fell apart. It cannot be argued, of course, that southern travelers in the North were solely responsible for spawning the South's half of the "blundering generation" that plunged the nation into war. It can be argued, as the evidence in this book suggests, that the South's seasoned travelers must share some of the blame for creating a climate in which reasonable discourse was no longer possible and in which suspicion and even paranoia replaced confidence and trust.

I am greatly indebted to many persons and institutions for their generous assistance in the preparation of this work. The staffs of many libraries and manuscript collections were most helpful, and I am very grateful to them. Among them were the Library of Congress, the Duke University Library, the University of North Carolina Library, the North Carolina Department of Archives and History, the South Carolina State Archives, the Howard University Library, the Tulane University Library, the Brooklyn College Library, the Library of the Illinois State Historical Society, the New York Public Library, and the Regenstein Library of the University of Chicago. Ottis C. Skipper of Huntsville, Alabama, and David O. Whitten of Auburn University shared with me the results of their research on the antebellum South, as did Winfred Thompson and Joe Timmons of the University of Chicago. My students and research assistants, among them Richard P. Fuke of Wilfrid Laurier University, Loren Schweninger of the University of North Carolina at Greensboro, Paul Finkelman and Joseph Castrovinci of the University of Chicago, were of inestimable help in performing many tasks and in raising important conceptual questions. My wife read the manuscript in its entirety and offered valuable observations and criticisms. I have also received invaluable assistance from critical readings by Ann F. Scott of Duke University and Arthur Mann and Barry Karl of the University of Chicago. My secretaries, Nancy B. Helmy of Palo Alto, California, and Margaret Fitzsimmons of the University of Chicago, provided critical judgment as well as efficient typing. I am deeply grateful to all of them.
In the course of my research and writing I held fellowships from

the John Simon Guggenheim Memorial Foundation and the Center for Advanced Study in the Behavioral Sciences. The University of Chicago has been generous in its leaves of absence and supportive of my work in numerous other ways. It is difficult to express my obligation and gratitude to these several institutions.

In 1972 I delivered the Walter Lynwood Fleming Lectures at Louisiana State University; the lectures were an earlier version of three chapters in this book. The audiences were unfailingly generous in their helpful criticisms and suggestions. Louisiana State University Press graciously permitted me to expand the lectures into this present form. While my thanks go to all these people, I must reserve for myself the responsibility for the contents of this work.

John Hope Franklin

February 1, 1975

A
Southern
Odyssey

1

The
Grand
Tour

Touring the North in the antebellum years became a favorite pastime for many southerners of means. They went as early and as often as time and resources would permit. Whatever their objectives or purposes, the enterprise took on some of the attributes of a "Grand Tour." It was a grand tour in the sense that it involved the expenditure of much time, energy, and money. It was a grand tour in the sense that it provided experiences that were novel, exhilarating, and even educational. It was a grand tour in the sense that it opened new vistas, provided new insights, and created new relationships—not only with northerners but among southerners themselves—that rounded out the "education" of southerners who could make the journey. Indeed, it appeared at times as if they were compelled to make the journey.[1]

Early in the nineteenth century the South was settling into the type of existence that was to characterize it for the next two generations. It was not that the South would not change during that time; for indeed, and perhaps without fully understanding what was occurring, it would experience dramatic economic and social changes in the antebellum years. Rather, it was that the way southerners lived would become so fixed, so much a part of the landscape itself, that even the more dramatic and significant de-

---

1. Some southerners did make *the* grand tour of Europe, but a much larger number went to the North. In the preparations for the trip and in the reactions, during and after the experience, it seemed a satisfactory substitute for the longer journey.

1

velopments would be absorbed without the slightest indication that profound changes had taken place. Central to all these developments, though not altogether responsible for them, was the planter who could take much credit for giving the impression that his region was the very essence of stability.

Southerners were slow to make distinctions among various parts of the South or their several ways of life. But there were clear distinctions if one cared to look for them. Virginia and the Carolinas in, say, the 1820s were the epitome of stability and quiet repose, when compared with the hustle and bustle of the cotton and sugar plantations of the lower Mississippi Valley during those same years. It was long after the fact, in the midst of great economic change, that southerners and their northern critics saw the full impact of the social stratification that had become so much a part of the southern way of life. And, together with a very special economic system, it was this social stratification—the sharp differentiation among classes and between the races—that would, in the long run, give the appearance of a South that was so internally similar and yet so different from the rest of the country.

Whatever the changes and however dramatic and far-reaching they might appear to later generations, or even to contemporaries, life in the South was relatively simple and unadorned—in part because of a stubborn resistance to change that was an article of faith by which southerners lived. It was not that their social order was perfect, or nearly so, as many would claim. Rather they feared that the delicate mechanism linking together their economic, social, and political structure would tolerate no revamping, lest the whole apparatus collapse. The southerner's simplistic and unsophisticated approach to life itself was singularly resistant to the forces for change which were transforming the Northeast.

The South, essentially a rural section, had not yet experienced the complexities of urbanization that Jefferson and his contemporaries had long since decried. If it permitted the favored ones to earn a good living, it was notably deficient in the man-made facilities of a more sophisticated life. It was a world, as Wilbur Cash pointed out rather extravagantly, "in which not a single factor operated to break up the old pattern of outdoor activity laid down on the frontier, in which, on the contrary, everything conspired to perpetuate it."[2] Its interior had, "on the whole, a very wild appearance," and even an older eastern city, such as Norfolk, had "no lyceum or public libraries, no public gardens, no galleries of art" and "no public resorts of healthful and refining amusement."[3] Indeed, its towns and cities were few and generally undeveloped. Not even Baltimore or Charleston or New Orleans offered many opportunities for exciting diversions; and unhappily for those who sought something in the way of splendor or charm, or even the usual urban amenities, the cities were merely, or largely, service centers for the vast agricultural interior.

Meanwhile, the North was becoming more diversified in its economic pursuits and in the makeup of its population; and the contrast with the South was becoming more marked with every passing year. Industry was developing, and commerce was flourishing. Immigrants from Europe were coming in at an increasing pace; and even if some older Americans had misgivings about "opening the floodgates," the newcomers did add flavor and color—and a valuable work force—to the population. Older cities—New York, Philadelphia, and Boston—were far more developed than any urban centers of the South. New cities—industrial, commercial, and transportation centers such as Rochester, Detroit, and Chicago—were springing up all around. New or old, for better or worse, northern urban centers seemed to be the wave of the future, the promised land, the meccas where innovation and excitement and diversion and entertainment were as

2. Wilbur J. Cash, *The Mind of the South* (New York: Alfred A. Knopf, 1941), 96.
3. For a description of the towns and countryside of the antebellum South, see James Stirling, *Letters from the Slave States* (London: John W. Parker and Son, 1857), 177–78; James S. Buckingham, *The Slave States of America* (2 vols.; London: Fisher and Company, 1842), I, 188, 251; and John Hope Franklin, *The Militant South, 1800–1861* (Rev. ed.; Cambridge: Harvard University Press, 1970), 20–21.

common as the cotton and sugar crops, and even the wilder-
nesses, were in the South.

This was the North that became especially attractive to southerners in the antebellum years. In time the attraction would be
transformed into utter dependence. Southerners who could afford
to do so would look to the North for much of their education and
recreation, as well as for cultural, physical, and spiritual refreshment. In time they would depend on the North for numerous
kinds of finished goods—furniture, household articles, clothing,
food and drink. Few southerners, however, were willing to go as
far as North Carolina's Hinton Rowan Helper did in his 1857
description of the extent of dependence:

> In one way or another we are more or less subservient to the North
> every day of our lives. In infancy we are swaddled in Northern mus-
> lin; in childhood we are humored with Northern gewgaws; in youth
> we are instructed out of Northern books; at the age of maturity we
> sow our "wild oats" on Northern soil; in middle life we exhaust our
> wealth, energies and talents in the dishonorable vocation of entail-
> ing our dependence on our children and our children's children . . . in
> giving aid and succor to every department of Northern power; in the
> decline of life we remedy our eyesight with Northern spectacles, and
> support our infirmities with Northern physic; and, finally, when we
> die, our inanimate bodies, shrouded in Northern cambric, are stretched
> upon the bier, borne to the grave in a Northern carriage, entombed
> with a Northern spade, and memorized [sic] with a Northern slab![4]

There was, indeed, a variety of specific dependencies on the
North; and if southerners did not admit it in so many words, their
actions clearly indicated a recognition of their inferior position.
They sent an ever-increasing number of young men to northern
colleges and universities for an education.[5] In order to justify
slavery, many of the better southern physicians were engaged in
"research" on the ethnology, craniology, physiology, and "dis-

4. Hinton Rowan Helper, *The Impending Crisis of the South: How to Meet It*
(New York: A. B. Burdick, 1859), 22–23.
5. See below, Chapter II.

eases peculiar to the Negro."[6] Consequently, they spent insufficient time on the agues, fevers, and other maladies that
plagued the southern population, black and white. Thus many
southern men and women went North in the hope, sometimes
mistaken, that they could find there the cure for all their ills.

Southerners were in search of social diversions, moreover, to
relieve the monotony of the countryside and to compensate for the
meager attractions offered by even their best urban centers, which
Cash has characterized as "overgrown villages." The musical
tradition of Charleston's St. Cecilia Society and the literary tradition of the writers of New Orleans were clearly insufficient to
satisfy the tastes of those truly interested in the cultivation of the
mind. And the *nouveaux riches* and the "cotton snobs," as Daniel
R. Hundley called them, wanted much more excitement than
they could find in a local horse race or militia muster.[7] Such
people gravitated to the North for the exciting and satisfying
activities it seemed to have in great abundance. In the forty years
before the Civil War southerners developed the habit—scarcely
short of an addiction—of going north. They seemed unable to
resist the temptation, even when their better judgment, financial
resources, and wise leaders counseled against it.

Among the wide variety of wanderers through the North during
the antebellum years, none attracted more interest and attention,
none reacted more definitely to what they saw and experienced,
and none articulated more graphically their impressions than the
well-to-do southern planters and men of affairs and their families.
They had the means, either in money or credit, to make the trip
and take in whatever the North had to offer. They had the leisure

6. See, for example, S. C. Cartwright, "Diseases and Peculiarities of the Negro,"
The Industrial Resources, etc., of the Southern and Western States (New Orleans:
Offices of the *Review*, 1853), II.
7. For a discussion of the activities of "cotton snobs" in the North, see Daniel R.
Hundley, *Social Relations in Our Southern States* (New York: Henry B. Price, 1860),
196, 223–24.

that made it possible for them to remain for extended periods of time. Many merchants who went North on business took their families along to spend the summer at some nearby resort while the merchants spent their time "among the jobbers selecting what they wanted from the stocks of imported and domestic goods."[8] Those who lived along the southern coast or near the river banks believed that during the summer some sort of "miasma or disease breeding fog was given off by the marshes after sundown which spelled fever and possible death for white men." Some called the summer months "the sickly season" and only the foolhardy risked the exposure.[9] Some moved far enough back, to higher ground, to escape the miasma's deadly effects, which were actually caused by the malaria-bearing mosquitoes. Others regularly went north to escape it.

Well-to-do southerners were understandably bored by the drabness of life that seemed to them a depressing and painful contrast to their own resources and tastes. In reply to a query, one southerner on the lower Mississippi told Frederick Law Olmsted why many southerners went north rather than to some Kentucky resort. "They go North. To New York, and Newport, and Saratoga, and Cape May, and Seneca Lake. Somewhere that they can display themselves more than they do here. Kentucky is no place for that."[10] If they clearly saw the differences between themselves and other southerners, they were also the ones most likely to sense the contrasts between the North and South during a period of growing tensions. If they longed for excitement—at the water-

8. Robert Greenhalgh Albion, *The Rise of the New York Port, 1815–1860* (New York: Charles Scribner's Sons, 1939), 118.

9. Albert V. House (ed.), *Plantation Management and Capitalism in Antebellum Georgia: The Journal of Hugh Fraser Grant, Rice Grower* (New York: Columbia University Press, 1954), 11. J. Harold Easterby, *The South Carolina Rice Plantation as Revealed in the Papers of Robert F. W. Allston* (Chicago: University of Chicago Press, 1945), 9. For a discussion of contemporary views of the "sickly season," see Lawrence F. Brewster, *Summer Migrations and Resorts of South Carolina Low-Country Planters* (Durham: Duke University Press, 1947), 3—9.

10. Frederick Law Olmsted, *The Cotton Kingdom*, edited with an introduction by Arthur M. Schlesinger (New York: Alfred A. Knopf, 1953), 416.

ing places, at the theater and concert hall, in the museums, in viewing spectacular sights, natural or man-made, in the bizarre or otherwise—it could be found in the North. And the scheming, shrewd, accommodating Yankee made the pleasure-seeking southern traveler feel that the North had everything, especially if the southerner had the money to pay for it.

Many persons in the North and South—factors, commission merchants, and bankers—did everything possible to encourage and facilitate the journey and to make all arrangements for accommodation. Travel books, magazines, and newspapers gave ample information to assist prospective travelers in making their plans. In 1830 Gideon M. Davison issued the fourth edition of his detailed travel book to encourage and assist southern travelers who desired to go north. It was called *The Fashionable Tour: A Guide to Travellers Visiting the Middle and Northern States and the Provinces of Canada*. "The oppressive heat of summer in the southern sections of the United States," Davison said, "and the consequent exposure to illness, have long induced the wealthy part of the population to seek, at that season of the year, the more salubrious climate of the North." He then pointed out that the "gigantic internal improvements" in the northeastern and middle states had greatly facilitated travel and made it possible for southerners to combine the "sublime mountain scenery in New-York and New-England, with the various attractions presented in the large commercial cities." Thus, he commended to the prospective southern traveler his pocket manual and guide of more than four hundred pages, directing the traveler in his course, "and pointing out, as he passes, objects which most deserve his notice and regard."[11]

While Davison concentrated on those traveling by sea from Savannah to Philadelphia and points east, others gave attention to

11. Gideon M. Davison, *The Fashionable Tour: A Guide to Travellers Visiting the Middle and Northern States and the Provinces of Canada* (Saratoga Springs: G. M. Davison, 1830), 17.

prospective travelers from the lower Mississippi and Gulf regions.[12] Meanwhile, Dr. Daniel Drake gave attention to travelers who would take the inland route to the northern lakes and then east. In a lecture to the students of the Medical Institute of Louisville where he was a professor, Drake promoted the northern lakes as a most attractive destination for invalids as well as others from the South. Travelers for health or recreation, he argued, should seek "places and scenes that will be in contrast with their homes. The invalid cannot recover, nor the fashionable rusticate, in a crowd." He hoped that southerners would avoid the large crowds of the North. Consequently, he recommended the New York springs, Long Branch, Newport, Nahant, and "other watering and bathing places." Such visits should be topped off, he said, with a trip to the falls of Niagara and a voyage on the St. Lawrence to Montreal and Quebec.[13]

While there were no Cook's Tours or American Express deals, those in a position to know and to lend assistance provided abundant information on where to go, how to get there, where to stay, what to see, and what to do. Magazines such as *De Bow's Review* and the *Southern Literary Messenger* frequently published articles designed to instruct the prospective southern traveler or to share with him the experiences of those recently returned.[14] It

12. See, for example, Theodore Dwight, Jr., *The Northern Traveller, Containing the Routes to the Springs, Niagara, Quebec, and the Coal Mines* (New York: J. P. Haven [1841]), 241–42, where he discussed at length the several alternative routes from New Orleans. Some of the better accounts of visits could well have served as guide books. J. C. Myers, *Sketches on a Tour through the Northern and Eastern States, the Canadas and Nova Scotia* (Harrisonburg, Va.: J. H. Wartmann and Brothers, 1849) is such an account, written by a resident of New Hope, Virginia.

13. Daniel Drake, *The Northern Lakes: A Summer Residence for Invalids of the South* (Louisville, Ky.: J. Maxwell, Jr., 1842), 5–7. See, also, the favorable comments regarding Drake's work in the *North American Review*, LVII (July, 1843), 108–27. Drake had spent two months on the northern lakes in the summer of 1842.

14. See, for example, *De Bow's Review*, VI (September, 1848), 45, and VII (July, 1849), 46, and "Traits of a Summer Tourist," *Southern Literary Messenger*, II (October, 1836), 696–99. In 1848 James H. Harrison of Columbus, Mississippi, used his travels to teach his young daughter a geography lesson. In a letter to her he gave her his route of travel so that she could follow it on her map: "Columbus to Tuscaloosa, Elyton, Ashville, Rome on Georgia Railroad—thence to Augusta and Charleston, thence to

was entirely possible, moreover, to travel on credit. Some planters had credit in New York and were able to draw against it. Others could secure advances, if necessary, at local banks or from their factors and pay for the trip at the same time that they discharged other obligations.[15]

By every possible means southerners went to all parts of the North at all times, though the summer months were the favorite season for travel. In 1819 the new steamer *Savannah* made the voyage from New York to Savannah in eight days and fifteen hours. From that time on, the coastal trade between New York and southern ports on the Atlantic and the Gulf expanded steadily. By 1830 ships regularly departed from New Orleans, Mobile, Savannah, Charleston, and Norfolk with loads of passengers as well as cargo bound for the northern meccas. Between 1834 and 1838 five steam packets were placed, "two at a time on the New York-Charleston run." They sailed each Saturday night from each port and provided regular service for many years.[16]

Meanwhile, boats began to ascend the Mississippi and Ohio rivers, taking on passengers at various points between New Orleans and Cincinnati. William Johnson, a well-to-do free Negro

---

Wilmington, Weldon, Petersburg, Richmond, Fredericksburg and Washington City, thence to Newport, Boston, Cambridge and Lowell—back to Boston and from thence to Worcester, Springfield, Hartford and New Haven and to New York again—thence up the Hudson to Albany and from that to Saratoga Springs—thence to Lake George, Lake Champlain, and to St. Johns, Canada and Montreal—thence to Quebec and back—thence to Kingston, Oswego, Rochester, Lewiston and Niagara Falls. . . . From this place I intend to go to Buffalo, Cleveland, Sandusky, Cincinnati, Louisville, Lexington and to Nashville, Tenn., at which last place you and your ma must write to me." James T. Harrison to Regina Harrison, August 11, 1848, in James T. Harrison Papers, University of North Carolina, Chapel Hill. See also the description of a northern trip in R. D. W. Connor (ed.), *Autobiography of Asa Briggs, Including a Journal of a Trip from North Carolina to New York in 1832* (Raleigh: Edwards and Broughton, 1915), 41–50.

15. The plantation journal of Hugh Fraser Grant provides a record of how he financed northern trips for himself and family. On August 22, 1857, he drew on his factor, R. Habersham and Son, a draft of $850 for H. F. Grant, Jr., and his sisters who were going to New York. On January 1, 1860, Grant, then in New York, noted that he had received $200 in cash from the Habersham firm. House (ed.), *Plantation Management*, 224, 228.

16. Albion, *Rise of the New York Port*, 314–16.

barber in Natchez, frequently noted in his diary the departure and arrival of southerners traveling to and from the North. On October 9, 1850, he observed, "Judge S S Boyd arrived This Evening from the North, Came Down the River."[17] Some southerners, following the advice of Dr. Drake or someone else, made their way to the Great Lakes and approached the East via the Erie Canal. The route they took depended on their own location, their destination, and the mode of travel they preferred. If they went via Chicago, "boats of the first class, as to size and all other respects, offer, every other day, the means of continuing the route, through a series of lakes . . . by a voyage, ordinarily of five days, to Buffalo."[18]

Guide books provided detailed information about modes of travel, distances from place to place, and the approximate time it would take to get from one place to another. But they gave little or no information on the cost of travel. Perhaps it was assumed that this was a very minor consideration for southerners planning to visit the North. From time to time, however, *De Bow's Review* would provide information on fares. In 1848 one could travel by sea from New Orleans to Philadelphia for $35.00; and if one continued the journey to New York or Boston, the fare would be $40.00. In the same year the fare from New Orleans to Cincinnati and Pittsburgh, by rivers, was $15.00 and $23.00, respectively.[19] Travelers from the Southwest did not seem to regard the cost of

17. William R. Hogan and Edwin A. Davis (eds.), *William Johnson's Natchez: The Ante-Bellum Diary of a Free Negro* (Baton Rouge: Louisiana State University Press, 1951), 749. Among other pertinent entries are the following: August 17, 1842, "I loaned Mr. Morris to day $12.00 in Specie to pay for Passage Money. He has Just Got Home this Morning from Cincinnati." (p. 399); June 23, 1850, "Greate many of Our Citizens were at The Landing waiting To Get off on The Origon, and The Boat Came up Late in the afternon. Col. W. Robertson and St. Jno. Elliotte, Dr. Mercer and a number of others I don't recollect." (p. 730); June 24, 1845, "Great many Persons are Leaving for the North, and our City is remarkable Dull." (p. 528).

18. *North American Review*, LVII (July, 1843), 116. For an extensive discussion of the various routes to the Northeast from the lower South, see *De Bow's Review*, VII (July, 1849), 45.

19. *De Bow's Review*, VI (July, 1848), 62–63. In 1859 the fare from Natchez to New York by boat and rail was $50. Charles S. Sydnor, *A Gentleman of the Old Natchez Region: Benjamin L. C. Wailes* (Durham: Duke University Press, 1938), 278. Albion states that the cabin fare "including food and sometimes wine, was normally $30 from

travel as too high. A "Citizen of Albemarle" toured the northern lakes in 1837. He went on a "zigzag course" through New York to Chicago, a journey of thirteen days, and the cost of conveyance was "about $70." The return journey, via Pittsburgh, took twelve days and cost $55. "One can scarcely doubt," he remarked, "that the same journey would thirty years ago, have required twice the money and more than thrice the time."[20] In 1858 a young woman from Virginia was pleased to report that her fare from Richmond to New York with "dinner on board the Washington boat, hack hire in Philadelphia, and here" came to only $14.50.[21] The trip by packet from the South Carolina and Georgia ports fluctuated between $15.00 and $20.00. In 1860 the trip from Augusta to New York cost Henry William Ravenel $17.50.[22]

Once in the North these sojourners used as many modes of transportation as were available in order to get from one place to another. They traveled by boat, stage coach, horse-drawn omnibus, railroad, and by foot. There were, of course, the usual inconveniences; and there were some dangers, though perhaps not as great as one Mississippi man imagined. When he arrived in New York in 1853, in the company of three ladies, he congratulated himself to his wife:

> There is scarcely a day that passes without some railroad or steamboat disaster and wholesale murder in this free country.... But I have performed the hardest *labor* for the last month ever I did in

Charleston and $80 or $90 from New Orleans." Robert G. Albion, *Square Riggers on Schedule: The New York Sailing Packets to England, France, and the Cotton Ports* (Princeton, N. J.: Princeton University Press, 1938), 229.

20. "Tour to the Northern Lakes," *Southern Literary Messenger*, III (December, 1837), 742. The traveler had kept a diary "for the amusement of my family and thinking that part of your readers might like to learn something of a tour, which though rarely taken till of late for either business or pleasure, is now becoming frequent and fashionable. I send you my notes for the use of your agreeable miscellany," from a subscriber to Mr. White, *Southern Literary Messenger*, III (November, 1837), 682. The "Tour" was printed in two parts in the November and December issues.

21. Ellen Mordecai to Samuel Mordecai, September 8, 1848, in Jacob Mordecai Papers, Duke University, Durham.

22. Arney Robinson Childs (ed.), *The Private Journal of Henry William Ravenel, 1859–1887* (Columbia: University of South Carolina Press, 1947), 26.

my life. The amount of travel has increased so that it is the next thing to an impossibility to get along with ladies at all, but for *one* gentleman like myself to have to take care not only of himself, but of three ladies and their baggage, is a downright impossibility.[23]

Inconveniences such as poor travel schedules and unsatisfactory living accommodations grated on the tempers of southerners, as they did on those of most travelers. Early in the century, on a journey from Schenectady to Albany, a Georgia physician had many complaints. "Bad roads and bad company in the stage," he moaned and "much crowded, and tired horses." Perhaps the sight-seeing on foot had been too much, for he added, "Taken on the way with acute pain and inflammation on the outer ankle of the left foot. Fever all night and no sleep till nearly day."[24]

Perhaps the weary traveler could have endured almost anything if, at the end of the long day's journey, he could obtain an attractive and comfortable room. He should have experienced no difficulty on that score, for the guide books not only listed the hotels but frequently ranked them. If one had a copy of Davison's *Fashionable Tour*, for example, he could learn that in 1830 New York's really "elegant establishment" was the Adelphi Hotel and that the first-class hostelries in Saratoga were Congress Hall, the Pavilion, and the United States Hotel.[25] Later in the decade he would learn that the New Astor House had eclipsed all other New York hotels and that by the midfifties the St. Nicholas had surpassed the Astor.[26] Sometimes conditions changed even faster than successive editions of the guide books, and reports of travelers were, at times, more up-to-date. Thus, prospective Natchez travelers could learn much from one of the town's young ladies who had stopped at the Astor shortly after it opened in 1836. "It

23. James T. Harrison to his wife, August 15, 1853, in Harrison Papers.
24. Adam Alexander, "Diary of a Trip to the North," June, 1801, in Alexander-Hillhouse Papers, University of North Carolina.
25. Davison, *Fashionable Tour*, 99, 163–65.
26. Europeans frequently commented on hotel accommodations, and southerners could well have been guided by such comments. See, for example, Ivan D. Stien, "Palaces for Travelers: New York City's Hotels in the 1850's as Viewed by British Visitors," *New York History*, LXI (April, 1950), 269–86.

occupies a whole square," she reported, "is elegantly furnished, and the living is delightful. All of us are very much at our ease, notwithstanding we are on Broadway."[27]

While South Carolina's William Bobo referred to the Astor as the "monarch of all hotels," he did not regard it as the only place for a southerner to stop in New York. In his effort to advise his southern friends who were determined to "spend their hard earnings among those who seek to destroy them, as well as their peculiar institutions," Bobo suggested other attractive places of accommodation. He thought Delmonico's was the best hotel in the city on the European plan, while the Clinton, quiet and orderly, with excellent cuisine, was the most successful hotel in the city. The Clinton was a favorite of southerners, "many of whom have been constant guests for more than twenty-five years." This was mainly because of the "excellence of the house," but the beauty and desirability of its location also added to its charm; "as it fronts on the park, in full view of Broadway, but just sufficiently removed from the great thoroughfares to avoid the unpleasant rumble and jar of the omnibuses and other vehicles which renders a sojourn in hotels located on those streets so disagreeable."[28]

In going north, southern travelers did not lose their ability to be discriminating or even critical of their accommodations. At times the cities were so crowded that it was difficult or impossible to secure satisfactory living quarters. When John Oxley of Clarksville, Tennessee, arrived in New York in 1853 during the Crystal Palace Exposition, he could get nothing better than "a miserable little room at the very top of the house, leading out of another room with three beds in it."[29] The fact that southerners

27. See excerpts of a letter from Mrs. James G. Carson to her father in John Q. Anderson, "Dr. James Green Carson, Ante-Bellum Planter of Mississippi and Louisiana," *Journal of Mississippi History*, XVIII (October, 1956), 247.

28. [William M. Bobo], *Glimpses of New York City, by a South Carolinian (Who Had Nothing Else to Do)* (Charleston: J. J. McCarter, 1852), 80–88. He also discussed hotels in Philadelphia and Boston and expressed the view that the Charleston Hotel was as good as any.

29. John S. Oxley to Tom Henry, October 1, 1853, in Gustavus A. Henry Papers, University of North Carolina, Chapel Hill.

came from a region where the temperature soared to uncomfortable heights during the summer did not mean that they would tolerate sweltering hotels and boardinghouses. "Viator," visiting Philadelphia in 1836, refused to be satisfied simply because his hot, uncomfortable room was in what was supposed to be a first-class hotel.

> Here we are, in the city of brotherly love, upon one of the very hottest days of the year, and upon asking for rooms at a new and much vaunted hotel, are ushered into a suite up three flights of stairs, and glowing, almost hissing, in weather to set the very mercury in the thermometer a bubbling. . . . What salamanders must be the people of the M——House! We could not stand it, and so, after one night's parboiling, we turned our backs upon the rectangular city, resolved never to "tarry" there, in summer time again, until she had her Tremont, her Page's, or her Astor's to receive and accommodate us.[30]

Neither dangerous modes of travel, unpleasant company, nor unsatisfactory rooms could discourage southerners who decided to make the journey. Most of them seemed quite willing to endure any of the hardships of travel to reach the northern El Dorado, where they could discard the cares and worries of a humdrum, drudgery-laden existence. They had each other, moreover, and they seemed to take heart and have greater confidence as they faced together the "strangers at the North." The happiest arrangement was when southern neighbors and friends traveled together. The experiences of the journey and the anticipation of what they would do when they reached their destination seemed to bind them together in a very special way. When the *Emperor* sailed from Savannah in 1830 there were thirty-three persons aboard from various parts of Georgia. One of the passengers described them as "generally a very sociable and friendly set" who "contributed much to render the situation of all agreeable and

30. Viator, "Traits of a Summer Tourist," *Southern Literary Messenger*, II (October, 1836), 697. The author was, perhaps, referring to the well-known Mansion House in Philadelphia. Tremont House was in Boston, Page's in Baltimore, and Astor's in New York. One discriminating visitor, Tyrone Power, had nothing but praise for Philadelphia's Mansion House. See Tyrone Power, *Impressions of America During the Years 1833, 1834, and 1835* (2 vols.; London: Richard Bentley, 1836), I, 70–73.

pleasant."[31] From Saratoga Springs a Charlestonian wrote his wife that he was fortunate to find about a dozen South Carolina families stopping at the United States Hotel, where he was registered. And he named them all! "The persons I have mentioned," he happily reported, "I am acquainted with and consequently I have sufficient society to render my time agreeable. . . . The evening I pretty much devote to the ladies. The last mentioned occupation I know you will be particularly pleased with for a man is always safe in the society of ladies."[32]

Southern travelers sought out persons from their area; and when they found them, their delight seemed inexpressible. The pleasure of a Richmond resident's excursion to Niagara was virtually assured when he met a group of southerners also going there. "On the steamer *Lady of the Lake*, there was on board a very agreeable company of Southerners, of whom I made the sixteenth. The party was composed of a bridegroom, a young and blooming bride and two other ladies from the broad savannas of Georgia; one middle aged and chivalric Orleanois, seven fine looking young Louisianians; 'all ardent as a Southern sun could make them'; three gentlemen who were well worthy of 'the Monumental City' [Richmond], and the writer, from Virginia."[33]

The New York Hotel where one Georgia lady was staying in 1853 was "full of strangers from the South and West, and all drink and do as they choose." Even if some of the westerners did not please her, she was obviously delighted to meet a fellow townsman, "Henry Moore of Augusta."[34] The city was crowded with visitors, for that was the year of the opening of the Crystal

31. "The Journal of Simri Ross, 1830," in Hermione Ross Walker Collection, University of North Carolina, Chapel Hill.

32. Christopher Jenkins to his wife, July 13, 1826, in Mrs. Christopher Jenkins Papers, Duke University, Durham. At Saratoga in 1860 Henry W. Ravenel encountered more than a dozen Charlestonians in one day. Childs (ed.), *Private Journal of Henry William Ravenel*, 27.

33. "Two Days at Niagara," *Southern Literary Messenger*, XI (December, 1845), 728. See, also, Barnes F. Lathrop (ed.), "A Southern Girl at Saratoga Springs, 1834," *North Carolina Historical Review*, XV (April, 1938), 159–62.

34. Sarah Gayle Crawford Diary, July 27, 1853, in the Gayle-Crawford Collection, University of North Carolina, Chapel Hill.

Palace Exposition. "Every hotel in the place is crammed," a Tennessean observed, but he had few complaints. At the opera he met many acquaintances, "mostly from New Orleans, and among them two very pretty Creole girls with whom I came up the Mississippi in the Eclipse."[35] A planter from Columbus, Mississippi, who made an extensive tour of the North that year saw friends from home as far north as the White Mountains. But it was in New York, he wrote, that "we have alighted upon the Town of Columbus." He then named thirty persons from Columbus, some with their families; and he happily wrote his wife, "So you see we have acquaintances on hand."[36]

If southerners were indeed clannish, as the records seem to suggest, they were most comfortable when in the company of others from their area. It is not surprising, therefore, to learn that some of them arranged their schedules of travel to make certain that they were with friends or acquaintances. A Charlestonian, for example, postponed his trip from New York to Saratoga for several days in consequence, he lamented, "of not being able to prevail on any of my South Carolina friends to go before that time."[37] Another, from Georgia, was moved to remark that while he found a few acquaintances in New York from his home state, he had encountered few others whom he had known there before.[38] Perhaps not many of them had the misfortune that Paul Hamilton Hayne had while in Boston seeing a book through the press. Writing in 1854 to his wife in South Carolina, the young poet complained that "not a single Christian in the shape of a South-

35. John S. Oxley to Tom Henry, October 1, 1853, in Gustavus Henry Papers.

36. James T. Harrison to his wife, August 15, 1853, in James T. Harrison Papers. Many years earlier Charles Fraser of Charleston had a similar experience in Boston. In a letter to his mother he said: "There are a great many Carolinians now in Boston, so many that I almost feel at home. Mr. Ball and his nephew are here, Mr. Hasell, Deas, Ingraham, and several others, so that I may be in Charleston whenever I please, as far as regards society." Charles Fraser to Mrs. Mary Fraser, August 29, 1800, in Mary Fraser Papers, Duke University, Durham.

37. Christopher Jenkins to his wife, July 5, 1826, in Mrs. Christopher Jenkins Papers.

38. "Journal of Simri Ross," in Hermione Ross Walker Collection.

erner has been here for weeks. I feel lost, somewhat I fancy like Sir John Franklin at the North Pole."[39]

Many southerners went north in search of cures for various maladies or, at least, a general improvement of their health. In their letters home southerners frequently complained of not feeling well, but much of this was doubtless due to the rigor and pace of travel as well as the rather drastic change in living habits. While any extensive sojourn that was not too arduous could properly be regarded as a diversion contributing to physical and spiritual well-being, some southerners went north for the specific purpose of seeking to improve their health. Here again, it is difficult to ascertain the extent to which poor or failing health prompted their journeys, for almost invariably the places where southerners sought treatment were also places that were most attractive for quite different reasons.

Southerners went north on the advice of their physicians or to seek medical services on their own. Dr. Thomas Cooper suggested to James H. Hammond that he go to Philadelphia in 1836 to consult a physician, who, in turn, advised him to get away from all his cares by sailing for Europe.[40] When Alexander Porter, the Louisiana planter, was serving in the United States Senate, he frequently went north to consult with physicians regarding his failing health. It was on one such trip that a Philadelphia physician told him that his condition was not only incurable but was rapidly deteriorating. The physician advised Porter to go to his Louisiana home immediately, and he died there a few months later in 1844.[41] Seven years later, Edmund Ruffin, who would not have considered a trip to the hated North for himself, was pleased to see his favorite daughter-in-law go to New York "on

39. Paul Hamilton Hayne to Mary Michel Hayne, September 30, 1854, in Paul Hamilton Hayne Papers, Duke University, Durham.
40. Elizabeth Merritt, *James Henry Hammond, 1807–1864* (Baltimore: Johns Hopkins Press, 1923), 40.
41. Wendell H. Stephenson, *Alexander Porter: Whig Planter of Old Louisiana* (Baton Rouge: Louisiana State University Press, 1934), 90, 113–14.

mendation of her physician," in search of a cure for her malady. The tiring journey was a futile one, for she died less than a month after her return to Virginia.[42]

Many of the water-cure establishments were most attractive and among the more romantic places for improving one's health. While partaking of the water's restorative powers, one could also indulge in a variety of pleasurable activities. As early as 1801 a Georgia physician was in Bulls Town (Balston Spa), and after he "commenced the cure of the waters" he became "immediately fonder of them than any liquid I ever tasted." Within a week he was well enough to take "a jaunt with a party of ladies and gentlemen to the Congress [Hotel] at Saratoga Springs." Even if his aches and pains remained, he apparently had been cured of strong drink—or almost. He said that he had tasted no kind of spirits since arriving at the Springs. "One glass of wine at a Hopp and a few glasses of porter in the whole of the last six days is all that I have drank nor had I the least inclination for it, and this sudden distaste for strong Drinks has been attended with no inconvenience that I can perceive."[43]

Clement Clay, an Alabama lawyer and a sufferer from chronic asthma, was a devotee of the water cures. In 1850, after his persistent cough remained despite treatment by a Dr. Jackson in Philadelphia, Clay went to Rockaway and tried sea bathing; but that did not agree with him at all. Then he decided to go to the much-heralded Hydropathic Palace in Brattleboro, Vermont. He was immensely pleased and felt that he was improving. It was, in part, because of the kind of place it was.

> I have been to watering places and seen mirth and gaiety, merry laughs, and light steps; but these were the results of some inordinate excitement, such as wine, or music, or cards, and did not last long or seem habitual. . . . But here there appears no sinking of the spirits, no despondence, but a uniform elasticity of the mind and body; here are

42. William Kauffman Scarborough (ed.), *The Diary of Edmund Ruffin* (2 vols. projected; Baton Rouge: Louisiana State University Press, 1972), I, 78, 81.

43. Alexander, "Diary of a Trip to the North," June, 1801, in Alexander-Hillhouse Papers.

seen no morning long faces after nights of merry making. . . . It is attributable to our mode of life, to our obedience to the dictates of nature, instead of those of fashion or custom.[44]

Two years later Mrs. Clay, at her husband's urging, returned to an earlier haunt of theirs, the Orange Mountain Water Cure in New Jersey. This time she was with her brother-in-law, Hugh Lawson Clay. The latter suffered from none of his brother's ailments. Using the watering place as a base of operation, he frequently went into New York City to call on merchants for whom the Clays collected overdue bills from Alabama customers.[45] As late as 1861 the Clays were in Minnesota where the air "was supposed to have a phenomenally curative effect upon the victims of asthma." Clay's health improved appreciably, and he even began to gain weight. But they felt compelled to leave on April 22, when they learned of Lincoln's call for troops.[46]

It will be recalled that Dr. Daniel Drake, the professor at the Medical Institute of Louisville, strongly advised southerners to seek their water cures in places that would be in contrast to their homes and to avoid the places that were primarily recreational spots. "The amusements and dissipations in which they abound, often tempt the infirm into unhealthy indulgences," he said. He then recommended a number of places on such northern lakes as Ontario and Superior that would help to restore health "in many chronic diseases, especially those of nervous character, such as hysteria and hypochondriasm." In his enthusiastic endorsement of the northern lakes, Dr. Drake sounded at times more like a travel agent than a professor of medicine. He discussed in great detail such places as Detroit, Port Huron, Chicago, Milwaukee, Greenbay, the Sault or Rapids of St. Mary, and Mackinac Island. Where else in the Union, he asked, "can the invalid and patriot

44. Clement Claiborne Clay to Clement Comer Clay, August 12, 1850, in Clement Comer Clay Papers, Duke University, Durham.
45. Virginia C. Clay to C. C. Clay, June 10, 1852, and Hugh Lawson Clay to C. C. Clay, June 25, 1852, both in Clement Comer Clay Papers.
46. Ada Sterling (ed.), *A Belle of the Fifties: Memoirs of Mrs. Clay of Alabama* (New York: Doubleday, Page and Company, 1905), 153–55.

roam, to find localities so opulent in varied and affecting recollections—so accessible—so arranged upon the thread of travel! We may fearlessly affirm, that in this respect, the lakes of the North take precedence over any other region of our beloved country."[47]

Happily, most southern travelers were not invalids, and even if they had been, they would not have been inclined to take Dr. Drake's advice. They did not travel hundreds or thousands of miles to find quiet isolation. They wanted excitement and diversion; and when they went north they sought it avidly. In one way or another, most of them found it. Imagine the thrill of anticipation that Arthur Morson of Fredericksburg, Virginia, tried to convey when he wrote his father from New York in 1818: "When we had procured lodgings and taken our dinner we sallied forth in search of adventures."[48] The first sensation of young Morson and thousands of other southerners was the grandeur and magnificence of the big northern city. As one contributor to *De Bow's Review* put it:

> The splendor, animation, and crowded population of the northern cities excite, bewilder, and delight southern men and their families. Compared with the calm, easy indolence of their own communities, a painful sense of inferiority depresses them when they go back to their own homes. The difference is as between a magnificent panoramic view, and a dark still landscape; life in action and life in repose.[49]

A sense of wonder, or awe, enveloped most southerners visiting the North for the first time and even on later occasions. "The most indifferent traveller," declared the editor of the *Southern Literary Journal*, "cannot pass through the growing and populous portions of our country, without seeing and hearing much that is calculated to excite the imagination, to warm the heart, to interest the feelings and instruct the understanding."[50]

47. Drake, *The Northern Lakes*, 5, 6, 19.
48. Arthur A. Morson to Alexander Morson, September 17, 1818, in Morson Papers, University of North Carolina, Chapel Hill.
49. *De Bow's Review*, XIX (July, 1855), 38.
50. *Southern Literary Journal*, III (November, 1836), 229.

It was New York City, more than any other northern mecca, that aroused such sensibilities. A visitor from Terre Bonne, Louisiana, was almost rhapsodic in his appraisal:

> What an empire, or rather what a world is this New York City, and how insignificant do all other places appear when compaired [sic] to this, with its thousand omnibuses thundering through the streets eighteen hours out of the twenty four, its many thousand hacks, and countless drays, with its hundreds of magnificent hotels, crowded with traveling millions, with its numerous steam boats constantly moving loaded with passengers, also the railroads that radiate from the city with their long train cars . . . then walk through her endless streets and observe the vastness of her constantly increasing commerce, the miles of sidewalks filled up with boxes and bales of merchandise, turned out to be shipped to all parts of the world "and the rest of mankind."[51]

Many southerners who visited New York attempted to capture its spirit and character and convey their impressions to others. Some impressions were naive and uninformed; others were incisive, even critical. All of them, in their own way, captured the very essence of the city, at least as it affected them. There was a bit of envy, some admiration, and some apprehension in the observations of virtually all of them. One senses many of these reactions in the comments of J. C. Myers, a seasoned Virginia traveler who had much to say about New York and its people:

> The traveller on walking the pavements of these winding streets, which present one of the most singular and animating scenes of any other city in the Union, is often much annoyed by the eager shopmen, who from every door will beseech him with bows and gentle violence, and will promise to sell cheaper than his neighbors. Among the moving throng he will be able to discover ladies and gentlemen who are bred in the lap of luxury, who employ and practice all the accomplishments and seductive arts that most enchant society. The ladies have much vivacity of mind, grace of manner, and display the most exquisite taste in all appertaining to dress. Among the gentlemen may be found some possessing all the moral, intellectual, and religious training and cultivation necessary to develope the nobler faculties of our nature, while others may be pointed out, more distinguished for their wit and

51. A. F. Rightor to Andrew McCollam, August 19, 1851, in Andrew McCollam Papers, University of North Carolina, Chapel Hill.

pliability of mind than for their attainments in sound philosophy; while still another class may be observed who are almost destitute of everything calculated to adorn.[52]

No city could be as dazzling as New York; even so, southerners were greatly impressed by other northern cities. Philadelphia, with its special place in the nation's history, had won the hearts of many southerners even before they arrived. And seldom were they disappointed. James H. Hammond of South Carolina was serving in the House of Representatives when he visited Philadelphia in 1836. He was completely entranced and seemed never to tire of walking and looking. "The streets are so clean," he wrote his wife, "the shops so fine and the houses so beautiful that one never gets tired here. I never was in so delightful a city." He thought that Chestnut Street surpassed anything he had ever seen in the way of "commercial elegance." He could not bear to think of returning to Washington, he confessed, "and were you not there I am not sure I should ever go back."[53] The people of Philadelphia were also impressive. To one shrewd observer, the ladies were not only handsome, they were also "intelligent and accomplished." Nor were the men and women cold and reserved, as had been argued by some. This was true only if one visited the city "and left it without remaining sufficiently long to become known. Strangers who bring letters of introduction, or persons whose family, education, and manners are such as to entitle them to move in their circles, will, when acquainted, have the most marked attentions paid them."[54]

To visit Philadelphia was to make a pilgrimage, to see the sights associated with the nation's early history. The Mint, the Old State House (Independence Hall), the Liberty Bell, the his-

---

52. Myers, *Sketches on a Tour*, 57–58.
53. James H. Hammond to Catherine Hammond, April 17, 1836, in James H. Hammond Papers, University of North Carolina.
54. J. Q. P., "Extracts from Gleanings on the Way," *Southern Literary Messenger*, IV (April, 1838), 251. The author was from Elizabeth City, North Carolina.

torical paintings—all claimed the attention of visitors; and those from the South were no exception. Their feeling, a sense of being in the presence of the most precious relics of the nation's founding, was expressed quite well in 1850 by Clement Clay: "When I struck the old cracked bell that pealed the first warning to arms in defence [sic] of our rights as a free people," he wrote his brother, "and when I sat in the chair occupied by John Hancock . . . I felt my patriotism grow warmer and pulse beat quicker."[55]

But as long as there was a Boston, Philadelphia could not claim all the patriotic affections of southern travelers. And they dutifully went to the Commons, the Navy Yard, the State House, and Bunker Hill. They reconstructed, in their own minds, the scene of the "massacre" of 1770 and the "tea party" three years later. One visitor was greatly moved by the sight of "that noble structure, Faneuil Hall Market" with its impressive and magnificent surroundings.

> Nor can any sight be more delicious or inspiring than that which the spectator enjoys as he stands near the antique and venerable State House, and looks down from Beacon Street over Boston Common, taking in a fine view of the water and of the beautiful environs of the city in the distance. . . . The whole of this country is beautiful as the Garden of Eden, and there is not a spot of it which does not revive interesting associations, or which is not distinguished by remarkable traits.[56]

While Boston's first impression "made upon the mind of a stranger" might be unfavorable—with its streets that were "narrow and crooked, and the houses crowded together"—it was nevertheless "the Athens of our Republic, a place where literature is more emphatically a profession, and a profession that commands greater respect and patronage than in any other part of the Union." Most visitors, while remarking on the unattrac-

---

55. C. C. Clay to Hugh Lawson Clay, July 22, 1850, in Clement Comer Clay Papers.

56. *Southern Literary Journal*, III (November, 1836), 231–32.

tive aspects of Boston's physical appearance—"being entirely
destitute of a handsome street of one hundred yards in length,"
as one observer put it—they did not dwell on the physical
aspects of the city.[57] They were much too awed by Boston's
history, its monuments, its institutions, and its people. On the
whole, they thought that its physical appearance was "interesting" and, indeed, worthy of its great past and the people who
lived there.

Even if areas outside Boston were not quite the Garden of
Eden that one observer saw, southern travelers found them
most attractive and sometimes downright exciting. A tour
through New Jersey and Pennsylvania did not consist alone of
seeing its picturesque and delightful scenery, though there was
plenty of that. In viewing the countryside, one sojourner in
1818 was moved to remark that it "generally has the appearance
of great fertility and seems to be well attended to. The *large
barns* with small dwelling houses appeared very frequently in
the country through which we passed."[58] But there were also
"those thrilling associations which pass in rapid review over the
mind when gazing on the many battlefields, rendered memorable for that martial strife which resulted in the overthrow of
British oppression over the colonies."[59]

In some ways the area north of the great metropolis was as
attractive and tantalizing as any that the southern traveler had
ever visited. There was nothing in the South with which to
compare New York. But the farms and villages of Upstate New
York were not beyond comparison with the South; and the result was not at all favorable to the South. Surely, every southerner who journeyed up the Hudson or traveled across the state
on the railroad or the Erie Canal saw much that, in some ways,
should have been within his reach but obviously was not. But

57. Myers, *Sketches on a Tour*, 311.
58. Arthur Morson to Alexander Morson, September 17, 1818, in Morson Papers.
59. Myers, *Sketches on a Tour*, 43.

the attractiveness of the area was fully as irresistible as that of the big city. As one of them said,

> Let him accompany us in our route up the beautiful Hudson, and feast his longing gaze upon the picturesque and sublime scenery that towers its borders;—let him admire the monuments of quiet beauty and healthful activity that greet his observation in the peaceful villages on the way;—let him pursue his course over that most perfect of American railroads, which, commencing at Albany, has Buffalo for its contemplated limit, passing through the beautiful valley of the Mohawk, and the romantic and bewitching scenery of Little Falls, where nature seems to have exhausted her art in presenting to the eye and the mind a picture of nearly unrivalled magnificence.

By the time that he reached Niagara Falls, the writer had so exhausted his powers of superlative description that he merely remarked, "Where, on the face of the earth, has Nature combined in one view, so many of her attributes of grace and sublimity!"[60]

It was the great sights of the North that southerners never tired of visiting. The much-publicized monuments, the widely heralded public buildings, the natural and man-made wonders, and even the cemeteries drew them like magnets. In Philadelphia, it was Independence Hall, the Bank of the United States—"How ponderous, how fine, how chaste!"[61]—the Schuylkill Water Works, Girard College, the Academy of Fine Arts, and Laurel Hill Cemetery. In New York it was the city hall, "a most stupendous building, the front of which is formed entirely of marble"; the Stock Exchange, " where members paid $400 per year for the privilege of buying and selling stocks"; the state prison; Croton Reservoir; Greenwood Cemetery, "twenty times as large as that of Laurel Hill"; the numerous retail shops; and, of course, the places of entertainment and amusement.[62] In

60. *Southern Literary Journal*, III (November, 1836), 229.
61. "A Trip to Niagara," *Southern Literary Messenger*, III (November, 1837), 658.
62. Arthur Morson to Alexander Morson, September 17, 1818, in Morson Papers;

Boston and environs it was the State House, Faneuil Hall, the Commons, Harvard College, and Bunker Hill. In other places they visited colleges such as Princeton and Yale, factories such as Lowell and Haverhill, natural attractions such as the falls and watering places, as well as churches, alms houses, and asylums.

No grand tour was complete or successful without a visit to one or more of the fashionable watering places—Saratoga Springs, Balston, Newport, or Cape May. Some southerners spent their entire time away from home at Saratoga or Newport, while some were there for only a few weeks or days. Even if the places to visit were few or if the time available was short, the spas were high on any traveler's list. The prospect of "bad roads, almost impassable streams, and slovenly accommodations" was nothing, since, as one commentator remarked, the southern travelers regarded "the exhibition of themselves for such a brief time there a full compensation for all perils and privations encountered while outward and homeward bound."[63] Saratoga's chief attraction was neither the mineral waters nor the salubrious climate, but the "gay and ever-changing company . . . from all parts of the Union . . . the rich merchants from New Orleans, and the wealthy planter from Arkansas, Alabama, and Tennessee, with the more haughty and more polished landowner from Georgia, the Carolinas and Virginia."[64] When the watering places were fashionable, the southern visitors did their part in making them so.[65]

If drinking the mineral waters was not their principle objective in visiting Saratoga, many did "take the water cure"; and one suspects that at least some of them hoped that it would

---

[Bobo], *Glimpses of New York*, 40–41; and James T. Harrison to Regina Harrison, July 17, 1853, in James T. Harrison Papers.

63. *North American Review*, XLVII (July, 1843), 112.

64. James Silk Buckingham, *America, Historical, Statistic, and Descriptive* (3 vols.; London: Fisher, Son, and Co., 1841), II, 435.

65. Brewster, *Summer Migrations*, 116–17. In the 1836 season there were many southern visitors at New Lebanon Springs, New York: "Traits of a Summer Tourist," *Southern Literary Messenger*, II (October, 1836), 699.

fortify them against the maladies to which they were susceptible in the southern environment. In 1826 a well-to-do Charlestonian began to drink the water upon arrival, but he admitted to
his wife that he was feeling quite well and spent most of his
time playing billiards and enjoying the company of friends.[66] A
Georgia planter went there in 1828 with some doubts about the
curative powers of the water. His wife, writing from New Haven, urged him to be patient. She added, somewhat wistfully,
that she hoped he would think of her often as he moved
"amongst all the beauties" in Saratoga.[67] When R. F. W. Allston,
the South Carolina rice planter, visited Saratoga in 1838, all
members of his family, including his two small sons, drank the
waters of Congress Spring. Allston very much hoped that it
would prove beneficial to his wife whose "nerves and muscular
system are still very unstrung." With that in mind, he extended
his visit a week longer than he had planned.[68]

There were many who did not even use the waters as an
excuse for visiting Saratoga. The distinguished personages, the
sightseeing trips to Sharon Springs, Balston Spa, and the Fair
Grounds, the "hops" or balls where the women could display
their finery were more than enough to justify the presence of
pleasure-seekers, young and old. One young lady from North
Carolina was frank enough to admit that she was not happy at
Union Hall, "where all the religious and sick people put up,"
and consequently persuaded her friends to join her in moving
to Congress Hall, "which is much the gayest and most fashionable house in the place." On their first two nights, there were
glittering balls and, of course, plenty of excitement.[69] At Con-

66. Christopher Jenkins to his wife, July 5 and July 13, 1826, in Mrs. Christopher
Jenkins Papers.
67. Sarah Alexander to A. Leopold Alexander, July 30, 1828, in Alexander-Hillhouse
Papers.
68. R. F. W. Allston to Elizabeth Frances Blyth, July 11, 1838, in Easterby, *The
South Carolina Rice Plantation*, 77.
69. Lathrop (ed.), "A Southern Girl at Saratoga," 960. See, also, Hugh Bradley, *Such
Was Saratoga* (New York: Doubleday, Doran and Company, 1940), 131 ff.

gress Hall and at the United States Hotel, one could see many of the South's most distinguished persons. These were the places frequented by such leaders as Henry Clay of Kentucky, John Slidell of Louisiana, Benjamin Perry and Joel R. Poinsett of South Carolina, and Richard Henry Wilde of Georgia. At one time in 1858 there were thirty-four Charlestonians spending their holiday in Saratoga.[70] As late as 1860, during a morning walk, Henry William Ravenel of Charleston encountered some fifteen people from South Carolina.[71]

It should be added that not every southerner found Saratoga as exciting and pleasurable as most did. One critical observer insisted that the southerner of means was courted by the obsequious innkeepers and others only until someone with greater wealth, such as a northern banker or manufacturer, came along. At such a time, the southerner gradually subsided from the "sublime nabob to an ordinary, civil-spoken and well-behaved gentleman."[72] Another said that the daily routine of life at Saratoga was but a "dreary repitition of the dissipations of winter in the metropolis—with this difference to its disadvantage—that there one sees all the petty coteries of 'society' brought together upon a theatre disagreeably narrow, each striving to outshine the other in dress and display."[73] It may well be that these two critics looked back on unhappy experiences at the great spa; but it can hardly be gainsaid that many northerners did, indeed, regard their southern visitors as inferior people who tended toward ostentation.[74]

Newport was so popular with southerners that even before the War for Independence it was known as the "Carolina Hospital." While, for the most part, it lived down this reputation in

70. Brewster, *Summer Migrations*, 101–102.
71. Childs (ed.), *Private Journal of Henry William Ravenel*, 27.
72. *Southern Quarterly Review*, XXVI (October, 1854), 437–38.
73. "Domestic Tourism," *Southern Literary Messenger*, XVII (June, 1851), 377.
74. See, for example, the account of the lecture given at Saratoga by one Dr. Curtis of South Carolina in Buckingham, *America*, II, 446. Although many thought it in bad taste, if not coarse, there was no inclination to remonstrate with the lecturer, for no one seemed really surprised that a southerner would perform in such a way.

later years, as it attracted more and more people who were not invalids, southerners in the nineteenth century enjoyed being in this "old fashioned town, where rides were handsome, the air pure and the girls beautiful."[75] As a matter of fact, Saratoga attracted the throngs, but Newport prided itself in attracting a more select group of the socially acceptable. And even if southerners tended to spend more time in Saratoga, the more sensitive and socially ambitious among them went to Newport to pay their respects and hopefully be anointed by the respectable. Southern visitors in Newport constituted something of a summer colony, some of them purchasing homes or living in rather modest rented houses.[76] If they preferred, they could live in hotels, described by one guide book as "ample and of a good character, affording every inducement to the invalid and seeker of pleasure to make this place a summer residence."[77]

Surely the pleasure-seekers from the South found much in Newport to attract them and, indeed, to keep them there for extended periods. Hugh Ball of Charleston did not mind the fact that in the summer of 1831 the town was crowded with "upwards of a thousand strangers." He expected to "weather it out one month more," since he much preferred Newport to New York.[78] He and the other visitors were entranced by the brilliant balls that were regular features at the major hotels, especially the Bellevue, Ocean House, and Atlantic House. The pace of the social life was a bit too much for one southern planter who said that he had come to Newport to "rusticate, but instead of that we are in a volcano of dissipation, and I am Completely tired of it," although he admitted that it was most

75. J. A. Maxwell to Adam L. Alexander, September 6, 1822, in Adam L. Alexander Papers, Duke University, Durham.

76. Mrs. John King van Rensselaer, *Newport: Our Social Capital* (Philadelphia: J. B. Lippincott Company, 1905), 30–31.

77. *The Eastern Tourist: Being A Guide Through the States of Connecticut, Rhode Island, Massachusetts, Vermont, New Hampshire and Maine* (New York: John Disturnell, 1848), 31.

78. Hugh S. Ball to John Ball, Jr., September 2, 1831, in John Ball, Sr., and John Ball, Jr., Papers, Duke University, Durham.

difficult to bring his daughters to accept a "peaceable life."[79]
Perhaps it was such "dissipation" that moved one southern visitor to remark,

> We must say that whenever we have attended church services at
> Newport or Saratoga, during our loitering there, we have felt
> (perhaps wickedly) inclined after witnessing a week's exhibition of
> heartlessness and folly, to throw an unusual emphasis into the supplication of the liturgy—"From pride, vainglory, and hypocrisy;
> from envy, hatred and malice, and from all uncharitableness, Good
> Lord deliver us."[80]

Perhaps somewhat more edifying were the artistic accomplishments of northerners in which many southerners manifested a pronounced interest. They delighted in visiting the
numerous museums and galleries and viewing the paintings,
sculptures, tapestries, and other art objects. In Princeton,
Joseph Brevard greatly admired the "excellent painting in the
College Hall done by Peale of the Death of General Mercer
who was killed here in 1777, in which there is a good likeness
of . . . President [Washington]."[81] A young Virginian visiting
Philadelphia in 1818 was very much impressed by a "celebrated picture" of Benjamin West. "The different characters can
almost be known by their different countenances," he reported
to his father. "I wished you and Mother and all my sisters and
brothers could have been present." After spending "about an
hour in contemplating it," he went on to see the "Panorama of
Paris," a representation of the battle "between the allied powers
and the French at the city of Paris . . . on the whole no contemptible painting."[82] In New York there was much to see. One of
the most important art centers was the Dusseldorf Gallery of

79. L. A. Taveau to his son, 1842, quoted in Brewster, *Summer Migrations*, 34.
80. "Domestic Tourism," 377. For descriptions of the "hops" at Newport see [Hiram Fuller], *Belle Brittan On A Tour, At Newport and Here and There* (New York: Derby and Jackson, 1858), *passim*. Fuller, the Massachusetts-born owner of the New York *Daily Mirror*, wrote under the pen name of Belle Brittan, a young southern lady.
81. "Joseph Brevard's Diary," June, 1791, in Alexander and Joseph Brevard Papers, University of North Carolina, Chapel Hill.
82. Arthur Morson to Alexander Morson, September 14, 1818, in Morson Papers.

paintings and statuary which attracted a group of southerners who saw and admired, among other things, Eduard Steinbruck's *Adoration of the Magi*, William R. Barbee's *Fisher Girl*, and Benjamin Paul Akers' *Lost Pearl Diver*.[83]

Among the things that many southerners enjoyed and of which they had so little at home were opera and other professional musical performances. When in the North they passed up no opportunity to satisfy their musical tastes. The winter of 1838 in Philadelphia had been made "uncommonly gay" by the performance of several operas, *Masaniello*, *Fra Diavolo*, and *La Somnambula*. The principal singers, one southern listener thought, had "fine voices," which they used with "great taste and power" and gave the "greatest satisfaction."[84] A Tennessean writing to a friend had nothing but praise for the operas and theaters of New York, "and above all to remind one of Drury Lane are Jullien's concerts, announced in flaming red placards, and Jullien himself, as I have just seen him got up in white waistcoat, embroidered shirt front, white tie, and hair curled within an inch of his life."[85] Among the delights of one southern editor's holiday in New York in 1853 was a performance of *Don Giovanni*, with Henriette Sontag in one of the leading roles.[86] The following year, while in Boston, Paul Hamilton Hayne told his wife that "one of the best opera troupes, ever in this country, perform tonight at the Howard Theatre. I wish dearest you were with me to enjoy the treat."[87]

Concerts by famous and accomplished singers were always a delight. In 1852 Hugh Lawson Clay of Alabama took time out,

83. Childs (ed.), *Private Journal of Henry William Ravenel*, 28. See also, the Sarah Gayle Crawford Diary, July 27, 1853, in the Gayle-Crawford Collection.

84. J. Q. P., "Extracts from Gleanings on the Way," 251. For a parody on a southerner attending a Philadelphia opera see the account by William T. Thompson's legendary figure, Major Jones, in Warren S. Tryon (ed.), *A Mirror for Americans: Life and Manners in the United States, 1790–1870, As Recorded by American Travelers* (3 vols.; Chicago: University of Chicago Press, 1952), I, 198–202.

85. John Stewart Oxley to Tom Henry, October 1, 1853, in Gustavus A. Henry Papers.

86. *Southern Literary Messenger*, XIX (August, 1853), 518.

87. Paul Hamilton Hayne to Mary Michel Hayne, August [29], 1854, in Paul Hamilton Hayne Papers.

during his visit to the Orange Mountain Water Cure, to go to New York to hear Marietta Alboni sing. Since he was preoccupied with business matters, he left it to his sister-in-law, Mrs. Clement Clay, to give the details of the concert.[88] Everyone, of course, wanted to hear Jenny Lind, the "Swedish Nightingale." Doubtless many southerners were as fortunate as Mrs. Clement Clay, who heard her in one of her several concerts at Castle Garden, where the "cantatrice" sang before ten thousand people.[89] Among those not so fortunate was Alabama Congressman Henry W. Hilliard, who arrived in New York in 1850 after Miss Lind had completed her series of concerts there. Upon learning that she would sing in Philadelphia a few evenings later, Hilliard wrote the proprietor of his Philadelphia hotel requesting two tickets for him and his son, a student at Princeton. When Hilliard reached Philadelphia, he discovered, to his dismay, that there were no tickets to be had. But P. T. Barnum, who had brought Miss Lind from Sweden, was in the hotel, and Hilliard called on him and pleaded for tickets. Barnum told him that every seat had been taken except one fifty-dollar box for five persons, overlooking the stage. Hilliard took it and then sold three seats to a congressional colleague, Lewis C. Levin of Pennsylvania. It was worth all the trouble:

> In the evening, on entering our box, I found Mr. Levin and two ladies of his family, and in looking over the audience I felt already repaid. I had never witnessed such a scene; the audience was brilliant, and the animation already irrepressible.... I heard Grisi and Persiani in Paris, but the singing of Mlle. Jenny Lind, as I heard her in Philadelphia, was to me a revelation in music.

Of Miss Lind's singing "The Last Rose of Summer," Hilliard

88. Hugh Lawson Clay to C. C. Clay, July 25, 1852, in Clement Comer Clay Papers. If Mrs. Clay wrote an account of the performance, it does not survive. In her own memoirs, however, she said that during the fifties she and her friends often went north "in order to hear to advantage some particularly noted star." Among others, she heard Grisé and Mario, the "Lovely Bozio," and Jenny Lind, "the incomparable Swede, whose concerts at Castle Garden were such epoch-marking events to music-lovers in America." Sterling (ed.), *A Belle of the Fifties,* 101.

89. Sterling (ed.), *A Belle of the Fifties,* 101.

said, "I shall not forget that song while I remember anything."[90]

In many ways the Crystal Palace Exposition that opened in New York in July, 1853, symbolized the attraction that the North had for southerners on the "Grand Tour." Despite the fact that the building was a poor replica of its London model, that the leaky roof damaged many of the displays, and that many of the exhibits were never completed, southerners went in droves daily. Surely they were not responsible for its dwindling attendance and ultimate failure. One Mississippi planter, regretting that he was not among the invited guests for the grand opening that was attended by President Pierce and three members of his cabinet, had to content himself with "an outdoor view." He gained admission after the opening ceremonies, however, and immediately pronounced the Palace itself "the most beautiful building on this side of the Atlantic."[91]

The Exposition was the principal object of interest on the schedule of virtually every southern visitor to New York in 1853.[92] Sarah Gayle Crawford was happy that there were friends with whom she could go, since her husband did not feel well enough to take in the sights. "It was a grand spectacle to my uninitiated eyes," she declared.[93] On the morning after Sue Henry arrived from Clarksville, Tennessee, she went with friends to the Crystal Palace and remained for about three hours. "I never saw as much in so short a time in my life," she exclaimed. "I looked over with my eyes and mouth both, wide open."[94] When "Cecilia" returned

90. Henry W. Hilliard, *Politics and Pen Pictures at Home and Abroad* (New York: Putnam's, 1892), 242–44.
91. James T. Harrison to Regina Harrison, July 17, 1853, in James T. Harrison Papers.
92. For a discussion of the throngs of southern merchants and planters at the Exposition in 1853 see Philip S. Foner, *Business and Slavery: The New York Merchants and the Irrepressible Conflict* (Chapel Hill: University of North Carolina Press, 1941), 1–4.
93. Sarah Gayle Crawford Diary, July 27, 1853. A few days later Mrs. Crawford returned to the Exposition with her husband, who was much better by that time. See the entry for July 30, 1853. Diary in Gayle-Crawford Collection.
94. Sue Henry to Mrs. Marion Henry, September 25, 1853, in Gustavus A. Henry Papers.

to her "quiet Southern home," the memories of her several visits to the Exposition remained vivid. "The Crystal Palace must characterize New York," she said. "What a wilderness of objects! Statues and statuettes, silks and satins, china and glass, furniture of all descriptions, and for all uses. What bright colors! What never ending glitter! What crowds of people! What questions they ask, and how strange their criticisms!"[95]

The editor of the *Southern Literary Messenger*, who visited the Exposition with the distinguished writer Joseph G. Baldwin, was not quite so specific in his enthusiastic description of what he saw:

> The editor need say nothing of the Crystal Palace as an architectural effort, his New York correspondent having done entire justice to it in preceding pages of the Messenger. Of the articles contained in it—the treasures of silver-work and tapestry and sculpture, the rare specimens of Parisian taste—and the wonderful contrivances in mechanics, he need say quite as little, as they will be set forth in exquisite wood engraving by Mr. Putnam in his official Illustrated Catalog. . . . Those who desire to know what the Crystal Palace contains should go and see it.[96]

Other Virginians joined the editor in urging friends and relations to visit the Exposition. Alfred Mordecai of Richmond said that he "derived so much gratification from seeing the exhibition . . . that I wish for all who I think would be alike pleased with it, to enjoy the same pleasure. It is with this view that I now write a line to try to induce you to come here," he wrote his brother, "if there is no insuperable obstacle to prevent your doing so." He was so enthralled by the displays that he remained from ten o'clock in the morning until nearly nine at night, "without sitting down the whole time, except for a moment to buy an Austrian chair. . . . In two days I think you could get a pretty good view of all, if pursued systematically, and you need not take two consecutive days for it."[97]

95. *Southern Literary Messenger*, XX (January, 1854), 29–30.
96. *Ibid.*, XIX (August, 1853), 518.
97. Alfred Mordecai to Samuel Mordecai, November 11, 1853, in Jacob Mordecai Papers.

Within a week, Ellen Mordecai, Alfred's sister, was also writing from New York urging her other brother in Richmond to come and visit the Exposition. She had even reserved a room for him and held the Commissioner's tickets "which Alfred left with me" and which would admit the two of them, "so that really my dear brother your only expenses would be the travelling and by land coming immediately on as we did from Washington, it only cost me $14 and some cents. . . . I am thus explicit to remove every impediment in my power between you and the pleasure that I am *sure* awaits you." She concluded her plea by pointing out that he should come before the first of December in order to see everything before the beginning of the dismantling. "The two most valuable pieces of tapestry are still there. Of other articles some have been purchased but nothing can be delivered before 1st December."[98]

There were times when southerners were so excited by the things they saw and the things they did that they made no clear distinction between the Exposition, on the one hand, and Christy's Minstrels, the Hippodrome, Barnum's, and the Bearded Lady, on the other. They frequently mentioned all these attractions virtually in one breath. It was not that they did not always see the differences or even that they did not value one kind of spectacle over another. Rather, it was that they were caught up in the excitement of witnessing the most unique things they had ever seen; and the recounting of the experience to friends and acquaintances was not the occasion for making "fine distinctions." The Exposition, like Barnum's or Saratoga or Niagara Falls or Laurel Hill Cemtery, was part of the Grand Tour—itself a great learning experience—for which they needed both time and perspective in order to sort it all out.

It can hardly be said that southern travelers were not in a position to pay whatever was required or that, with rare exceptions, they were unwilling to do so. Despite the financial

98. Ellen Mordecai to Samuel Mordecai, November 17, 1853, *ibid.*

difficulties that some southern planters and businessmen were said to have been experiencing, the travelers all appeared well prepared to pay their way, however exorbitant the costs. One doubts that, as a rule, they carried large amounts of cash. Many of them had excellent credit ratings and drew on their accounts at home or in the North, whenever they required additional funds. But one hapless Charlestonian was so unfortunate as to lose $800 which, after paying some bills, he carelessly placed in his coat pocket. He never recovered it.[99]

If others did not lose their money in this way, they found it going through their fingers at an astonishing rate; and some were compelled to make unanticipated arrangements. A Charleston matron, who thought that she had left home with ample funds, found it necessary within a few weeks to request that her son send her additional funds. Despite her imperfect grammar and spelling, she had no difficulty in making clear her desires. "My dear Eff," she confessed, "my demands on you has been great but I hope not more than my arrangements could meat and as I wish to get me a chaise and a few articles and to have my plate made up anew I shall stand in nead of more than I thought when I first left home. If it is possible I could wish you to send me Eight Hundred Dollars more. I am sure I can't do with less without running in debt to Henry or Mr. Schenck. They are very polite and kind but I could not on any account wish to make my obligations greater to them, than what they are already."[100]

The lengthy sojourns in the North were inevitably expensive by any standards. Some southerners frequently extended their trips, in terms of time and places visited, beyond their original plans. There were more things they wanted to do in the North, or the "sickly season" had not yet ended at home. They stopped at the best hotels and dined at the finest restaurants. Some of them

99. Paul Hamilton Hayne to Susan Hayne, August 8, 1843, in Paul Hamilton Hayne Papers.
100. Ann Wagner to Effingham Wagner, August 15, 1818, in Cheves-Wagner Papers, University of North Carolina, Chapel Hill.

rented cottages at resorts or homes in the cities and brought their slaves to provide the many services they required.[101] Like the Charleston matron, they made purchases that far exceeded their intentions, and they went to the theater, concerts, and numerous other places of entertainment.[102] When the trip was over, if they were exhilarated by what they had seen and done, they were also sobered, at least for the moment, by the experience of counting up the costs.

Young southern travelers were as extravagant in their spending as their elders. William Morson, a young Virginian studying at Yale, had some difficulty explaining to his older brother Arthur, who had charge of the family estate, how he had spent so much in so short a time. "Though I acknowledge myself guilty of some acts of extravagance," he said, "still I flatter myself, that on a critical investigation of the subject, you will find that they have proceeded from indiscretion rather than wanton prodigality. You say that you furnished me with the sum of $825, I was under the impression that it was $725." Working from his own figure rather than his brother's, young Morson then proceeded to justify his expenditures. He spoke of the books and supplies he had purchased in New Haven and pointed out that they would have cost more had he purchased them in Fredericksburg. He then asserted that he had spent only $380. "And on the supposition that I shall not return before July my board and ticket of admittance to Professor Olmsted's lectures will not exceed $120 and all other expenses both here and on my return to Virginia will amount to about $150. Agreeably to which calculation all my expenditures from the time I left Virginia until I return will not exceed $650."[103]

Arthur Morson's troubles were relatively simple compared to those of John Ball of Charleston, whose two younger brothers were in lively competition in disposing of the family fortune in the

101. For a discussion of southern masters and their slaves in the North, see below, pp. 130 ff.
102. Shopping tours are discussed below, pp. 89–99.
103. William Morson to Arthur Morson, January 23, 1826, in Morson Papers.

North. In 1825, Hugh Ball, who had been a student at Wesleyan University, quit that institution and went to New York to study medicine. For this undertaking he drew heavily on his brother for some two to three hundred dollars at a time. Within a few months, however, he decided that Europe was the proper place to study medicine; upon request the older brother sent Hugh's fare to Vienna, but Hugh did not go. Instead, he spent the summer of 1826 in Saratoga, Niagara, and other attractive places. There was still another factor delaying his studies. Although only eighteen, Hugh had become engaged to the daughter of Boston physician Walter Channing. Shortly thereafter he sent for $800, and a few weeks later he requested another $600. Upon making the last remittance, the older brother wrote with obvious dismay, "In complying with this last demand you will have received at my hand the aggregate sum of three thousand three hundred and fifty dollars since last October."[104]

If that was not enough to place a strain on the family resources, the older Ball received the following missive from another younger brother in Newport:

> About two months ago, when on my return from traveling, I was at New York, I wrote you a letter apprising you of having drawn a draught on you for five hundred dollars and of having received five hundred from you about the same time. I also requested you to send me five hundred more as my traveling expenses, and the expense of buying a pair of horses had reduced my purse very considerably. After a months wait and I had not received an answer I began to think that you had not received the letter. So I wrote to you again (from this place) increasing my demand to a thousand dollars. I have now waited for the answer to this last letter a week over the time and fearful that that was also lost or miscarried I have written this to inform you that poor "Pilgarlick" (as you used to call me) is at low water mark. I had to go upon "tick" to the tune of better than three hundred. I hope if you have not sent the money you will hasten to relieve me from so disagreeable situation.[105]

104. John Ball, Jr., to Hugh Swinton Ball, October, 1826, in John Ball, Sr., and John Ball, Jr., Papers.
105. E. O. Ball to John Ball, Jr., September 15, 1830, in John Ball, Sr., and John Ball, Jr., Papers.

One is not surprised that the records do not indicate the nature of John Ball's reply to his younger brother.

The big spenders from the South had few complaints about what they received for their lavish outlay of funds. Now and then, a traveler would grumble about the meager services for which servants expected handsome tips. At a hotel near Niagara Falls one traveler's patience was sorely tried by a porter's demand for a gratuity for baggage he claimed to have handled but which, in fact, he had not touched.[106] Another complained of the "catch-penny ways of extracting money from visitors throughout all this Northern country."[107] It was left for the hard-bitten South Carolinian, William Bobo, to level the most adversely critical comments regarding the manner in which northerners "fleeced" southern travelers. His "proper classification of Yankees" follows:

> The New-Yorker will skin you and then kick the body out of the house because the hide was not worth more, or that he can make no further use of it.
> A Connecticut Yankee fleeces you, from principle, and if he fails or neglects to do so, does not rest easy at night; his conscience chides him; he has departed from the true faith.
> The Down-Easter, who has, by the way, more soul, gives at least half the worth of your money in amusing you while you're under the operation. Now and then you find a warm heart in a Down-Easter, in the other two never.[108]

Whether they did so cheerfully or begrudgingly, southern travelers annually spent enormous sums in the North. Today it is impossible to make any estimate of the expenditures that would approach reliability, although many contemporaries were willing

---

106. G. F. W., "Notes by the Way," *Southern Lady's Companion*, II (January, 1849), 218.

107. James T. Harrison to his wife, July 31, 1853, in James T. Harrison Papers.

108. [Bobo], *Glimpses of New York*, 143. In 1801, when Dr. Adam Alexander of Brunswick, Georgia, visited Providence, he did not think that the bed and board of $1.50 at Mrs. Sabin's Boarding House was reasonable, since the supper for three consisted of "about 3 ozs. fryed skinny Ham bread and coffee," but he "paid without a word as it was a young lady." Adam Alexander, "Diary of a Trip to the North," in Alexander-Hillhouse Papers.

to do so. Clement Clay of Alabama was a close observer of southern spending habits, since a part of his law practice involved
representing northern business houses against southerners
whose accounts were in arrears. By 1850 he was so disgusted with
southern extravagance that he exclaimed to his brother:

> I am so opposed to helping these northern folks with my money, that I
> am reluctant to spend a cent with them. I have seen this city of New
> York swarming with Southern tourists or invalids, seeking pleasure
> and health in the midst of our enemies, and disbursing among them
> $2,000 annually . . . instead of expending it in the South to aid and
> advance our own institutions and our own people![109]

William Gregg, anxious to promote local industries in South
Carolina, estimated that southerners annually spent at least
twelve million dollars in the North. And his fellow South Carolinians contributed their full share. "Go where you may," he
exclaimed, "in the city or out of it . . . and you can scarcely set your
foot into a rail-road car, in which you will not find some half dozen
persons from this State. The register book of every fashionable
hotel that I visited, exhibited a large share of names, with South
Carolina attached to them." He observed, moreover, that such
people were not known for their economical habits, "as the bar-
keepers will inform you that their wine bills exhibit liberality
even to wastefulness. You may see them flying around cities, in the
finest and most costly equipages that money can procure, and
while a *millionaire* of New York is content to ride in an *omnibus* . . . many of these persons not worth ten thousand dollars,
would be ashamed to be seen in such vehicles."[110]

Although the redoubtable editor, James D. B. De Bow, had no
precise figures on what southern travelers were spending, he
feared that it was a staggering amount. After suggesting in 1851
that perhaps the South was losing some eighty millions annu-

---

109. Clement C. Clay to Hugh Lawson Clay, July 22, 1850, in Clement Comer Clay
Papers.
110. William Gregg, *Essays on Domestic Industry* (Charleston: Burgess and James,
1845), 10.

ally to the North in transportation and manufactures, he added:

> But that is not all. How much more does the North annually receive from us in support of her schools and colleges, her editors and authors—her Saratogas and her Newports? . . . And this, too, without reciprocity; for who of the North reads a Southern book, or attends a Southern college, or visits a Southern watering place, or brings the accumulated earnings of years to invest in Southern improvements?[111]

De Bow should have known, for despite his protests and remonstrances, he was one of the South's big spenders in the North.[112]

When Hinton R. Helper looked at the problem in 1857, he blamed much of southern spending in the North on southern merchants. "You are the channels through which more than one hundred twenty millions of dollars . . . are annually drained from the South and conveyed to the North," he told them. "You are daily engaged in the unmanly and unpatriotic work of impoverishing the land of your birth. . . . Your conduct is reprehensible, base, criminal." Having stimulated and promoted southern tastes for northern products and northern amusements, southern merchants were responsible for the consequent steady flow of southern capital northward. "Let them scrutinize the workings of Southern money after it passes north of Mason and Dixon's line. Let them consider how much they pay to Northern railroads and hotels, how much to Northern merchants and shop-keepers, how much to Northern shippers and insurers, how much to Northern theatres, newspapers, and periodicals." He had no doubt that the result of such prodigality was the "injury and impoverishment of almost every individual in the South."[113]

In the troubled year of 1860 some southern observers were even more specific than Helper regarding the spendthrift habits

---

111. *De Bow's Review*, XI (November, 1851), 544.
112. See below, p. 107.
113. Helper, *The Impending Crisis*, 334–35.

of southerners in the North. J. A. Turner, for example, was inti-
mately acquainted with the habits of numerous planters; and
his *Cotton Planter's Manual*, published in 1857, gave practical
advice on the improvement of cotton culture. Turner now proposed to give practical advice to southerners about conserving
their resources. Based on some shocking facts about their wasteful habits in the North, he advised them not to visit the North.
He estimated that about one hundred thousand southerners visited New York each summer. Some authorities had estimated
that the ordinary expenses of a visitor in the North would be
five dollars per day. Southerners, Turner contended, would not
be satisfied to part with mere ordinary expenses. "People who
have seen tourists from Southern States, scattering their money
among newsboys, porters, cabmen, and the whole host of street
blood-suckers who can scent a Southern man from afar, and
who recognize immediately one who will bear bleeding—to
say nothing of gambling shops and other shops—those who
have witnessed all this, will readily believe that most of the
class of travelers spoken of spend twice five dollars per day."
Even if they spent only five dollars per day, Turner was appalled to conclude that "we have the snug little sum of a
half million dollars, expended by Southerners, in that city
alone, each day during their stay in it."[114]

Perhaps only one-third of the southern travelers were in New
York City at any given time. The others, Turner surmised,
would be in other cities, at the spas, or even on "foot tours." If,
then, two hundred thousand southerners were wandering about
the North and spending as much as five dollars per day, their
aggregate expenditures would come to approximately one million dollars per day. "Suppose each of the tourists . . . goes on at
this rate for thirty days," Turner argued, "then the fact stands
that Southern travelers, as such, leave in the Northern States, in

114. J. A. Turner, "What Are We To Do," *De Bow's Review*, XXIX (July, 1860), 73.

the course of one summer, forty-five millions of dollars."[115]

Thomas P. Kettell, editor of *Hunt's Merchants Magazine*, arrived at a somewhat different figure by estimating that 50,000 southern travelers annually spent on the average of $1,000 each. He concluded that they left in the North the tidy sum of $53,360,394.[116] It was folly, Kettell contended, for northerners to agitate the slavery question when they were benefiting so handsomely from southern wealth.

Some southerners had the good fortune to have northern friends or relatives whom they could visit and from whom they could gain some perspective on what they had seen and done. The R. F. W. Allstons could visit in Cambridge their uncle, Washington Allston, the distinguished painter, and learn from him a good deal about the ways of people in the North.[117] John Slidell could visit August Belmont, whose wife was Slidell's niece and in whose New York home he was always welcome.[118] Hugh S. Legaré's dearest friend was Professor George Ticknor of Massachusetts, whom he visited many weeks each summer and in whose home he died in 1843.[119] If one had political connections such as those enjoyed by Henry Hilliard and Clement Clay of Alabama or William Aiken and Joel R. Poinsett of South Carolina or Benjamin L. C. Wailes and John A. Quitman of Mississippi, he could be certain of a cordial reception and, consequently, a view of the North that other southerners could not possibly have. There were those, moreover, who had culti-

---

115. *Ibid.*

116. Thomas Prentice Kettell, *Southern Wealth and Northern Profits, As Exhibited in Statistical Facts and Official Figures* (New York: George W. and John A. Wood, 1860), 75.

117. For a moving description of R. F. W. Allston's reunion with Uncle Washington, see R. F. W. Allston to Elizabeth Frances Blyth, September 25, 1838, in Easterby, *The South Carolina Rice Plantation*, 82–83.

118. Louis M. Sears, *John Slidell* (Durham: Duke University Press, 1925), 11, 19, 75, 80.

119. Linda Rhea, *Hugh Swinton Legaré: A Charleston Intellectual* (Chapel Hill: University of North Carolina Press, 1934), 173, 181, 216.

vated friendships over the years with northerners in the academic, business, and religious communities.[120] Discussions among such friends did much to help southerners understand what they had seen and done.

Most southerners had no such entrees into northern life. While in the North they spent most of their time alone—or with each other—on packets, railroad cars, stage coaches, in hotel lobbies, restaurants, museums, concert halls, trying to fathom the mysteries and meaning of the civilization and culture of Yankeeland. Or, perhaps, they simply took in what they saw rather passively, with little or no effort to sort out the meaning of their experiences. Under such circumstances, their understanding was, perhaps, no better than the understanding of southerners that a New Englander ventured in 1831:

> Behold him then in New England, where he disburses liberally the remnant of the splendid income, that rains, droughts, storms, and tariffs have left him. Our arts, stages, steam-boats, hotels, and shops, have all a share of his property, and all who know him esteem his frankness, his social qualities, and his high feelings. The individual is honored but the class is contemned.[121]

120. See below, pp. 51–53.
121. *The New England Magazine*, I (September-October, 1831), 340–41, quoted in Brewster, *Summer Migrations*, 34.

II

Learning
in
Yankeeland

The ultimate value of travel depended in the antebellum years, as it does today, on the extent to which the traveler was willing and able to profit from new experiences. But almost any person who went to the trouble of exposing himself to a culture in many ways different from his own was likely to acquire some new ways of looking at life and its problems, regardless of how strenuously he may have resisted any modification of his own views and habits. It seems safe to say that few adult southern travelers went north for the express purpose of adding to their fund of knowledge about how to live, work, or even enjoy themselves. But the very act of venturing into a strange and different land and of taking with them some lingering, if unarticulated, doubts as to the essential qualities of their own way of life weakened their defenses and rendered them susceptible to the new influences they met on every hand.

How could southern travelers possibly be impervious to the invigorating influences of the hustle and bustle of life in the big northern cities, even as they weakly protested the evils of big-city living? How could they entirely reject the miraculous, if monotonous, operations of northern factories, when their own communities provided no efficient methods of producing a wide variety of goods that they found indispensable? How could they ignore northern educational institutions on which they depended so heavily for the collegiate and professional training of their youth? How could they honestly condemn the

marvelous modes of entertainment which, more than anything
they could imagine, satisfied their tastes and their passions for
diversion? They could demur or mouth some feeble objections;
but they could and did learn from observing and even par-
ticipating in the unique and even outrageous practices that
were everywhere around them in Yankeeland.

Perhaps few southerners went north for the specific objective
of seeing and studying the agricultural work of northerners. It
was difficult, nevertheless, to avoid seeing how northern farmers tilled the soil and made a life for themselves in the northern countryside. After all, southerners had to pass by the farms
en route to the big cities; and they were constrained to react to
what they saw. One young Virginian, on his way to New York,
could not resist the opportunity to comment on the "seats on the
river" as he made his way to New Brunswick, through Trenton
and Princeton. "Many of them are beautiful," he said; "the
country generally has the appearance of great fertility and
seems to be well attended to. The large barns with small dwelling houses appeared very frequently in the country through
which we passed . . . and served to warn us, we were on foreign
ground."[1]

The neat appearance of northern farms and the abundance of
the crops were admittedly the result of hard work, which southerners seemed to admire in northern farmers even if they had
no serious intention of following their example. A Louisiana
planter, traveling in Upstate New York, remarked that everything along the road bore "the mark of industry and good taste,
almost every farm had neat and tasty buildings tastefully arranged, and comfort was conspicuous everywhere."[2] A Virginian viewing the same region complimented the New York
farmers for embellishing their "grounds and habitations," which

    1. Arthur A. Morson to Alexander Morson, September 17, 1815, in Morson Papers,
University of North Carolina, Chapel Hill.
    2. A. F. Rightor to Andrew McCollam, July 25, 1851, in Andrew McCollam Papers,
University of North Carolina, Chapel Hill.

was "not inconsistent with the highest regard to profit. . . . In travelling over this great agricultural region, I could not but feel a regret that the renowned Old Dominion should be found so far in the rear in the great agricultural art."[3]

Whether on a foot tour, a journey to the watering places, or a visit to the cities or the lakes, southerners were impressed with the skill and success of northern farmers in cultivating their crops and beautifying their homes. Perhaps the most indelible impression they received was the disarming hospitality of Yankee farmers and their willingness to show others how they were able to accomplish so much. "I found the hospitable and intelligent proprietors had no disposition to conceal any part of their excellent mode of agriculture," J. C. Myers reported, "but to all appearance were ever as ready and willing to give information as the stranger could possibly be to ask it, in all matters concerning their prospering system of agriculture."[4] It was, of course, pardonable pride on the part of northern farmers; and it was, at the same time, a most instructive experience for visitors from a land that boasted of its accomplishments in the field of staple-crop agriculture.

While many of the comments regarding northern agriculture were general in nature, some of them indicated that there were, indeed, many specific things that could be learned from northern farmers. Myers, the Virginia traveler and planter, was so impressed with northern agricultural methods that he devoted many pages of his travel book to describing ways in which southerners could benefit from northern farming methods. He was especially eager to instruct his readers regarding "muck heaps," ashes, and lime as fertilizers; the importance of cultivating wheat, corn, and other grains for foodstuffs; and the desirability of rotating crops to prevent land sterility. "Why the far-

3. J. C. Myers, *Sketches on a Tour through the Northern and Eastern States, the Canadas and Nova Scotia* (Harrisonburg, Va.: J. H. Wartmann and Brothers, 1849), 123, 139.
    4. *Ibid.*, 123.

mers of Virginia do not practice as a general thing a better mode of agriculture I am unable to say, unless we attribute it to negligence. Would that the famous Old Dominion would wake from her slumber on the subject, and no sooner than she would, we would hear no longer the great cry of Westward, Westward." Myers hoped that Virginia and the South would follow New York by raising the profession of agriculture to its proper dignity, where it would be as respectable as law or medicine or business.[5]

It was in the area of industrial pursuits that the southerner conceded his total inferiority and expressed, meanwhile, his doubts regarding the salutary results of such an undertaking. Such exotic industrial pursuits as the silk industry were especially impressive; and even when four-year-olds were among the workers, one Virginian saw it as a "beautiful picture of cheerful industry and good order."[6] Perhaps this was not a typical southern impression of northern industry, for even before William J. Grayson published his celebrated poem, *The Hireling and the Slave*, many southerners believed that the southern system of labor was more humane and more efficient than that of the North. In Willimantic, Connecticut, one southerner saw four or five hundred operatives in a textile mill "trooping to their prisons. . . . They work twelve hours or more, daily. No schooling except when withdrawn from work. No lyceum, or library, or association for their improvement, even if they had time. Last evening I saw several samples of a most degraded population about the tavern."[7]

The favorable impressions persisted, however. One southerner who had long held the view that northern industry was oppressive and inhumane found his opinions modified by personal experience and observation. He confessed that he visited

5. *Ibid.*, 123–40. See also pp. 154–59.
6. A Virginian, "One Day of a Foot Tour in Connecticut," *Southern Literary Messenger*, XIV (June, 1858), 384.
7. *Ibid.*,

New England hoping to have his opinions confirmed that the textile mills could not possibly house so many persons together "without a large result of licentiousness and vice. . . . In some places, I heard and saw confirmation strong; but in most—and those the chief seats of manufactures—my inquiries resulted directly otherwise." The laborers, he said, seemed "as moral as any other class of the population." He spoke of their attending common schools and Sunday schools, lectures, and libraries. "Wherever these good effects appear, be it observed, the proprietors and superintendents . . . have taken the greatest possible care to produce them. And where the unfavorable appearances occurred, there seemed to have been a corresponding neglect on the part of owners and agent."[8]

Not the least of those who saw and admired northern industry was David Crockett, who made his celebrated tour of the North in 1834, during his last term in Congress. Among the many objects that attracted his attention, none excited him more than the textile mills of Lowell. "I had heard so much of this place," he wrote, "that I longed to see it; not because I had heard of the 'mile of gals' . . . but I wanted to see the power of machinery, wielded by the keenest calculations of human skill. I wanted to see how it was that these northerners could buy our cotton, and carry it home, manufacture it, bring it back, and sell it for half nothing; and in the mean time, be well to live, and make money besides." He saw more than he expected: a bustling city, nine meetinghouses, free schools, and the miracle of efficient, profitable textile production. "I never witnessed such a combination of industry," he concluded, "and perhaps never will again. I saw the whole process, from the time they put in the raw material, until it came out completely finished. . . . I regret that

8. "Letters from New England—4," *Southern Literary Messenger*, I (February, 1835), 273. The author, "a Virginian," wrote five of these letters, and they were published in succeeding issues of this journal from November, 1834, through April, 1835. For clarity, breadth, and understanding these letters are far superior to most commentaries on northern life.

more of our southern and western men do not go there, as it
would help to do away with their prejudices against these manufactures."[9]

Some southerners were willing to learn from their northern
hosts in still other ways. "In all the cities, and many of the larger
and middling towns . . . " reported one traveler, "there are
Lyceums, Young Men's Societies, Library Societies, or associations under some such name, for mental exercise and improvement."[10] Whatever their intellectual tastes or interests,
southerners could find much in the northern pulpit, platform,
or forum to stimulate them. Some went to Brooklyn to hear
Henry Ward Beecher, whose tone "was on the whole mild, if sar-
castic" as he prayed for those "steeped in the guilt of slavery"
and who made one such person "feel a livelier sense of" his
"individual depravity than ever before."[11] Another, who listened
to some abolitionist speakers in New Hampshire, concluded
that "their impracticable schemes produce the most mischie-
vous effects in society."[12]

Southerners were not quite so uneasy when they listened to
public discussions of some other important matters, such as
temperance. A large meeting in Boston in 1841 attracted some
three thousand persons, including a southerner who listened
with rapt attention as speaker after speaker flailed the audience
with the evils of strong drink. One of the speakers was most
persuasive. "Never did a speaker so agreeably surprise me," the
other visitor from Virginia recalled. "For three quarters of an
hour, he chained my attention as it had not been for years before . . . and the attention of the whole audience," as he told of

9. Davy Crockett, *An Account of Col. Crockett's Tour to the North and Down East,
Written by Himself* (Philadelphia: Carey, Hart and Company, 1835), 91. For an unfavorable view of the Lowell Mills, see the *Southern Literary Messenger*, III (November,
1836), 233. For an extensive discussion of northern industrial and other economic
influences on southern travelers, see below.
10. "Letters from New England—4," 273.
11. *Southern Literary Messenger*, XX (January, 1854), 60.
12. Myers, *Sketches on a Tour*, 380.

the effects of drunkenness upon a husband and a father, "the beggared, ill-taught, vitiated children—the abused sorrowing, heart-broken wife." After resolutions were passed pledging all those present to work for the cause of temperance, the southern visitor "went away . . . congratulating myself on having come to this Temperance meeting, instead of going to a cotillion party at Mrs. F's in C., to which I was bidden some days ago."[13]

Southerners with scholarly or scientific interests took advantage of their sojourns in the North to meet and discuss their interests with northerners from whom they could learn. One of them, who prided himself on his accomplishments in the study of Greek, called on Professor Perdicaris at Yale, who received him cordially and read to him a portion of the *Iliad* "in his native melody." He was especially delighted to receive a personal invitation from the professor to attend his lecture on the literary and political history of modern Greece. "It was marked by a rich yet chaste imagination," the southerner reported, "a generous glow of patriotic enthusiasm, and the eloquence which they naturally inspire."[14] Another, Dr. Thomas Nelson of Richmond, journeyed to Worcester to visit Elihu Burritt, the learned blacksmith. The physician was astonished to learn how this humble man had taught himself some fifty languages through self-discipline and perseverance. Burritt hastened to point out that he had not studied all of them critically and that he yet had much to learn about them. The meeting, at the initiative of Dr. Nelson, resulted in a lively exchange of letters in which Burritt supplied Nelson with additional details regarding his study habits and the languages he had mastered.[15]

Among the men of science who had much to learn in the North, perhaps none could profit more than physicians. Some, like Dr. Daniel Drake of Louisville, advised their patients to

13. "Eloquence in New England," *Southern Literary Messenger*, VIII (January, 1842), 68–69.
14. "Letters from New England—5," 421.
15. *Southern Literary Messenger*, VI (March, 1840), 202.

visit the North. Others, like Dr. Adam Alexander of Brunswick, Georgia, went north themselves to visit physicians and hospitals. Dr. Alexander visited Philadelphia in 1801 by appointment of his "attentive friend Dr. Chalwill." Apparently he saw everything of any importance that the city had to offer in the field of medicine and medical services. He saw the hospital, "a very elegant pile and under good regulations," and by Dr. Jacobs was "politely shown the anatomical preparations that appeared to be extremely well executed and in high preservation." Through Dr. Chalwill he met several other leading physicians of the city, including Dr. Woodhouse and Dr. Barton. There was no doubt in Dr. Alexander's mind that the entire experience was a most rewarding one.[16]

Henry W. Ravenel, the South Carolina botanist who made frequent visits to the North to consult with other scientists or to examine specimens, had experiences similar to those of Dr. Alexander. Ravenel spent considerable time, for example, in the herbarium of Lewis David de Schweinitz of Philadelphia, a pioneer student of American fungi. There is evidence of Ravenel's cordial relations with Philadelphia scientists in the permission that the Academy of Natural Sciences gave him to select some 150 duplicate specimens from its collection. These valuable contacts doubtless had much to do with Ravenel's becoming one of the leading mycologists in the United States.[17]

Benjamin L. C. Wailes, the Natchez planter with many interests in science and education, used his northern travels to extend his intellectual horizons and widen his contacts. In

16. Adam Alexander, "Diary of a Trip to the North," in Alexander-Hillhouse Papers, University of North Carolina, Chapel Hill. Dr. James Woodhouse and Dr. Benjamin S. Barton were both distinguished members of the faculty of the university, and Barton was professor of *materia medica*. Just before the University of Nashville decided to establish a medical school in 1850, faculty member John Berrien Lindsley, a graduate of the University of Pennsylvania Medical School, went north to study the organization, administration, and physical facilities of medical schools in Philadelphia and New York. John Edwin Windrow, *John Berrien Lindsley* (Chapel Hill: University of North Carolina Press, 1938), 32.

17. Arney Robinson Childs (ed.), *The Private Journal of Henry William Ravenel, 1859–1887* (Columbia: University of South Carolina Press, 1947), xv–xvii.

Philadelphia he learned from a workman how to make plaster casts, a technique he had earlier failed to master on his own. For many years he collected geological and other natural specimens which he housed in his small museum in the town of Washington, Mississippi. He made many contacts at the meetings of the American Association for the Advancement of Science, of which he was a charter member; and from time to time he sent specimens from his collection to Louis Agassiz and other scientists in the North. In 1854 he completed his exhaustive report on trees, crops, artesian and other wells, and the flora and fauna of Mississippi. While the report was going through the press in Philadelphia, Wailes, who had brought his manuscript there, worked at the Academy of Natural Sciences, consulted with Timothy Conrad, a fellow scientist in New York who had come to Philadelphia to see him, visited Agassiz in Cambridge, Benjamin Silliman and the widow and son of Eli Whitney in New Haven, and inspected some factories in Massachusetts and Connecticut.[18]

It was only natural that southerners would show a lively interest in northern educational institutions and practices. While there were numerous schools and academies in the South, they were privately and, for the most part, inadequately supported. By the time of the Civil War only North Carolina and Kentucky had made significant strides toward the establishment of statewide systems of public education. One may suspect that those southerners who traveled north were generally committed to private education, especially where their own children were concerned. Some were trustees of local colleges and

18. Charles S. Sydnor, *A Gentleman of the Old Natchez Region: Benjamin L. C. Wailes* (Durham: Duke University Press, 1938), 279, 190, 178, 196–99. John B. Lindsley, the Nashville educator, had similar contacts in the North. In 1848 he joined Dr. Gerard Troost, one of his mentors, in an extensive geological tour of the North, from St. Louis, Missouri, to Burlington, Vermont, with numerous stops en route. Windrow, *John Berrien Lindsley*, 14–15. See also the lively interest of R. F. W. Allston in the exhibits, animals, implements, and other things he saw at the Cincinnati fair in 1850. J. Harold Easterby, *The South Carolina Rice Plantation As Revealed in the Papers of Robert F. W. Allston* (Chicago: University of Chicago Press, 1945), 103–104.

academies and, on occasion, recruited northern teachers for the schools they served.[19] But these parochial activities did not diminish their interest in any and all forms and methods of education in the North, especially as they considered their own responsibilities to the general public. Thus, they learned as much as they could about northern schools from reading matter, including guide books, from conversation, and from observation. After visiting Massachusetts and seeing her colleges and every part of the state "spotted with school-houses," one southern observer was compelled "to come to the conclusion that there is no other region inhabited by the Anglo-Saxon race, containing 750,000 souls, where national education has been carried so far." He spoke admiringly of the state's commitment to education at every level and of the remarkable private support that the institutions received.[20] It was quite clear that he wished that Virginia, his own state, would do as well.

Another southerner who visited many schools in New England in 1835 reviewed in considerable detail the condition of education there. Manual-labor schools had not multiplied, he observed, perhaps because there was a tendency to blend labor with study, thus rendering such schools unnecessary. Infant schools appeared "to have sunk a good deal in esteem," and one Hartford lady explained that they were found be be "hurtful both to body and mind: To *body* . . . by over-exciting, and thus injuring the brain and nervous system; to *mind*, by inducing the habit of learning parrot-like, by rote . . . without exercise of the thinking power." He admired the common-school system "*as a system*," but feared that there was too much minutiae in its administration. "A pervading fault in the management of the common-schools, is a *false economy*; shown, in choosing

19. In 1838, while in the North, Robert F. W. Allston interviewed a prospective teacher, Rev. C. B. Thürmmel, for a parish school in South Carolina. After consulting with his colleagues at home, Allston hired Thürmmel, for $2,000 per year. Easterby, *The South Carolina Rice Plantation*, 80, 86.
20. Myers, *Sketches on a Tour*, 364.

teachers less by their proper qualifications, than by their cheapness." After pointing out that most common schools had wide latitude in constructing the curriculum, he made the following trenchant observation regarding study programs for females:

> Latin and mathematics are coming to be considered as a regular part of female education, throughout the North. But I have not ascertained satisfactorily, whether it is a mere smattering that is taught, or so thorough a course as may solidly improve the memory, taste, judgment, and the reasoning powers. In relation to women even more emphatically than to men . . . these studies are less to be prized, for any specific pieces of knowledge they furnish, than for the activity strength, acuteness and polish they give to the various powers of understanding. The Yankees are too shrewd, and too habitually observant of practical utility, not to perceive this truth, and act accordingly.[21]

One southerner, making his way through Connecticut by foot, could not resist the temptation to call at one of the common schools in Hampton village. In appearance, it resembled many that he had passed: "Framed—one story—twenty-four feet long by about eighteen wide, with a stove and four windows in the schoolroom." When he knocked at the door the teacher, "a pretty young woman of eighteen or nineteen," admitted him. Upon his asking permission to rest awhile and observe her mode of teaching she said, "if you please, sir," and gave him her chair. Meanwhile, she proceeded to listen to the recitations in spelling.

> On their coming up to recite, she would stamp with her foot, and say, "attend!" when each one dropped a curtsy, or made a bow, and forthwith the recitation began. The spelling was odd enough— letters and syllables mumbled over, yet with tempestuous loudness, so that I could only guess what the varlets were saying. A reading class actually got through five or six sentences, before I could with my best endeavors distinguish one word, or conjecture what the subject was.

The teacher remained standing or walking "to and fro rebuking

21. "Letters from New England—4," 274–75.

one, patting another to make him take his hands out of his breeches—soothing and encouraging." Finally, he spoke admiringly of the young teacher whose "countenance betokened much decision of character and intelligence."[22]

Doubtless, some southerners were not content merely to admire the educational programs and methods in the common schools of the North. Christopher G. Memminger, who had long been interested in educational matters in South Carolina, was one of them. In 1834, in company with his friend, W. J. Bennett, Memminger visited a number of such schools in the North and collected much practical information regarding their administration. He was so impressed with what he saw that he and Bennett devised and introduced a plan for the schools in Charleston. An act of the state legislature was passed authorizing the city of Charleston to levy a special tax for educational purposes. Subsequently, the Charleston public school system was inaugurated and achieved considerable success. Memminger then attempted to secure a statewide adoption of his plan for common schools, but without success. In his efforts, nevertheless, he had the support of many influential editors and legislators.[23]

The admiration of southerners for northern schools did not lead them immediately to dispatch their younger offspring to New England common schools and academies. Few of them had living accommodations; and if they had, the distances were much too great for many southern parents to concede that any possibly superior training was worth parting with their children at a tender age. When Paul Hamilton Hayne of Charleston was thirteen years old, he was studying French in Northampton, Massachusetts; but his mother had come up to be with him. And they were there only for the summer months.[24] Some souther-

22. A Virginian, "One Day of a Foot Tour in Connecticut," 385.

23. Henry D. Capers, *The Life and Times of C. G. Memminger* (Richmond: Everett Maddey, 1893), 110–14. See, also, Lillian Kibler, *Benjamin F. Perry, South Carolina Unionist* (Durham: Duke University Press, 1946), 308.

24. Paul H. Hayne to Susan Hayne, August 8, 1843, in Paul Hamilton Hayne Papers, Duke University, Durham.

ners sent their young sons to military schools in the North. The most popular was Captain Alden Partridge's American, Literary, Scientific, and Military Academy at Norwich, Vermont, that had 80 students from the South in 1824, when the total enrollment was 480. In the following year, when the academy was moved to Middletown, Connecticut, there were 102 students from the South, representing more than one-third of the student body.[25]

Even some southern girls went north to school. In 1823 Christopher Jenkins of Charleston enrolled his nieces in Dr. Seidel's Academy near Bethlehem, Pennsylvania.[26] In 1846 George McDuffie's daughter was in school in Philadelphia, where Judge Augustus B. Longstreet visited her when he was en route home from New York.[27] At the age of fifteen Mathilde Deslonde, a French Creole girl from Louisiana, was sent to New York to learn English at the celebrated school run by Madame Chegaray. John Slidell's sister Julia was there at the same time studying French. The two girls became friends, which led to Slidell's acquaintance with and subsequent marriage to Mathilde.[28] When Benjamin Perry and his wife went north in 1857 to enroll their three oldest children in school, they placed one son in Harvard, another in the Naval Academy at Annapolis, and their daughter Anna in St. Mary's Hall in New Jersey.[29]

The really attractive educational institutions in the North were the colleges and universities, which southerners visited whenever possible. Some of the guide books for the period included the major institutions of higher education as important places to see, and southern travelers took their advice seriously.[30]

25. William Arba Ellis, *Norwich University, 1819–1911, Her History, Her Graduates, Her Roll of Honor* (Montpelier, Vt.: Capital City Press, 1911).

26. Christopher Jenkins to his wife, September 5, 1823, in Mrs. Christopher Jenkins Papers, Duke University, Durham.

27. John Donald Wade, *Augustus Baldwin Longstreet: A Study of the Development of Culture in the South* (New York: The Macmillan Company, 1924), 247.

28. Louis M. Sears, *John Slidell* (Durham: Duke University Press, 1925), 13.

29. Kibler, *Benjamin F. Perry*, 313.

30. Gideon M. Davison, *The Fashionable Tour: A Guide to Travellers Visiting the Middle and Northern States and the Provinces of Canada* (Saratoga Springs: G. M. Davison, 1830), *passim*; and Myers, *Sketches on a Tour, passim*. In discussing northern

They liked to visit Princeton, which was rapidly becoming an important educational mecca for southern youth. Perhaps it was because, as one visitor remarked in 1818, it had the "marks of being conducted with much regularity and decorum; there were none of the students on the green in front of the college, but seemed all to be in their rooms."[31] Girard College in Philadelphia was on the list of most southerners, perhaps to appreciate its Greek Revival architecture more than its academic program.[32]

If southerners visited many colleges—including Rutgers, Columbia, Yale, and Wesleyan—it was Harvard more than any other about which they spoke. Commencement there was always a great event, even if one had no son or nephew in the graduating class. In 1800 Charles Fraser of Charleston called it "quite a public festival . . . for people of all classes and descriptions." After the exercises, he attended, by invitation, "a very large entertainment . . . given by the father of one of the students who graduated."[33] Much later, in 1851, A. F. Rightor also attended the Harvard commencement, and he was very glad that he did. But after observing the proceedings, he was "well satisfied that large colleges with great reputation of long standing, are not the best places to educate boys." Out of the graduating class of some sixty young men, twenty-six spoke; "but their speeches were poorly written and worse spoken." He very much hoped that his own son's class at Wesleyan would do much better.[34]

It was not unusual for northern colleges and universities to

---

tours these volumes never failed to give due attention to the colleges and universities as major attractions. Davison also mentioned such academies as Groton and Andover and provided a full description of Captain Partridge's military academy.

31. Arthur A. Morson to Alexander Morson, September 17, 1818, in Morson Papers.

32. See, for example, the references to Girard College in C. C. Clay to Hugh L. Clay, July 33, 1850, in Clement Comer Clay Papers, Duke University, Durham. Girard College was, in fact, a precollegiate institution for orphan boys, but some southerners seem to have been misled by its name.

33. Charles Fraser to Mary Fraser, August 29, 1800, in Mary Fraser Papers, Duke University, Durham.

34. A. F. Rightor to Andrew McCollam, July 25, 1851, in Andrew McCollam Papers. After the Harvard commencement, Rightor went on to Middletown to attend his son's graduation exercises at Wesleyan.

honor distinguished southern visitors in a way that must have been quite gratifying. In 1836, when he was en route to Charleston from his diplomatic post in Brussels, Hugh S. Legaré stopped in Boston to visit his friend, George Ticknor, professor of French and Spanish at Harvard. It was the time of Harvard's bicentennial celebration, and Legaré was invited to speak. Although he had not made a speech in four years, he was highly complimented for his use of the theme of the Puritan exiles who, "like Solomon, sought wisdom above all things."[35] In 1842 Dr. S. H. Dickson, one of Charleston's leading physicians quite interested in cultivating friendships between the North and South, was invited to deliver the Phi Beta Kappa oration at Yale, from which he had graduated. He examined the question of whether the pursuit of knowledge leads to happiness. One writer praised his "boldness of inquiry and keenness of research which do not often appear in such performances."[36]

Several southerners received honorary degrees from northern institutions. In 1841, shortly after his *Georgia Scenes* was published in New York, Augustus B. Longstreet received the honorary degree of Doctor of Laws at Yale.[37] Upon his election to the position of chancellor of the University of Nashville, John B. Lindsley received a similar degree from Princeton.[38] When Davy Crockett visited Boston in 1834, he could not be persuaded to go to the Harvard commencement, "where they keep readymade titles or nicknames to give people. I would not go," he said, "for I did not know but they might stick an LL.D. on me before they let me go; and I had no idea of changing 'Member of the House of Representatives of the U.S.' for what stands for 'lazy lounging dunce,' which I am sure my constituents would have translated my new title to be, knowing that I had never taken any

35. Linda Rhea, *Hugh Swinton Legaré: A Charleston Intellectual* (Chapel Hill: University of North Carolina Press, 1934), 156–57.

36. An account of Dickson's address is in *Magnolia*, New Series, II (January, 1843), 64.

37. Wade, *Augustus Baldwin Longstreet*, 156.

38. Windrow, *John Berrien Lindsley*, 20.

degree. . . . There had been one doctor made from Tennessee already, and I had no wish to put on the cap and bells."[39]

The practice of sending southern youth to northern colleges and universities began in earnest about the time of the War for Independence. Before that time, explained the editor of the *Southern Review*, many southern youth studied law and the classics in England. With the coming of independence, however, the people of the South began to send their sons to northern colleges "where the standard of classical learning had never been high . . . because the fortunes of the people did not admit of their giving their youth a foreign education, and where, until very recently, it continued to be exceedingly low."[40] Even if the classical education in northern institutions was deficient, southerners patronized them in increasing numbers. In the early years of the nineteenth century, the visits to northern colleges and universities undoubtedly enhanced their reputation among southerners and stimulated them to send their sons there. And the sense of adventure that such an experience offered would surely elicit the enthusiastic cooperation of the prospective students.

For many southerners the most attractive educational institution in the North was the United States Military Academy at West Point. It was, in the words of one southerner, "the pride and ornament of our country," while John C. Calhoun, when secretary of war, said it was the "cheapest and safest mode" of promoting and perpetuating scientific knowledge.[41] No other institution in the world could give its graduates such a high status, one mother declared. "Other schools might even be better, but reputation is not won in a day and for success in this world, reputation

39. Crockett, *An Account of Col. Crockett's Tour*, 85. Crockett was referring to the fact that Harvard had conferred an honorary degree on President Andrew Jackson the previous year.

40. *Southern Review*, IX (November, 1829), 347.

41. *Southern Literary Messenger*, IX (November, 1843), 665–66; and John Calhoun to R. M. Johnson, January 15, 1819, in Richard K. Crallé (ed.), *The Works of John C. Calhoun* (6 vols.; New York: D. Appleton, 1853–57), V, 56.

is of vast importance."[42] Another southern mother, delighted that her son was at West Point, urged him to seize the opportunity to make important decisions regarding his future. "I think you had better stay at West Point till next December twelvemonth," she advised, "learn all you can, then choose a Profeshion [*sic*], study that two years in some Healthy Clime, then come home . . . and never be ashamed to enter any Company or meet your Father's Enemies or your own."[43]

The popularity among southerners of "The Point," as they called it, can be seen in the fact that between 1802 and 1829 some 1,913 young southerners sought admission, while the more populous North and West could boast of only 2,160 who sought training in the Academy. The South had more than its share of graduates, moreover. In 1820, for example, the sixteen southern graduates constituted approximately 53 percent of a graduating class of thirty. Thirty years later, when the southern states could claim only 35 percent of the population, the twenty-one southern graduates represented approximately 47 percent of the graduating class.[44]

Early in the nineteenth century young southerners went to northern colleges and universities in increasing numbers. John C. Calhoun, Cassius M. Clay, Augustus B. Longstreet, and Joseph E. Brown went to Yale. Robert W. Barnwell, Daniel R. Hundley, James H. Thornwell, and J. L. M. Curry went to Harvard. James McDowell, Nathaniel Macon, Andrew Jackson Polk, and Charles Fenton Mercer studied at Princeton, while John Chavis, a North Carolina free Negro, studied privately with

42. Mrs. J. W. Anderson to Edward Willoughby Anderson in Francis P. Sullivan (ed.), "Letters of a West Pointer, 1860–1861," *American Historical Review*, XXXIII (April, 1828), 609.

43. Charlotte Ann Allston to Robert F. W. Allston, September 27, 1818, in Easterby, *The South Carolina Rice Plantation*, 50–51.

44. The figures are compiled from George Washington Cullum, *Biographical Register of the Officers and Graduates of the U.S. Military Academy* (9 vols.; Boston: Houghton-Mifflin, 1891), I, II, *passim*. For a more lengthy discussion of southern interest in West Point, see John Hope Franklin, *The Militant South, 1800–1860* (Rev. ed.; Cambridge: Harvard University Press, 1970).

Princeton's President John Witherspoon. Robert Toombs went to Union College, William L. Yancey to Williams, Henry Wise to Washington College, Pennsylvania, and John M. Richardson to Lawrence Scientific School. But it was not merely the men of later distinction who received their education in Yankeeland. There were also the Natchez planter's son who went to Harvard, and the young man who went to Yale from Fredericksburg, Virginia, and the lad who went to Wesleyan from Terre Bonne, Louisiana, and the one who went to Princeton from Augusta, Georgia. The impressive thing was the number of young southerners who studied in northern colleges and universities.[45] In 1840 there were 14 young southerners at Harvard College in a class of 243. Twenty years later there were 20 in a class of 443. At Yale, in 1840, there were 53 southerners in a class of 438. Twenty years later the figure was 29 in a class of 521. Princeton led all northern colleges in the number of undergraduates from southern states. In 1840 there were 107 in a class of 226, and in 1860 there were 98 in a class of 314.[46] Others were attending Columbia, Rutgers, Brown, Dartmouth, Bowdoin, Hamilton, New York University, and other institutions.

Northern professional schools were the cherished goal of many young southerners; and in the early years of the century none was more popular than the law school at Litchfield, Connecticut, conducted by Judge Tapping Reeve and James Gould. During the colonial years large numbers of southern men studied at the Inns of Court in Britain.[47] The standards of politics and law that they maintained and their interest in oratory, litera-

45. It was said that at one time, in the late antebellum years, about one-half of the leading families of Natchez sent their offspring to educational institutions outside the South, particularly for their college training. D. Clayton James, *Antebellum Natchez* (Baton Rouge: Louisiana State University Press, 1968), 218.

46. The figures were compiled by John S. Ezell and presented in his "A Southern Education for Southrons," *Journal of Southern History*, XVIII (August, 1951), 310. See, also, Varnum Lansing Collins, *Princeton* (New York: Oxford University Press, 1914), 408; Edwin Mark Norris, *The Story of Princeton* (Boston: Little Brown and Company, 1917), 185–91.

47. J. G. de Roulhac Hamilton, "Southern Members of the Inns of Court," *North Carolina Historical Review*, X (October, 1933), 74.

ture, and manners had a profound influence on southern life in the late eighteenth century.[48] For a few years law students went to William and Mary College, where George Wythe and, later, St. George Tucker taught law. After about 1802, when the Federalist-Republican controversy involved Tucker, the program of legal education at Virginia's oldest college declined. Meanwhile, legal studies were not begun at Harvard until 1815, and they were not regularized at Columbia and Yale until 1824 and 1826, respectively.[49] Thus, for a time Judge Reeve's school was one of the few places where young Americans could obtain rigorous, first-class legal training. Miss Sarah Pierce's nearby Litchfield Female Academy was an added attraction for many young swains.

Southerners went to the Litchfield Law School in large numbers. Before it was closed in 1833, every southern state had sent young men there. Seventy had come from Georgia, forty-five from South Carolina, thirty-seven from Maryland, and seven from Louisiana. Among those who later distinguished themselves were John C. Calhoun, Augustus Baldwin Longstreet, Georgia's United States Senator Nicholas Ware, Francis L. Hawks, first president of the University of Louisiana, and William Cumming, the antinullification leader of Georgia. After 1833 the law schools at Harvard, Yale, and Columbia would claim those southerners who could no longer go to Litchfield because it had closed.[50]

Southerners aspiring to the medical profession were attracted to the North in even larger numbers than those who sought to become lawyers. After all, it was possible to qualify for the bar by reading law in a law office or with a judge. The study of medicine was not so simple. One needed anatomical laboratories, chemis-

48. William R. Taylor, *Cavalier and Yankee: The Old South and American National Character* (New York: George Braziller, 1961), 45.
49. Samuel H. Fisher, *The Litchfield Law School, 1775–1833* (New Haven: Yale University Press, 1933), 23–25.
50. *Ibid.*, 26–31.

try, materia medica, and many things that one could not possibly learn from a physician; and above all, one needed clinical facilities. The South lagged far behind the North in medical education. Despite the fact that more than twenty medical schools were founded in the South before the Civil War, only five prospered: the Medical Department of Hampden-Sydney College, the Medical Department of the University of Virginia, the Medical College of Virginia, the Medical Institute of Louisville, and the Medical Department of the University of Louisiana. Many were closed within a few years of their founding. All too often, financial difficulties and faculty disputes adversely affected the colleges' educational work. Most of them, with no adequate hospitals nearby, suffered from deficient facilities for clinical and anatomical instruction. Perhaps most important of all, "many of the men who trained in the North, particularly Philadelphia, sent their sons to and advised their pupils to study in the nationally known Northern schools."[51]

Thus, most southerners who ventured out of their section for medical training went to the well-established schools in Philadelphia, New York, and Boston. The most popular of all were two Philadelphia institutions: the University of Pennsylvania Medical School, founded in 1765, and the Jefferson Medical College, founded in 1832. It was not always a source of pride, but southern magazines and newspapers frequently published the statistics on southern students in northern medical schools. In 1846, for example, the Richmond *Enquirer* called its readers' attention to the fact that of the 170 students who graduated from the Jefferson Medical College that year 40 were from Virginia.[52] The following year a leading journal reported that there were 184 students from Virginia attending the Jefferson Medical College and the University of Pennsylvania Medical School.[53]

51. William F. Norwood, *Medical Education in the United States before the Civil War* (Philadelphia: University of Pennsylvania Press, 1944), 283.
52. Richmond *Enquirer*, March 31, 1846.
53. *Southern Literary Messenger*, XIV (August, 1848), 519.

Some southerners were always delighted to witness what they called the "spectacle" of medical education in the North. One of the most awe-inspiring experiences one Virginian had in 1841 was "wandering" into New York University's new medical school and spending some time "in the land of Calomel and Jalap, in the very region and shadow of pestles, and pill boxes, and purging." He wrote an article about his experience in which he said that the faculty was distinguished, the building and equipment "magnificent."[54] With such praise published in a widely read southern journal, there is small wonder that Virginians and other southerners continued to patronize northern medical schools. In a comprehensive report on students in medical schools in 1838–1839, southerners could clearly see the remarkable attraction that northern medical schools had for young men from that section. Of the 402 students at the University of Pennsylvania Medical School, 259 were from the slaveholding states. The Jefferson Medical College had 95 students out of 248, while the College of Physicians and Surgeons of New York, Harvard, Yale, the Medical College of Ohio, the Berkshire Medical Institution, and Bowdoin Medical School had a dozen students from the South. Even the Cincinnati Medical College, founded only three years before the survey, had 44 southern students in a total enrollment of 112. Meanwhile, there were some 439 students in all of the medical schools in the South. The Medical College of South Caro¹˙ ' ' with 151 students, and the Medical Institute of Louisv. .. as second with 120. The others were in schools in Virginia, Georgia, and Louisiana.[55] Even as southern medical colleges increased and improved, the strong preference for northern medical colleges continued. By 1860 the University of Pennsylvania and the Jefferson Medical College had graduated 9,945 physicians, of whom 6,841, or 68

54. *Ibid.*, VII (July, August, 1841), 551.
55. T. Romeyn Beck, "Statistics of the Medical Colleges of the United States," *Transactions of the Medical Society of the State of New York* (Albany: J. Munsell, 1839), *passim*.

percent, were from the South.[56] In that year James De Bow estimated that "fully a thousand young men from the South attend the medical colleges of the North."[57]

For the most part, southern youth seem to have fared well in northern colleges and professional schools. At Captain Partridge's military school the strict discipline was too much for some young southerners accustomed to greater freedom. In 1824 the commandant had his problems with the Ball brothers, Alwyn and Elias Octavus, of South Carolina. They left the village of Norwich without permission, and upon being found guilty of improper conduct, were suspended. They seemed genuinely remorseful when the Captain told them how serious the offense was; but a few days later the young men left again, without the Captain's consent or knowledge. Some three weeks later the commandant learned that they were in New York; he declared to their older brother and guardian that he did not know why they left and assured him that they were not unduly restrained at the academy.[58]

In collegiate and professional schools academic matters were of greater concern than discipline. Some students had difficulty,

56. Norwood, *Medical Education in the United States*, 282.

57. *De Bow's Review*, XXIX (September, 1860), 396. For an earlier discussion of southerners "spurning" their own medical school see the *Southern Literary Messenger*, VIII (October, 1842), 643–44. There are numerous references, in both contemporary writings and secondary literature to southerners in northern medical schools. See, for example, John Q. Anderson, "Dr. James Green Carson, Ante-Bellum Planter of Mississippi and Louisiana," *Journal of Mississippi History*, XVIII (October, 1956), 243–67; Amey Robinson Childs, *Planters and Businessmen: The Guignard Family of South Carolina, 1795–1830* (Columbia: University of South Carolina Press, 1957); and Anne Firor Scott, *The Southern Lady: From Pedestal to Politics, 1830–1930* (Chicago: University of Chicago Press, 1970), 26. At Harvard, in 1846, even a law student from Charleston was attending the lectures on anatomy and physiology which he found "interesting and instructive." John Siegling, Jr., to his father, April 8, 1846, in John Siegling Papers, Duke University, Durham.

58. Alden Partridge to John Ball, January 8, 26, 1824, in John Ball, Sr., and John Ball, Jr., Papers, Duke University, Durham. Strict discipline at West Point caused trouble for some southerners as it did for northerners. A young South Carolinian wrote his cousin that he had been dismissed in 1835 for two offenses: "One for having used a dagger too freely in a *personal* contest; and the other for having made an *unprovoked* attempt to

in part, perhaps, because the studies required the kind of self-discipline to which many young southerners were not accustomed, but also because the course requirements tended to be more exacting than anything they had previously experienced. One student complained bitterly of the difficult course of study at the University of Pennsylvania Medical School. "It is enough to kill a horse almost to get eight hours study every day upon hard benches," he reported. "I feel very much like resting at night but there is no rest for the wicked—or righteous here, all fare alike. I have no time to think about the girls scarcely if I even felt disposed. You know that never was my disposition. It is one anatomic-surgico-physicochemical Sing Song from morning to night; if Job himself was here his patience would be wearied."[59]

A Louisiana planter had some real doubts about how much his son had really learned at Wesleyan. "I do not think he has much knowledge of engineering, he barely passed his mathematical examination." But the father was quite pleased that at the commencement exercises his son was considered the best speaker "and his oration was pronounced to be the best written."[60] The planter's son was not alone in the difficulty he was having with mathematics. When Hugh Blair Grigsby of Virginia was at Yale in 1824 his constant complaint was about the study of mathematics, and he tended to place the blame on the college and its professors. "I must say," he wrote his parents, "that the faculty at Yale are a diminutive and low-minded set" who seemed more interested in a student's performance in mathematics than anything else. "To get an honor at Yale, one must be a dull plodding mathematician, as torpid and lifeless as our inanimate Presi-

---

shoot a man, who had let fall some unguarded words, hostile to my feelings." John Lidell to John G. Guignard, February 25, 1835, in Childs, *Planters and Businessmen*, 67.

59. Neil McNair to Annabella McNair, November 15, 1838, in Annabella McNair Papers, Duke University, Durham.

60. A. F. Rightor to Andrew McCollam, August 9, 1851, in Andrew McCollam Papers.

dent." Near the end of the academic year, Grigsby leveled a parting shot at the institution: "The best passport to Yale College is a New England appearance and a knowledge of mathematicks."[61]

A young Charlestonian, studying at Harvard in 1831, insisted that the method of teaching mathematics there had dulled his enthusiasm for the subject. In an imaginary letter to his professor, which he recorded in his diary, Jacob Rhett Motte said, "You have been the cause of more agony to me, and loss, than any man of the faculty. To you may be ascribed my late aversion to mathematics, my favorite study. . . . Oh that I had but received a commission to enter West Point. . . . There everything would coincide with my taste: military and mathematical studies could have been indulged in to the extent of my almost unlimited inclination for those pursuits."[62] Grigsby graduated, as did the others who complained. Perhaps their apprehension merely reflected their determination to overcome the obstacles that they felt were their unhappy fate.

The students were not unlike their traveling parents and other southerners who were determined to get as much as possible out of their northern sojourn. They would learn as much as their time and abilities permitted; but even as they learned and even as they benefited from the intellectual experiences in the northern institutions, they did not overlook the nonacademic features of life in the North. "My studies do not employ the whole of my

61. These letters to Grigsby's parents are quoted in Fitzgerald Flourney, "Hugh Blair Grigsby at Yale," *Virginia Magazine of History and Biography*, XXII (April, 1954), 166–90. Arthur Morson of Fredericksburg, Virginia, also at Yale, informed his father that during the vacation period he would study Euclid, "as that will make my time much easier next year in college." Arthur A. Morson to Alexander Morson, September 8, 1819, in Morson Papers.

62. Arthur H. Cole (ed.), *Charleston Goes to Harvard: The Diary of a Harvard Student of 1831* (Cambridge: Harvard University Press, 1940), 63–64. Ralph Waldo Emerson was most critical of southern students at Harvard. In 1837, some years after his own graduation, he said, "The young Southerner comes here a spoiled child, with graceful manners, excellent self-command, very good to be spoiled here, but good for nothing else,—a mere parader." E. W. Emerson and W. E. Forbes (eds.), *The Journals of Ralph W. Emerson* (10 vols.; Boston: Houghton, Mifflin Company, 1910), IV, 312.

time," one Virginian wrote his father; "and I have some leisure for reading and exercise." He then shared with his father his plans for study and for the May vacation. In the following fall, when he was admitted to the sophomore class after an examination of about "five hours and a half," the young man was off for another holiday in New London and points south.[63] A young Princeton student from Augusta, Georgia, assured his father that he was enjoying the quiet of the village, which was conducive to study. He was not implying that he did nothing else. "Absolute seclusion," he said, "would be rather irksome, and in spite of all the pleasures to be derived from a contemplation of the beauties of nature, I think our Sicilian and Arcadian swains, unless they occasionally grazed with their sheep, must have been sadly at a loss for methods of killing time." Doubtless he found other ways and methods of "killing time."[64] A young Virginian's experience as a medical student in Philadelphia must have been most rewarding, for upon graduation he wrote, "The only portion of life upon which I can look with unqualified satisfaction is that which has been passed here."[65]

Many students spent their holidays, between academic terms, traveling in the vicinity of their northern colleges—alone, or in the company of parents or friends. In 1843 Andrew J. Polk of Raleigh, North Carolina, left Princeton to spend the Christmas holidays with friends in Philadelphia. Christmas Eve and Christmas Day on Chestnut Street were memorable experiences, especially the large "egg Nogg parties gratis" that every public house dispensed. In addition, he had "a superabundance" at his hotel.[66] Many students went to Saratoga, Newport, or New

63. Arthur A. Morson to Alexander Morson, February 23, and September 8, 1819, in Morson Papers.

64. W. C. Cumming to Thomas Cumming, April 19, 1805, in Alfred Cumming Letters, Duke University, Durham.

65. Solomon Mordecai to Sam Mordecai, April 9, 1822, in Jacob Mordecai Papers, Duke University, Durham.

66. Andrew J. Polk to Sarah Polk, January 12, 1844, in Polk-Yeatman Collection, University of North Carolina, Chapel Hill.

York for their spring or summer holidays.[67] Jacob Motte was content to spend his holidays from Harvard at New London, "that delightful place, famed for pretty girls and fine fishing lines."[68]

One student on holiday was pleasantly surprised to discover that he could enjoy himself about as much in the North as he could in his southern homeland. Everywhere he found the people warm and friendly. "There is no land," he reported, "where the stranger is more welcomed, or where the hand of friendship is more freely extended." At the end of the college term, he and his friends, "believing that the mountain air and rural sports would have a beneficial influence over their health concluded to pass a short time in some neighboring village; and after consultation, settled upon L____, in distance, only a short day's ride from the university and beautifully situated near Long Island Sound." Much to his surprise, he and his friends not only enjoyed the hospitality of the "pillars" of the village, but had the congenial company of many of the fair maidens as well.[69]

Even if some young southern students had the most pleasant association with their northern hosts both in the colleges and in the communities, an increasing number of their elders became apprehensive about those educational sojourns in the North. To be sure, they valued some of the education that the North had to offer, especially the skills in such professional fields as medicine and law.[70] But some began to question the value of a northern

67. See, for example, a Yale student's account of his summer excursions to Saratoga Springs, Boston, and Newport in J. A. Maxwell to Adam L. Alexander, September 6, 1822, in Adam L. Alexander Papers, Duke University, Durham.

68. Cole (ed.), *Charleston Goes to Harvard*, 18.

69. A Southron, "Vacation Scribblings; Or, Letters from a College Down East," *Southern Literary Messenger*, IX (July, 1843), 437–41. See, also, the Nashville *Republican Banner*, March 6, 9, April 6, 10, 1846, for letters from a southerner at Harvard regarding his vacations in New England as well as accounts of life at Harvard.

70. When he addressed the New England Society of Charleston in 1854, Dr. S. H. Dickson was quite enthusiastic about his Yale education. "And although I did not, perhaps, profit as much as I ought, by the strict lessons of precision and morality which I received in my Connecticut Alma Mater, yet it is impossible that a youth, brought up 'at the feet of Gamaliel,' under the eye of the venerable Timothy Dwight, should not have

exposure and wondered if the risk of moral and psychological contamination was really worth it. Thomas Jefferson was among the first to sense the dangers of a northern education for southern youth. During the Missouri controversy he was appalled to learn that almost half the student body at Princeton was from the South. He feared that southerners at Princeton and other northern institutions would imbibe "the lessons of Anti-Missourianism" and would return home "deeply impressed with the sacred principles of our holy alliance of Restrictionists."[71]

A generation later another Virginian, R. H. Garnett, would invoke the views of Jefferson to support his contention that too many southerners were studying in the North. The strongest generation of southerners—Jefferson, Randolph, Mason, etc.—was educated in the South, he argued.

> The men of the next generation were greatly inferior to their fathers in learning, and the few who received education at Northern colleges, brought back their second-hand history and shallow philosophy. They joined the place-hunting politicians in an outcry against Southern indolence, and its fancied cause, Southern slavery; they pointed us to Northern opulence and the growth of Northern cities, not as what they really are, the fruit of tribute that has dwarfed our own cities, but as examples of their superior enterprise and industry until at last we began to believe, what was so often dinned into our ears, that slavery was the moral, social and political evil they pretended. Mr. Jefferson saw this danger, and designed the University [of Virginia] to avert it.[72]

Garnett was so carried away with his argument that he seems to have overlooked the fact that in that "next generation" such men as Calhoun, Longstreet, Yancey, and Judah P. Benjamin, scarcely "inferior to their fathers in learning," were educated in the North.

---

been in some degree moulded and impressed by the circumstances in which his ductile adolescence was passed." S. H. Dickson, *Address Delivered before the New England Society of Charleston, S.C.* (Charleston: J. Russell, 1855), 184.

71. For an exposition of Jefferson's views, see Nathaniel F. Cabell (ed.), *Early History of the University of Virginia as Contained in the Letters of Thomas Jefferson and Joseph C. Cabell* (Richmond: J. W. Randolph, 1856), 178, 201, 202.

72. R. H. Garnett, "Education in Virginia," *De Bow's Review*, X (April, 1851), 476.

A fairly strong argument against educating young southerners in the North was that it drained the South of resources that southern educational institutions sorely needed. In 1848 the editor of the *Southern Literary Messenger*, in praising the medical department of Hampden-Sydney College in Richmond, decried the fact that many young Virginians preferred a northern medical education. This resulted, the editor lamented, in the withdrawal of an "enormous sum . . . from the economical interests of our own State." It was all the more astonishing when one considered "the facilities afforded by the excellent school of our own University, the school at Winchester, and the Metropolitan school, with all its clinical and anatomical advantages."[73] In 1856 a resident of Norfolk, Virginia, estimated that between 1810 and 1855 the "startling amount of $13,988,124 had been sent out of Virginia to the North for medical education alone." It was the same in everything, he concluded. "We give our support to northern schools, and *northern papers*, and northern merchants, and mechanics, and manufacturers, because they are a little more celebrated, or because they are less modest than we, in trumpeting their own praise. . . . We believe that as thorough a medical education can be received in Richmond as in any northern school and much more *practical* in relation to the prevalent diseases of the South."[74] Arguments like his simply did not convince young would-be physicians or their parents.

A much more forceful argument against southerners studying in the North, especially as undergraduates, was the possible sinister influence that a northern education would have upon

73. *Southern Literary Messenger*, XIV (August, 1848), 519. When the editor wrote this, Winchester Medical College was less than one year old, hardly in a position to compete with Jefferson Medical College in Philadelphia. In 1842 the editor estimated that Virginians were annually spending more than $76,800 on medical education in the North. *Ibid.*, VIII (October, 1842), 643.

74. "Educational Reform at the South," *De Bow's Review*, XX (January, 1856), 75–76. The article had originally appeared in a Norfolk newspaper. For a discussion of the economic aspects of southern patronage in the North, including education, see Chapter III.

their character and point of view, especially with regard to slavery. To be sure, there were, in the early 1830s a few southern students, not more than five, in that hotbed of radical abolitionism, the Lane Theological Seminary. One of them was William T. Allan of Alabama, a slaveholder's son. After struggling with his conscience, "his noble soul broke loose from his shackles" and he became president of the local antislavery society in Cincinnati.[75] From time to time there were a few southerners at Oberlin College: two in 1836, one in 1840, and one in 1860.[76] These were the two institutions in the North where sentiment against slavery was quite strong. Obviously, their influence on southern students was minimal.

Interestingly enough, there is the possibility that some southerners sent their sons north to school in order to prevent their early involvement in the more sordid aspects of slavery. Frederick Law Olmsted said that he learned that the sexual crossing of the color line and all the ill-feeling that it created, especially among white women, was an important reason for sending young men to school in the North. "A large planter told me, as a reason for sending his boys north to be educated, that there was no possibility of their being brought up in decency at home." All white men had black concubines, he said; and as a result, "there is not an old plantation in which the grandchildren of the owner are not whipped in the field by his overseer." On another occasion, Olmsted said, "In spite of the constant denunciations by the Southern newspapers, of those who continued to patronize northern educational institutions, I never conversed with a cultivated Southerner on the effects of slavery, that he did not express a wish or intention to have his own children educated where

75. Theodore Weld to Lewis Tappan, March 18, 1834, in Gilbert Barnes and Dwight L. Dumond (eds.), *Letters of Theodore Dwight Weld, Angelina Grimké Weld, and Sarah Grimké 1822–1844* (2 vols.; New York: Appleton Century Company, 1934), II, 132.
76. Robert Samuel Fletcher, *A History of Oberlin College* (2 vols.; Oberlin: Oberlin College, 1943), I, 508–10.

they should be free from demoralizing association with slaves."[77] It was a matter which southerners did not freely discuss, but it is entirely possible that not a few of them were influenced by the considerations to which Olmsted referred.

In the campaign to persuade southerners to educate their youth at home, no one was more active than James De Bow. In the final decade before the Civil War the pages of his *Review* bristled with regular admonitions to its readers about the dangers of a northern education. The North, De Bow argued, was committed to having its own way, even it if meant the annihilation of the South or the violent disruption of the Union. Its evil designs could be seen in the way the press, the churches, political parties, and even the schools and colleges participated in the campaign against southern rights.

> And it is just precisely into the hot-bed of political heresy and "higher law" that we are hurrying our children, the moment they assume the toga virilis, if not much earlier, to be trained to the duties of manhood, the rights of republicanism, and the defences of their firesides, their altars, and their homes. There they go, crowding Dartmouth and Harvard, and Brown and Yale, and Amherst and Middlebury, and Hamilton,—the sons of the men who have raised throughout all the South a storm they cannot still, and carried into Africa a war to be ended God only knows when.
>
> This is Southern consistency, and it is thus that the North wisely laughs at our silly boastings which end with the breath that utters them. They make the songs, and may well be indifferent if *we* have a part of the laws. Granted that our institutions of learning are inferior, in endowment and celebrity, and for argument, even inferior in scholastic attainments and merit, which last, if true, would make the humiliation of the South still greater, better would it be for us that our sons remained in honest ignorance and at the plough-handle than that their plastic minds be imbued with doctrines subversive to their country's peace and honor, and at war with the very fundamental principles upon which the whole superstructure of the society they find at home is based.[78]

77. Frederick Law Olmsted, *The Cotton Kingdom*, edited with an introduction by Arthur M. Schlesinger (New York: Alfred A. Knopf, 1953), 240, 475.

78. *De Bow's Review*, X (March, 1851), 362. For a review of the campaign for southern education, see Ezell, "A Southern Education for Southrons," 303–27.

A few years later, while praising a new work on the history of the University of Virginia, which clearly showed that institution's high standing, De Bow said, "It is time to call home our youth from north of Mason and Dixon's line. Subject them no more to the poison of Yale and Amherst, and even Harvard."[79]

De Bow was not alone in the campaign to stop southerners from studying in the North. Indeed, there were many prominent southern leaders and organizations that stood with him. John Perkins of Louisiana, a graduate of Yale who had studied law at Harvard, said in 1855 that no southerner could any longer study at northern schools and escape the pernicious influences of abolitionism. In advocating a southern education for southern youth, Perkins associated himself with the views of another distinguished southerner who had been educated in the North. "It was the advice of Mr. Calhoun, himself a graduate of Yale and therefore speaking from experience, that boys intending to reside at the South, should be educated at the South."[80]

If such was possible, C. K. Marshall of Vicksburg, Mississippi, was even more vigorous than De Bow in advocating a southern education for southern youth. Speaking before the Southern Convention in New Orleans in 1855, Marshall pleaded with southerners to support southern colleges and universities:

> We are in the habit of sending our sons and daughters to the north, far from their homes and home influences, there to be exposed to those which we believe dangerous to our interests, and damning to our peace. . . . It was not possible for southerners to be safely educated at the north. They cannot come back with proper feelings towards their families and their people. Our sons and daughters return to us from their teachings and influences against the institution of slavery with erroneous religious opinions on the subject, and with the idea that it is a sin to hold slaves.[81]

Two years later Marshall, unable to be present at the Southern

79. *De Bow's Review*, XXI (October, 1856), 440–41.
80. John Perkins, Jr., "Southern Education for Southern Youth," *De Bow's Review*, XIX (October, 1855), 464–65.
81. C. K. Marshall, "Home Education at the South," *De Bow's Review*, XVIII

Convention in Savannah, sent a letter calling for the entire education of southern children at home, with suitable teaching materials. This, he said, was the only true protection for the educational interests of the South, "in thus guarding the threshold we may preserve the citadel. Our citizens have, for years together, lavished their wealth by the unknown thousands upon institutions and faculties who esteem it a condescension to teach Southern pupils, and spurn their parents and guardians as graceless barbarians."[82]

As southerners met in convention during the final decade before the Civil War to assert their rights as southerners and to promote southern commercial and industrial growth, they did not neglect education. At the Charleston convention in 1854, the members adopted a resolution warning parents and guardians against sending their children out of the South for their education. If they persisted, their action was "fraught with peril to our sacred interests, perpetuating our dependence on those who do not understand and cannot appreciate our necessities and responsibilities, and at the same time fixing a lasting reproach upon our own institutions, teachers, and people."[83] In the same year a group of Richmond citizens noted that some of the most distinguished opponents of the Kansas-Nebraska bill were northern professors. Surely, such persons were the avowed enemies of the South; yet, they were teaching young southerners. Consequently, the assemblage passed a resolution calling on the people of Virginia and the entire South "to encourage and patronize Southern schools, colleges, or institutions."[84]

In 1851, a committee appointed to call a convention to meet at Savannah emphasized the importance of considering southern education at the forthcoming meeting. After praising southern education and the flourishing state of institutions in most of the

(March, 1855), 430–31. The address was printed in full in the Review for May, 1855.
   82. Ibid., XXII (March, 1857), 312.
   83. Ibid., XVI (June, 1854), 639.
   84. Ibid., XVI (May, 1854), 551.

southern states, the committee asked, "Must the youth of the South be longer doomed to exile in uncongenial climes, where the most sacred associations of their homes are denounced as those of the savage and the barbarian, the heritage of guilt and crime, and where grave and Reverend professors and Clergymen leave the pulpit and the desk to sign and circulate incendiary political addresses, substituting rifles for Euclid and the Bible and finding in Kansas, fields more classic and consecrated than were ever before furnished to them by Attica or Palestine?"[85]

When the convention met in Savannah in 1856 it dutifully urged parents to send their children to southern schools and even dutifully used the precise language of the 1854 Charleston convention in pointing out that attendance at northern institutions would be "fraught with peril to our sacred interests."[86] The convention went beyond its imitation of the Charleston body and appointed a committee to prepare textbooks for southern use, hoping thereby to emphasize the striking difference between education in the North and in the South. The committee could hardly have been more distinguished, composed as it was of Albert T. Bledsoe and William H. McGuffey of the University of Virginia, David L. Swain of the University of North Carolina, Augustus B. Longstreet of the University of Mississippi, Stephen Elliot of Georgia, and Charles E. A. Gayarré of Louisiana.[87] If southerners remained at home and used southern textbooks in schools and colleges, William H. Stiles believed that the resulting independence in education would prove to be not only more important than the financial and commercial independence of the South, but an essential prerequisite to it. Speaking at the Cherokee Baptist College in 1858, Stiles warned his listeners that the time was fast approaching, "nay, is already at hand," when the South would need the aid of all her sons. "Southern minds, educated and disciplined in the South, would do much to

85. *Ibid.*, XXI (November, 1856), 552.
86. *Ibid.*, XXII (January, 1857), 100.
87. *Ibid.*, 100.

vindicate her peculiar institutions not only before our Federal councils, but in the judgment of the world."[88]

Southern spokesmen like Stiles, Perkins, Marshall, and De Bow hoped against hope that southerners would heed their advice and stop sending their sons and daughters to northern educational institutions. As early as 1852 the editor of the *Southern Quarterly Review* thought that he could discern a happy reversal of the trend. Down to a comparatively recent period, he said, "the alma mater for the Southern youth was still sought in New England, and the mental nurture of our young was thus derived from a region which necessarily mingled a large infusion of bitter, if not poison, with the food which it bestowed. But the progress of natural events, which might be, and indeed was, predicted, necessarily wrought a rescue for us from this pernicious habit, and led, or is leading our people to better sources of education, in a more thorough independence of their foreign and frequently hostile teachers."[89]

This was more wishful thinking than accurate reporting. There had been no significant decline in the enrollment of southern students in northern schools by 1852.[90] The persistence of southern students in the North dismayed De Bow, who, after giving the figures for 1856, promised to "obtain the Catalogues and publish the lists of Southern students at Northern colleges."[91] He did not do so; and one suspects that the reason was that the figures were too depressing, from De Bow's point of view. Southerners watched for any sign that suggested the defection of their students from northern schools and colleges. At Beechwood, Edmund Ruffin's Virginia refuge to which he had returned after witnessing the execution of John Brown, Ruffin's Christmas in 1859 was made more joyful by the news that "267 of

88. William H. Stiles, *Southern Education for Southern Youth* (Savannah: n.p., 1858), 4–5, 13, 25.

89. *Southern Quarterly Review*, XXII (July, 1852), 236.

90. See, for example, the statistics given in Ezell, "Southern Education for Southrons," 310.

91. *De Bow's Review*, XXI (December, 1856), 660.

the southern medical students at the two colleges in Philadelphia, have, by agreement left those institutions, though they had paid their fees, and came on to the Medical College of Richmond."[92] He could have added that the young men were not required to pay any tuition or fees in Richmond.[93]

In 1860 De Bow rejoiced that "The exodus of Southern students recently from Colleges of the North is a matter of public congratulation. There has been no reason for many years why Southern students should betake themselves to such inhospitable climes, seeing that our own institutions of learning are not surpassed by any on the continent."[94] Apparently it took little to cause De Bow to rejoice. The number of students at Princeton had dropped from 107 to 98 between 1840 and 1860 while the number at Harvard had actually increased in all departments from 37 to 59 for the same period. Indeed, there were still 222 southerners in a student body of 528 at the University of Pennsylvania Medical School in 1860—after the withdrawal of those who entered the Medical College of Richmond.[95]

If northern educational institutions were centers of abolitionism and other activities that were inimical to the interests of the South, they did not seem to affect southern students in their esteem for southern institutions and the southern way of life. Even when the slavery question was discussed on northern campuses, it did not mean that abolitionism necessarily carried the day. Abolitionism was more in the minds of De Bow, Marshall, and Stiles than in the educational and other programs at Yale, Harvard, and Princeton. Yankee educators were much too shrewd to offend their affluent southern patrons. And not a few of them, such as Agassiz at Harvard and Silliman at Yale, had

92. William Kauffman Scarborough (ed.), *The Diary of Edmund Ruffin* (3 vols. projected; Baton Rouge: Louisiana State University Press, 1972), I, 384.
93. Norwood, *Medical Education in the United States*, 282. Norwood, p. 274, says that 140 students, not 267 as Ruffin claimed, migrated from northern to southern medical colleges after John Brown's raid.
94. *De Bow's Review*, XXVIII (February, 1860, 243.
95. Ezell, "Southern Education for Southrons," 310.

genuinely warm feelings toward southerners and their way of life. In any case, Calhoun, Longstreet, Toombs, Yancey, Perkins, and other southerners educated in the North could hardly have been more loyal to the South had they been educated at home. They went north for what they believed was a superior education, and if, anywhere along the line, someone served them a dose of abolitionism, it is quite obvious that they rejected it.

This is what De Bow could not see. Neither he nor his colleagues seemed to understand the remarkable hold that northern educational institutions—like cities, watering places, industry, and commerce—had on the people of the South. Nothing short of an all-out war could keep them at home. Only in the midst of such a tragedy could they come to appreciate fully the southern institutions and way of life to which they had paid only lip-service for more than a generation.

III

A Special
Economic
Relationship

When Captain Basil Hall, the British traveler, visited the United States in 1827, he was intrigued by the fact that Boston annually shipped no less than three thousand tons of ice to the South. It was a fact, he said, "which affords a curious illustration of the power of commerce to equalise and bring together, as it were, the most distant climates."[1] In the same decade William Crafts, a Charleston resident, wrote, "The periodical emigration to the North makes rapid progress; and the idle, the gay, and the luxurious fly before our scorching sunbeams, in quest of cool and fashionable leisure."[2] In their own respective ways, Hall and Crafts were commenting not only on the climatic differences between the two sections but also on the manner in which the economy of one section complemented that of the other.

Southern travelers in the North were important factors in an intersectional relationship that, under favorable circumstances, could flourish. What southerners saw and experienced in the North and how they reacted to it had an important effect on the development of a complementary economy. If they became convinced that there was more to northern travel than sightseeing for themselves and education for their offspring, it would be pos-

1. Captain Basil Hall, *Travels in North America in the Years 1827–1828* (Edinburgh: Robert Cadell, 1830), 128–29. The shipment of ice from Boston grew from 40,125 tons in 1848 to 110,000 tons in 1854. Edward Ingle, *Southern Sidelights* (New York: T. Y. Crowell, 1896), 127.
2. Lawrence F. Brewster, *Summer Migrations and Resorts of South Carolina Low-Country Planters* (Durham: Duke University Press, 1947), 117.

sible for them to cultivate a relationship that would be economically beneficial to both sections. J. C. Myers hoped that his fellow Virginia planters would take lessons from the great farmers of western New York "and return using their influence and exertions in sustaining and carrying forward the great agricultural improvements" in the Old Dominion.[3] William Gregg hoped that South Carolinians would emulate New Englanders in the construction of cotton mills, if for no other reason than to contribute to the stability of a region "in which the cream of a virgin soil is hardly exhausted before the owner is ready to abandon it, in search of a country affording new and better lands."[4] Even more important, perhaps, were the unmistakable signs of wealth and prosperity that they saw in the North. The passion for gain or the "pursuit of temporal advantages" was a quality in northerners that their southern visitors greatly admired, for it would lead to the accumulation of wealth that southerners could use for the advancement of their own section. For opulence, observed a southern editor, "where people are intelligent, is the nurse of Taste, and draws after it in its train every species of refinement and mental cultivation."[5] It was, indeed, something worth acquiring, most southerners thought.

In the early antebellum years there was a clear disposition on the part of southerners to cultivate every possible economic relationship that would not compromise the integrity of their section. They were willing to travel, to see, and to learn. They were willing to make purchases, to trade, and to enter into arrangements for future economic ties. But it appeared, at least to some, that each new relationship created new imbalances in favor of the North at a time when southerners very much wanted parity. Where were the northern travelers in the South? Why

3. J. C. Myers, *Sketches on a Tour through the Northern and Eastern States, the Canadas and Nova Scotia* (Harrisonburg, Va.: J. H. Wartman and Brothers, 1849), 158.
4. William Gregg, *Essays on Domestic Industry* (Charleston: Burgess and James, 1845), iv.
5. *Southern Literary Journal*, III (November, 1836), 235.

were there no northerners in Charleston and New Orleans, at the watering places of Virginia and Kentucky, in institutions such as William and Mary and the Collge of Charleston? Were northerners ever willing to do more than receive southern raw materials, process them, and sell them back to the South at a very high price? And regardless of whether the new imbalances were real or fancied, they had the effect of creating a sense of disadvantage as well as dissatisfaction on the part of southerners. Thus, any move to establish and maintain a truly balanced economic relationship would become increasingly difficult to sustain as the years went by.

Among the things that greatly impressed southerners were the energy and zeal with which northerners went about their numerous tasks and the industrial innovations that were transforming the economy of their section. Anne Royall never saw "more industry, or more general application to business of every description" than in New York City. "Turn which way you will, mechanics, carvers, carpenters, bricklayers, ship-carpenters, cartmen, all is one continual bustle, from morning till ten o'clock at night."[6] No one seemed afraid of work or unwilling to engage in it. In New England a Virginian was astounded to see men of position and means engaged in ordinary work. One, a justice of the peace and former member of the legislature, was harvesting his crop of hay himself. Two of the richest men in the village were busy with hoe and rake. The wife of a Rhode Island tavern keeper, whose establishment was worth $40,000, prepared the traveler's breakfast and waited upon him with a briskness such as he never saw equaled. "In the household economy of these thrifty and industrious people, it were endless to specify all the things worthy of our imitation," he concluded.[7]

The likelihood of southerners imitating northerners in the

6. Anne Royall, *Sketches of History, Life, and Manners in the United States* (New Haven: privately printed, 1826), 261.

7. "Letters from New England—2," *Southern Literary Messenger*, I (December, 1834), 167–68.

performance of menial tasks was remote, indeed. To do so would have been to reject an important principle on which Southern civilization was based, namely the idea that the use of slaves freed the masters to engage in more edifying cultural, social, and political pursuits. Even so, the absence of servants in considerable numbers pointed up an aspect of the diversity of the northern economy that was most impressive to the southern visitor. Everywhere servants were growing "more fastidious and intractable" because of the increased demand for labor and higher wages offered by the numerous manufacturing establishments. Consequently, the spirit and the habit which "oblige one to do so much for himself within doors, produce corresponding effects without. Useful labor is nowhere disdained in New England, by any class of society."[8]

As southerners came to admire the growth of industry in the North, they were painfully aware of the possible impact that a similar development in the South might have on the labor force there. And if this awareness restrained some of them from advocating an extensive program of industrialization for the South, it did not prevent a few from seeing in industry an effective vehicle for equalizing the economies of the two sections. It would be a calculated risk, of course, but for those who viewed staple-crop agriculture as a dead end that was certain to impose a permanent colonial status on the South, it was a risk worth taking.

The leader in the movement to increase the South's industries was William Gregg, the South Carolina silversmith and watchmaker. Gregg was doubtless influenced in his thinking by the Philadelphia economist, Henry C. Carey. A frequent visitor to Philadelphia, where his mother was born, Gregg probably attended some of the weekly gatherings at Carey's home, where, according to Gregg's biographer, there were animated discussions of economic theories and policies.[9] In any case, Gregg

8. *Ibid.*, 167.
9. Broadus Mitchell, *William Gregg, Factory Master of the Old South* (Chapel Hill: University of North Carolina Press, 1928), 19–20.

shared Carey's views regarding the importance of economic diversity, the linking of agriculture and manufactures, and a dislike of England's economic domination. Gregg became convinced, after visiting northern industries in 1844, that the future growth of the South depended on its becoming committed to a program of industrialization. Upon his return he published a series of articles in the Charleston *Mercury*; and in 1845 the articles were published in a volume called *Essays on Domestic Industry*. He was also a contributor to *De Bow's Review* and other periodicals.

Gregg remonstrated with southerners not merely for their deep and virtually exclusive commitment to agriculture, but also for not discovering and appreciating northern industrial and commercial genius, even when they traveled in the North. He knew so well that when most southerners visited the North they spent much of their time enjoying each other's company, frequenting the fashionable shops, and seeing the sights suggested in the guide books.

> He who confines his walks to the fine streets of New York, Philadelphia, and Boston, can have but a faint idea of what is going on in these worlds of trade. To get a knowledge of these things, one must go into the garrets and cellars—into the by-ways and alleys, where he will find thousands of nativeborn Americans as well as foreigners, from all parts of the globe, engaged in various branches of the mechanic arts. In articles of steel and iron, there is nothing which the world produces, that is not now being made in this country.[10]

In the North Gregg had seen shop after shop busily turning out products for the southern market. It was especially mortifying to him to find a small shop in Philadelphia busily engaged in producing large quantities of velocipedes for the southern market. Even in the mountainous districts of Massachusetts, Con-

---

10. Gregg, *Essays on Domestic Industry*, 55. As late as 1860 Edward Ingle decried the South's almost exclusive commitment to agriculture. "The fashion of the South has been to consider the production of cotton and sugar and rice the only rational pursuits of gentlemen, except the professions, and, like the haughty Greek and Roman, to class the trading and manufacturing spirit as essentially servile." Ingle, *Southern Sidelights*, 67.

necticut, Vermont, and New Hampshire, Gregg saw and admired
a remarkable number of people engaged in industrial pursuits,
especially the manufacture of cotton products. "Wherever it
finds its way, all other branches of industry follow" and give
increased value to property. Every waterfall was used, and the
forests yielded lumber for many purposes.

What impressed Gregg most, perhaps, was the manner in
which the northern manufacturers utilized steam power so ex-
tensively, at a time when southerners were not even using the
water power that was available in so many convenient places. In
the North almost everyone used steam, or seemed to. In Philadelphia, he said, "I visited a *last maker*; his shop was in the
fourth story of a house near Market between Fourth and Fifth
Streets; his lathes were also driven by a steam engine, the fur-
nace for which was an iron stove, with the boiler on top of it, the
smoke pipe entering the chimney. He had more power than he
needed, and rented the surplus to a carpenter, in the fourth story
of a house, on the opposite side of a narrow street, the power
being communicated by a belt." This was the kind of enterprise
that brought stability, prosperity, and economic independence
to the North. If, therefore, the South desired to "cure the evil" of
dependence on the North, it would need to resolve not to purchase northern articles of manufacture and to produce its own
axhandles, wagons, wheelbarrows, and the like.[11]

Gregg was convinced that the true secret of the South's
difficulties lay "in the want of energy on the part of our capitalists,
and ignorance and laziness on the part of those who *ought* to
labor."[12] The South, if its leaders would only lead, would have
advantages that the North had never enjoyed. When Massachusetts and Rhode Island sought to develop manufacturing,
Gregg recalled, they could get no assistance or cooperation from

11. Gregg, *Essays on Domestic Industry*, 54–55. Myers had a similar admiration for
the North's use of steam. "What a proof is steam of the high destiny that awaits our
species!" Myers, *Sketches on a Tour*, 75.
12. *De Bow's Review*, VIII (February, 1850), 134–35.

England, which forbade the export of machinery and obstructed the emigration of artisans. It would be quite different for an aspiring South. "We find no difficulty in obtaining the information, which money could not purchase for them, and which cost them years of toil. The New England people are anxious for us to go to spinning cotton, and they are ready and willing to give us all the requisite information." The South had available to it, therefore, not only the best machinery to be found anywhere in the world, but also the "best machinists and most skillful manufacturers to work and keep it in order."[13]

It was left for Hinton Rowan Helper to dramatize, through the use of statistics, the industrial and commercial superiority of the North that he hoped the South would attempt to overcome. In 1850, he reminded his readers, the value of manufactured goods in the North was $842,586,058 as compared to $165,413,027 in the slave states. And in other categories—such as exports and imports, bank capital, and post office operations—there were similar disparities.[14] "The North is the Mecca of our merchants," he declared, "and to it they must and do make two pilgrimages per annum—one in the spring and one in the fall. All our commercial, mechanical, manufactural, and literary supplies come from there."[15]

Thus, two southerners who knew the North well presented their case for change in the South. Gregg, deeply committed to a diversified economy, wanted the South to emulate the North in promoting the establishment of manufactures, wherever possible, and especially to provide labor opportunities for landless whites. Helper, deeply committed to abolishing slavery because of its adverse effect on nonslaveholding whites, insisted that

13. Gregg, *Essays on Domestic Industry*, 20. Helper tells about the visit to Richmond of Abbott Lawrence of Boston who was pleased to discover adequate water power for manufacturing and expressed a willingness to assist in the establishment of mills along the James River. In this case, however, the Richmond *Enquirer* criticized him for interfering in local affairs. Hinton Rowan Helper, *The Impending Crisis of the South: How to Meet It* (New York: A. B. Burdick, 1859), 106–108.

14. Helper, *The Impending Crisis*, 283–87.

15. *Ibid.*, 22.

once slavery was abolished the South could compete favorably with the North in achieving the objectives that Gregg had in mind. Change would not come quickly enough, either for Gregg or for Helper. Meanwhile, southerners would have to accommodate themselves to an economic relationship with the North in which they were clearly at a disadvantage; and as long as southern merchants and other businessmen set an example for others by spending much of their time and most of their money in the North, the South's position of economic dependence was likely to continue.

It was largely northern capital and initiative that provided the means and routes of transportation over which southern goods and people traveled. Steamers on the Atlantic and the western waters were the result of northern enterprise. And the same could be said of the development of canal and rail transportation. New York led all states, North and South, in creating a transportation revolution. "Her works are executed on a scale of imperial grandeur, the State almost literally executing what Xerxes the Great fancied in his threat to the mountain. We here see her for the purpose of obtaining artificial levels for her Railroads and Canals, hewing down hills and mountains and casting them headlong into sea and ravine, and spanning her noble rivers with bridges and aqueducts."[16] These massive transportation projects—in New York, Pennsylvania, and elsewhere in the North—greatly facilitated the flow of southern travelers and southern produce into the commercial centers of the North.

A principal figure in the special economic relationship between the North and South was the southern merchant, who could be relied upon to make one or two trips to the North each year. He has been described in a rather uncomplimentary manner by D. R. Hundley:

> When the Model Storekeeper goes abroad, (which is to say, when he visits the land of the Northerners,) despite his everlasting satin

16. Myers, *Sketches on a Tour*, 47–48.

waistcoat, he assumes to be a Southern gentleman, and so tries very hard to free himself of certain little telltale habits, which trades-people sometimes unfortunately contract in the shop. But not knowing precisely how the "thing" should be done, and possessing besides somewhat original and peculiar ideas on the subject, he endeavors to convey some notion of his importance to strangers by looking eminently grave and consequential, and picks his teeth along with those flashy *chevaliers d'industrie* who are wont to assemble in front of the St. Nicholas or the Girard, in the rather ludicrous convic-tion that such a dirty and ill-becoming practice makes him appear nonchalant and "up to snuff"—a vulgar phrase, this last, but sig-nificant of our meaning.[17]

William Gregg insisted that "almost every country merchant who visits Charleston has a through ticket for New York in his pocket." From all over the South the storekeepers swarmed to New York by the hundreds, and once there "they made a real visit of it, prowling from countinghouse to countinghouse of the jobbers to find the best bargains in what they wanted to fill their shelves for the coming year."[18] It has been argued that such semiannual pilgrimages to the northern meccas were neither desirable nor necessary. The "simple country merchant would be much more at home in some friendly Southern city than in the den of vice and iniquity—New York." And the merchant princes of New York, adroit, even cunning men who lived in matchless luxury would extort the most exorbitant prices from naive mer-chants from the interior, in order to maintain their sumptuous palaces on Fifth Avenue.[19] Nor were the semiannual treks a necessity, some argued; for the factors who bought their cotton and other produce could "also bring down anything needed and

17. Daniel R. Hundley, *Social Relations in Our Southern States* (New York: Henry B. Price, 1860), 109–10.
18. *De Bow's Review*, XXIX (December, 1860), 776. There were exceptions, of course. Merchants in Americus, Georgia, for example, dealt not only with New York houses but also with firms in Savannah and Macon. See Harold Woodman, *King Cotton and His Retainers* (Lexington: University of Kentucky Press, 1968), 79; and Robert Greenhalgh Albion, *The Rise of the New York Port, 1815–1860* (New York: Charles Scribner's Sons, 1939), 280.
19. Philip S. Foner, *Business and Slavery: The New York Merchants and the Irrepressible Conflict* (Chapel Hill: University of North Carolina Press, 1941), 11–12.

there were plenty of New Yorkers in Southern cities who carried a considerable stock."[20]

These arguments ignored several important considerations. In the first place, traveling North was a good excuse to get away from the South when the weather was hot and unhealthy. In doing so the travelers could visit places whose hotels, theaters, and other places of diversion made northern life attractive for most southerners who could afford the trip, including merchants. To be sure, not all southern merchants relished the long, arduous, and expensive trip to the eastern emporiums; and if they did not purchase, say, at least $5,000 worth of goods, it was hardly worth it.[21] Like it or not, they came to realize that the trip north was necessary if they were to become the efficient and successful businessmen they aspired to be. Even more important was the fact that the southern merchant could get better credit terms in the North than in the South. His own customers—planters, small farmers, and artisans—lived on credit during most of the year. Consequently, in order to accommodate them, the merchant, whether he was in Charleston or New Orleans or in some interior town or village, had to secure his merchandise on the most favorable credit terms. In the North he could secure six months of credit interest free and another six months of credit at low interest rates.[22] Not even the Charleston, Savannah, and New Orleans business houses could provide such favorable terms, since the southern banks were in no position to sustain them.

Finally, it was necessary that the merchant make the journey north in order to supervise directly all the stages of acquiring a

20. Albion, *Rise of the New York Port*, 118.
21. For a discussion of the merchants' own attitude toward their semiannual treks to the North, see Lewis E. Atherton, *The Southern Country Store, 1800–1860* (Baton Rouge: Louisiana State University Press, 1949), 137–38. For an account of Samuel Fowlkes, a Marion, Alabama, merchant who went to New York annually from 1847 to 1856 to purchase merchandise for his own store and supplies for his plantation and for his friends, see Weymouth T. Jordan, *Ante-Bellum Alabama, Town and Country* (Tallahassee: Confederate Publishing Co., 1957), 47.
22. Atherton, *The Southern Country Store*, 114–17. For a discussion of variations in the credit arrangement see Roy A. Foulke, *The Sinews of Commerce* (New York: Dun and Bradstreet, 1941), 153–54.

yearly supply of goods. He *knew* his customers, and he could select items that appealed to their tastes. He could then advertise in the local paper that he had recently received shipments from the northern markets, "which having been selected with particular care for the wants of the community and purchased for cash, enable us to offer them on very favorable terms."[23] Some of these goods may well have been purchased at auctions, where cash was needed, but where a wide variety of imported and American goods could be secured at unusually low prices. The Mobile merchants, Cullen and Smith, boasted in 1846 that they had acquired a rich assortment of Parisian goods, some of which had been purchased at New York auction houses at cheap prices. It mattered not that some competitors scorned goods bought at auction as "seconds" or "tendered goods." They were truly "bargain" items and, what was more, they bore the stamp of "New York" on them, thus appealing to those fastidious customers who did not consider themselves in fashion if their clothing or other personal items did not come from the empire city.[24]

Most advocates of the notion that southern merchants should make their purchases in the South argued that the better bargains were in the South. There was the feeling that southerners, especially backward merchants, would somehow lose in any transaction with a northern mercantile establishment. "New York is the last place to which an inexperienced, impractical merchant should venture to purchase a stock of goods," one of them said.[25] Even if they were not "taken" in the North, it was still uneconomical for them to trade there, De Bow asserted. On merchandise sold in New York at $123.50, some $18.16 "exclusive of expenses of traveling to the North," could be saved if it were purchased in Charleston, he contended.[26]

Such arguments simply did not prevent southern merchants

23. Atherton, *Southern Country Store*, 74.
24. *Ibid.*, 124. See also Foner, *Business and Slavery*, 12–13.
25. *De Bow's Review*, XXIX (December, 1860), 777.
26. *Ibid.*, IV (December, 1847), 498.

from venturing North, and New York soon became virtually synonymous with the North as far as trade was concerned. By the forties New England mills were sending their products to New York for the convenience of their southern customers. Gotham was the hub of trade between the North and the South as well as other parts of the country and, indeed, the world. Small wonder that Davy Crockett called New York "the London of America, the Big Prairie of the North, the Mississippi of Commerce."[27] Myers called it a "great theatre of commerce" where "we behold conspicuously the new era which has come upon us . . . in the greatest emporium of the western hemisphere."[28] The passion for gain, the chief impression that New York made upon one southern editor, "awakens in the dormant breast an indomitable spirit, which covers no difficulties or dangers, and which makes action—persevering action—a peculiar element in the character of our countrymen."[29]

If the southerner who did not make the northward trek was a consumer of northern goods, as he was very likely to be, he had the southern merchants to thank. Those energetic and enterprising persons never missed an opportunity to secure items in the North that would satisfy their southern patrons. In 1850 one Richmond house spent $100,000 for shoes from the North. In the same year the *Southern Planter* estimated that Virginia purchased $500,000 worth of northern brooms, apples, and hay.[30] When the Savannah packet *Louisa Matilda* was wrecked near Hatteras in 1827, she was laden with a cargo valued at between $350,000 and $400,000—goods purchased in the North by Georgia merchants.[31]

If southern merchants, through whom many southerners trav-

27. Davy Crockett, *An Account of Col. Crockett's Tour to the North and Down East, Written by Himself* (Philadelphia: Carey, Hart and Company, 1835), 44.
28. Myers, *Sketches on a Tour*, 426–27.
29. *Southern Literary Journal*, III (November, 1836), 134–35.
30. Quoted in Ingle, *Southern Sidelights*, 127.
31. Albion, *Rise of the New York Port*, 118.

eled north vicariously, could not resist making purchases in the North, it was too much to expect those private individuals, who made the trip on their own, to resist the temptation to purchase goods while on their tour. They believed, as did the merchants, that they could get better bargains during their northern sojourns. A Mobile resident told Olmsted that he found it cheaper to have all his furniture and clothing made for him in New York than to purchase such items in Mobile.[32] In 1843 even thirteen-year-old Paul Hamilton Hayne was impressed with New York's low prices. "You can buy a knife or anything of that kind for half the price you can in Charleston," he wrote his cousin.[33] One is not persuaded by the assertions, here and there, that southern shoppers were actually searching for bargains. They seemed as interested in quality or uniqueness as they were in low prices. When James Hammond had made some purchases in New York in 1840, he told his wife that he did not get any of the items from an auction house. "I might have got it cheaper, but they are *good articles* and cheap enough. I hope they will pleasure you."[34]

Some southern shoppers dealt largely through their factors, either in the North or at home. The transactions of the Allston family of South Carolina provide examples. When young Robert Allston entered West Point in 1817, Charles Kershaw, the well-known Charleston businessman and factor, assured the Allstons that he would see to it, through his friends in New York, that Robert "shall not want for anything while he is there." Consequently, he had one Mr. Cary in New York to advance Robert "one hundred and fifty dollars to purchase what is necessary for himself and the Furniture of his Room Bed etc. as he says his pay

32. Frederick Law Olmsted, *The Cotton Kingdom*, edited with an introduction by Arthur M. Schlesinger (New York: Alfred A. Knopf, 1953), 220.

33. Paul Hamilton Hayne to Susan Hayne, July 3, 1843, in Paul Hamilton Hayne Papers, Duke University, Durham.

34. James H. Hammond to Catherine Hammond, September 2, 1840, in James H. Hammond Papers, University of North Carolina, Chapel Hill.

will not commence until he receives his Warrant."[35] Later, when Robert Allston was the head of the family, he made numerous purchases on his frequent visits to New York. During one of his visits, the Charleston firm of Lewis and Robertson was delighted to hear from Allston after wondering if his long silence meant that he had dropped them and made other arrangements. "Your drafts shall meet due honor," the firm wrote him. "None have yet come in. Pray let us know what discount you pay. Exchange in New York here is at 1½ prem. You can judge whether you are best served by drawing, or our remitting, for either way is the same to us, as long as you are satisfied."[36]

The shopping lists of southerners were long and contained items ranging from horses to rifles to spiritual tests. Allston's factor, Alexander Robertson, asked him to do him the favor of purchasing a pair of horses for one of his customers.[37] A friend asked Allston to get him a pair of horses and a Colt's patented repeating rifle "with equipment, etc. complete."[38] James H. Hammond sent money to William Gilmore Simms and requested him to secure "spiritualistic tests and questions, which he was to ask four or five mediums, and he [Hammond] regarded the results as absolute proof." Hammond declared that "spiritualism is a great and glorious thing. . . . These phenomena demonstrate a future life for us. . . . We *now* know that we live after death."[39]

Most shopping lists contained less esoteric matters and usually dealt with quite practical things such as wearing apparel and household goods. Mrs. Clement Clay, in recounting her years in Washington society, observed that in the fifties "our home manu-

35. Charles Kershaw to Charlotte Ann Allston, December 19, 30, 1817, quoted in J. Harold Easterby, *The South Carolina Rice Plantation As Revealed in the Papers of Robert F. W. Allston* (Chicago: University of Chicago Press, 1945), 365–66.

36. Lewis and Robertson to R. F. W. Allston, October 20, 1838, *ibid.*, 408.

37. Alexander Robertson to R. F. W. Allston, November 14, 1838, *ibid.*, 410.

38. Joshua W. Ward to Robert F. W. Allston, September 28, 1838, *ibid.*, 83

39. Elizabeth Merritt, *James Henry Hammond*, 1807–1864 (Baltimore: Johns Hopkins Press, 1923), 111.

facturers contributed but little." She purchased most of her clothing as well as accessories in New York, and supplemented those purchases with the help of friends and relatives in Spain and Italy.[40]

Few southern women had the resources or the connections of the "Belle of the Fifties," Virginia Clay, wife of the Alabama senator. Those who did not were nevertheless as anxious as she was to dress in the latest fashions and to enjoy the admiration of the men and the envy of the women. Some of them who did not make the northern journey themselves entrusted to their husbands the all-important task of purchasing new dresses for them. Christopher Jenkins of Charleston took his assignment seriously; but in attempting to carry it out, his own tastes came into conflict with the fashions of the times, as he reported to his wife:

> The mantle I will purchase for you but as regards the frock I think you would not be pleased with the fashion here, it is true the pleats in front may do very well particularly for a mother who is often in the family way, but from the upper parts of the hips down they are made so scant that a ladys figure is shown more distinctly than decency warrants. In addition to that the upper part is so tight that the bosoms of the wearer is so much compressed as to destroy the bust giving them in that particular part the appearance of a girl twelve years old. This may do very well for the New York ladies almost all of whom are about the bosom as flat as a journey cake board, who stoop a great deal and have very small hips, but our southern ladies whose bosoms and hips are almost invariably of a good size and who so far from stooping are remarkably upright, I cannot think it will suit, for I certainly think a fine bust and good hips gives always to the possessor a dignified and majestic appearance without which a full grown lady is not very interesting.[41]

Most southerners seemed convinced that the only places to get

40. Ada Sterling (ed.), *A Belle of the Fifties: Memoirs of Mrs. Clay of Alabama* (New York: Doubleday, Page and Company, 1905), 90. See also, p. 22, her account of the purchase of a hat in the North while en route to Dr. Wesselhoeft's Hydropathic Institute in Brattleboro, Vermont.

41. Christopher C. Jenkins , September 25, 1823, in Mrs. Christopher Jenkins Papers, Duke University, Durham.

superior furnishings for the home were the great stores in the northern cities. Ann Wagner, whose son was a Charleston merchant, wrote him from Providence that she wanted to purchase a new carpet. She wished to know what the price was of the best Brussels carpeting in his stock "and weather I had better get it here or in Charleston. If you think I had better get it in New York I will thank you to measure how much it will take to cover the Room and how much Bordering. . . ." One wonders if she would even have raised the possibility of getting it in Charleston if she had not asked her son, earlier in the same letter, for "Eight Hundred Dollars more to get me a chaise and a few articles and to have my plate made up anew."[42] At the end of his New York shopping spree in 1840 James Hammond was quite pleased with himself for having purchased "all the furniture" and also for having obtained such furnishings as marble mantles, linens, draperies, and blankets and shipped the greater portion of them on the *Sutton*.[43]

Most of the items on display at the Crystal Palace Exposition were for sale, but there is little evidence that southerners made many purchases there. Perhaps they were too enthralled with "the wilderness of objects" that they saw and did not take the time to make purchases. One Virginian reported his own activities at the Exposition: "I went there yesterday at 10, worked with my Jerry from 11 to 4, then joined Leslie Ellen and stayed until nearly 9 P.M. without sitting down the whole time, except for a moment to buy an Austrian chair."[44] Perhaps the items were generally too expensive. A Mississippian wrote home, "Molly and Sis were most struck with the rich variety of articles of *Silver ware*, and I must confess that I was rather carried away with them

42. Ann Wagner to Effingham Wagner, August 15, 1818, in Cheves-Wagner Papers, University of North Carolina, Chapel Hill.

43. James H. Hammond to Catherine Hammond, September 2, 1840, in James H. Hammond Papers.

44. Alfred Mordecai to Samuel Mordecai, November 11, 1853, in Jacob Mordecai Papers, Duke University, Durham.

myself. But when I reflected upon the cost I steadied myself very soon."[45]

If they tended to make few purchases at the great Exposition, one can be certain that this conduct was not typical of southerners in the North. William Gregg considered the frenzied pace at which they made purchases in the North as nothing less than a spectacle, and a sad one at that. "You cannot step into a furniture store, carpet warehouse, or dry goods establishment, where fine silks and laces are sold, without meeting persons from our State, making lavish expenditures and purchasing thousands of articles of wearing apparel, which are not worn until they return home, where the same articles can be obtained in the stores of our own tradesmen, at cheaper rates than those at which they were purchased at the North." Gregg reported that one Boston tailor sold $50,000 worth of goods to Charlestonians the previous year and he expected the sales to reach $80,000 in the current year. If one added this to the huge sums that Charlestonians also spent for clothes in New York and Philadelphia, Gregg was certain that it would be sufficient to support three or four fashionable establishments in Charleston.[46]

A dozen years later Hinton Rowan Helper decried the penchant of southerners for northern goods. "We should not run to New-York, to Philadelphia, to Boston, to Cincinnati, or to any other Northern city, every time we want a shoe-string or a bedstead, a fish-hook or a handsaw, a tooth-pick or a cotton gin."[47] In his insistence that northern merchants were more principled than southern consumers, Helper claimed that the better class of merchants had "too much genuine respect for themselves to wish to have any dealings whatever with those who make merchandise of human beings."[48] This seemed un-

45. James T. Harrison to Regina Harrison, July 17, 1853, in James T. Harrison Papers, University of North Carolina, Chapel Hill.
46. Gregg, *Essays on Domestic Industry*, 10–11.
47. Helper, *The Impending Crisis*, 357.
48. *Ibid.*, 358.

likely. There were not many New York merchants who were as uncompromising in their opposition to slavery as Arthur and Lewis Tappan or, indeed, as Hinton R. Helper. The vast majority of them were pleased to receive southern money, regardless of how it was made.

Some northern merchants did become somewhat reluctant to do business with southerners, but the considerations were more practical than idealistic. Despite the liberal credit terms they obtained, some southern merchants were habitually in arrears with their northern creditors, and at times the latter had real difficulty in making collections. Merchants in New York, Boston, Philadelphia, and some southern cities regularly retained agents to collect outstanding debts. Hugh Davis, himself a prominent planter, was a collector in central Alabama for several firms.[49] Clement Clay, also of Alabama, made the rounds of business houses in Philadelphia and New York in 1850 offering his services to collect accounts that were in arrears. Two years later his brother, Hugh Lawson Clay, was advised by James Brown, of the banking firm of that name, that it was better first to learn with whom the Alabama merchants dealt. Brown would then introduce Clay to the houses with whom the Alabama merchants did business, and they would, perhaps, in turn retain the Clays as collectors.[50]

There was some decline in the number of southern merchants and shoppers in the North after the panic of 1857. The South had become overstocked with goods due to the "bargain prices" caused in part by the reduced buying power in the West and the large inventories in northern mercantile establishments. Some New Yorkers suggested that southerners stayed away because they could not pay their debts.[51] There is no evidence to support

49. Weymouth T. Jordan, *Hugh Davis and His Alabama Plantation*. (University, Alabama: University of Alabama Press, 1948), 14–15.
50. C. C. Clay Memorandum, July 22, 1850, and Hugh Lawson Clay to C. C. Clay, July 25, 1852, both in Clement Comer Clay Papers, Duke University, Durham. Some northern firms sent their own employees into the South to collect bills. See Atherton, *Southern Country Store*, 127.
51. Helper, *The Impending Crisis*, 358.

this claim. Not until the months preceding the election of 1860 did any considerable number of northern houses show any serious reservations about continuing to extend credit to southern merchants.

While it was always possible for southerners to purchase wearing apparel, household goods, and even horses in the southern market, many of them, for a variety of social and economic reasons, preferred to make such purchases in the North. There was one area, however, where competition between the northern and southern markets was virtually nonexistent. In printing and publishing, the clear preference for the North, growing out of its several advantages, was so great as to obscure any sound reasons why anyone should have favored having southerners perform these tasks. The printing presses in the South were not only few in number but most of them were unsophisticated in their operation; and they could scarcely handle any large or complex orders. The few publishers that did operate in the South were inadequately staffed and had little of the facilities for advertisement and distribution that would commend them either to authors or readers. Small wonder that a special relationship developed between northern printers and publishers and their southern customers and authors.[52]

One of the real ironies of the period is that James De Bow, who made a career of promoting southern commercial and industrial enterprise, had to print his celebrated *Review* in the North. For a while he tried two New Orleans printers, but they were unreliable, and he had to turn to a New York house where the third and perhaps all of the fourth volumes were stereotyped. As De Bow observed the amazing size and daily output of the New York houses he decided to purchase a large Adams press on which he could print his own *Review* and do job printing as well. Unfortunately, he had neither the technical skill nor the capital to carry out his plans. Beginning in November, 1848, he again shifted the

52. In 1857 Helper estimated that there were three hundred publishers in the North and only twenty-four in the South. *Ibid.*, 390.

printing of the *Review* to New York City where, except for one or two years, it was printed until the beginning of the Civil War. Understandably, he did not inform his readers of his reliance on northern printers, lest they might also be encouraged to patronize northern business houses.[53]

At least three-fourths of the advertisements in *De Bow's Review* were from northern firms despite De Bow's persistent and vigorous advocacy of southern business. In one issue, where he discussed New York at length, he sought to justify the extensive use of his *Review* by northern advertisers which, incidentally, he cultivated assiduously. He said that since southerners did trade outside their section, they should know which merchants in the free states "adhere to the compromises of the Constitution, and refuse to devote their time or their means to the unholy crusade which is waged there against our rights and institutions." He assured his readers that he would accept patronage only from such men.[54]

Even when southern printers had some equipment and facilities, they had difficulty competing with northern firms for southern business. Northern printers had both the experience and the volume of business that gave them a clear advantage over their southern competitors. Even some of the southern state governments placed their printing orders in the North, where they could get the best price. When John Millington and Benjamin L. C. Wailes completed their report on Mississippi's natural and

53. Ottis C. Skipper, *J. D. B. De Bow, Magazinist of the Old South* (Athens: University of Georgia Press, 1958), 24–25, 125. The opportunity to serve as assistant editor of *American Ephemeris and Nautical Almanac* led William Ferrel, Nashville teacher and meteorologist, to spend his summers in Cambridge, Massachusetts. When this proved unsatisfactory Ferrel gave up his Nashville school post and moved to Cambridge. F. Garvin Davenport, *Cultural Life in Nashville on the Eve of the Civil War* (Chapel Hill: University of North Carolina Press, 1941), 51–52.

54. Davenport, *Cultural Life in Nashville*, 127–28; *De Bow's Review*, XXI (August, 1856), 216. While the *Southern Literary Messenger* was printed in Richmond, it is clear that the editor's admiration for northern printing facilities suggested that he would be delighted to improve his own situation. After a visit to New York in November, 1847, he told his readers much about the remarkable presses and other machinery used by Harper and Brothers and other New York houses. *Southern Literary Messenger*, XIV (January, 1848), 57–58.

industrial resources, the state appropriated $2,500 to have it printed. Apparently there was no firm in Mississippi that could do the job for the amount available; and Wailes went North in search of a printer. He found the prices too high in New York City. Finally he was able to make a contract with Lippincott in Philadelphia, who took the job for $2,200.[55] There was, of course, the additional expense of remaining in the North to see the book through the press.[56]

The works of most of the major southern writers were published by northern houses, and this frequently entailed extended trips by the authors to negotiate with northern publishers and see their works through the press. Perhaps it was less because he had exhausted every opportunity in Richmond than because of one of his numerous estrangements from his foster father, John Allan, that Edgar Allan Poe went to Boston in 1827 to find a publisher. He chose Boston because of its reputation as a literary and publishing center; and he succeeded in arranging with an obscure young printer to bring out his first volume, *Tamerlane and Other Poems*.[57] This was for Poe the beginning of many years of personal negotiation with northern publishers. In 1829 he went to Philadelphia in an attempt to get Carey, Lea, and Carey to bring out his second volume, *Al Aaraaf*; and when Allan refused to put up even a small subvention as a guarantee against losses by the publisher, Poe had to be content with publication by Hatch and Dunning of Baltimore.[58] When he was dismissed from West Point in 1830, Poe proceeded immediately to New York City and arranged with Elam Bliss to publish *Poems by Edgar A. Poe*.[59]

55. Charles S. Sydnor, *A Gentleman of the Old Natchez Region: Benjamin L. C. Wailes* (Durham: Duke University Press, 1935), 196. In the same period Mississippi engaged a Boston firm to print its session laws and made an appropriation of $3,000 to pay one of its members to go there to read proof and see the work through the press. Helper, *The Impending Crisis*, 391.

56. Wailes made excellent use of his time while waiting on the proofs. See above.

57. Arthur Hobson Quinn, *Edgar Allan Poe: A Critical Biography* (New York: Appleton Century-Crofts, 1941), 118.

58. *Ibid.*, 145, 152.

59. The West Point cadets had subscribed to the publication of the volume, thus making its appearance possible. *Ibid.*, 174.

Later Poe would live in Philadelphia and New York for long periods of time and would be able to arrange with Harper and Brothers for the publication of *The Narrative of Arthur Gordon Pym* and with Lea and Blanchard for the publication of *Tales of the Grotesque and Arabesque.*[60]

Paul Hamilton Hayne, the Charleston poet, went to Boston in 1854 to see his first book through the press. He anticipated some difficulty because of the rumored absence of James Thomas Fields, one of the partners in Ticknor and Fields. He was greatly relieved to learn, while visiting in New York, that this was one of the few years when Fields was not in Europe for at least a portion of the year.[61] He spent two months in Boston seeing through the press the volume of poems that was published early in the following year.[62] He fretted a bit about his tedious task. "Were it not that I have so much to do, I should feel very solitary here," he wrote his wife. "I am glad you sent me the names of the new books received. Continue to do so; for although, just at present . . . I absolutely *cannot* write for the paper, yet I shall be able to do so before my return."[63]

William Alexander Caruthers, a Virginian by birth, spent several of his early adult years in the North. After graduating from the University of Pennsylvania Medical School in 1823 and after an eight-year sojourn in Lexington, Virginia, he moved to New York, where for some six years he pursued a dual career of writer and physician. Although the cholera epidemic of 1832 gave him more medical experience than he expected to gain, his writings brought him the reputation and wide acquaintanceship that he enjoyed immensely. It was about the same time, 1832, that he arranged with Harper and Brothers to bring out *The Kentuckian in New York*, an epistolary novel of man-

60. *Ibid.*, 263, 287–88.
61. Paul H. Hayne to Mary Michel Hayne, August 25, 1854, in Paul Hamilton Hayne Papers.
62. Paul H. Hayne, *Poems* (Boston: Ticknor and Fields, 1855).
63. Paul H. Hayne to Mary Michel Hayne, September 9, 1854, in Paul Hamilton Hayne Papers.

ners which was at once a guide book to New York and an exploitation of the intersectional theme. Two years later Harper brought out his *Cavaliers of Virginia*, an historical novel laid in the seventeenth century and centering around Bacon's rebellion. Although Caruthers moved to Savannah, Georgia, in 1837, he maintained his New York connections. Indeed, he was back in New York in November of that year to attend to some details in connection with his writings and to make purchases for his Savannah residence. His final novel, *The Knights of the Golden Horseshoe*, was rejected by Harper and Brothers, who, because of the panic of 1837, had drastically cut the list of works appearing in their "Library of Select Novels." After running serially in 1841 in the Savannah magazine, *Magnolia: Or Southern Monthly*, it was finally issued in 1845 by one Charles Yancey, in the village of Wetumpka, Alabama.[64]

It was fitting that the most prolific and most successful writer of the antebellum South, William Gilmore Simms, should also have the strongest ties in the North, where he was well known and widely read. Simms was as much at home in the literary and publishing circles of New York as he was in the world of southern plantations and politics.[65] His large circle of New York friends was cultivated not only by his prolific pen but also by his regular trips to New York to visit with them and to attend to business with his publishers. "I am here, according to my wont, of a summer," he wrote a friend in 1853.[66] He usually stopped with an old friend, James Lawson, on 12th Street, but he spent much time with William Cullen Bryant, editor of the New York *Evening Post*, and Evert and George Duyckinck of Scribners. Simms was at least as busy during his weeks in New York as he

64. The information on Caruthers is derived largely from Curtis Carroll Davis, *Chronicler of the Cavaliers: A Life of the Virginia Novelist, Dr. William A. Caruthers* (Richmond: Dietz Press, 1953).

65. William R. Taylor, *Cavalier and Yankee: The Old South and American National Character* (New York: George Braziller, 1961), 267–68.

66. William G. Simms to Alfred Billings Street, September 15, 1853, in Mary C. Simms Oliphant and T. C. Duncan Eaves (eds.), *The Letters of William Gilmore Simms* (5 vols.; Columbia: University of South Carolina Press, 1954), III, 249.

was in South Carolina, where he wrote, supervised the work on his plantation, and edited the *Southern Quarterly Review*. "I am very busy with three volumes in press; but hope to be at home by Setpember 28 or thereabouts," he wrote a business associate in August, 1853.[67]

Over the years Simms dealt with several New York publishers, sometimes simultaneously, at other times successively. Harper and Brothers had published six works by him between 1833 and 1837. In 1853 he agreed to purchase the copyrights from Harper for $1,500.[68] By that time Wiley and Putnam were bringing out some of Simms's work, for in 1850 the house published *Wigwam and Cabin*.[69] In 1853 Simms used the Putnam offices as his headquarters during his New York visit, wrote letters back home on Putnam stationery, and entered into an agreement to serve as a contributor to a new venture, *Putnam's Monthly Magazine*.[70] Meanwhile, on his visit to New York in 1851 Simms took with him the completed manuscript of his tragic drama, *Norman Maurice*. After discussing the play with an actor and making some corrections, Simms turned it over to Justus Redfield, the New York printer, who brought out the play as well as a complete collection of Simms's poetry in two volumes. Subsequently, both works were reissued by the Charleston printer John Russell.[71]

In going north to have their works published, southern writers were seeking the very best arrangements they could find,

67. William G. Simms to Thomas A. Burke, August 14, 1853, *ibid.*, 248.
68. William G. Simms to James H. Hammond, June 20, 1853, *ibid.*, 240.
69. William G. Simms to James Lawson, June 7, 1850, *ibid.*, 47. See also the statement of Simms's account with John Wiley, *ibid.*, 50–52.
70. *Ibid.*, 199 and 200n.
71. *Ibid.*, 140n and 141n. Among other southern writers who had arrangements with northern firms were Augustus B. Longstreet, whose *Georgia Scenes*, first published in Augusta, Georgia, in 1835, became nationally known after Harper and Brothers brought it out in 1840; Nathaniel Beverly Tucker, whom Simms doubtless assisted in getting his *George Balcombe* published by Harper and Brothers in 1836; John P. Kennedy, whose *Swallow Barn* Peter Cruse, his friend, persuaded Carey and Lea to publish in 1832; John Esten Cooke, who received a check from Harper and Brothers in 1852 for his first novel, *Leather Stocking and Silk*, published in 1854; and Joseph G. Baldwin, whose *Flush Times in Alabama and the Mississippi* was published in 1853 by D. Appleton.

just as the southern merchants were doing. Even if a Russell in Charleston or a Yancey in Wetumpka made a bid for their works, the writers accepted them only as a last resort.[72] For the prestige, as well as the bulk of the reading public, was in the North. The stimulation was there, moreover; for where else in the country could one find a Bryant or a Longfellow or a Duyckinck willing to offer friendly and constructive criticism? Where else but in Philadelphia, New York, and Boston could one place his writings before such a variety of prospective printers, publishers, and agents? If their almost exclusive concentration on northern publishers created a great imbalance in the literary market in favor of the North, then the balance was somewhat redressed by the alacrity with which northerners read many of the works of southern authors. Perhaps it was further redressed by the attention northerners gave to still other products from the South.

If southerners had any desire to redress the economic balance, they had a peculiar way of going about it. Gregg, De Bow, and other spokesmen could decry southerners' lavish expenditures in the North.[73] Conventions in many parts of the South could call on southerners to remain at home and invest in southern manufactures, shipping, and publishing houses.[74] But southerners simply did not heed such admonitions. What is more, those who were in the vanguard in suggesting such sectional policies were among the worst offenders against such policies.

72. Hinton Rowan Helper, with no chance whatever of having his *Impending Crisis of the South and How to Meet It* published in the South, also had real difficulty in finding a publisher in the North. The manuscript was turned down successively by Harper, Appleton, Scribners, "and other reliable publishers, even when he offered it for nothing. These firms had a creditable Southern business which they did not wish to jeopardize. . . . Disappointed, dissatisfied, and disgusted, he finally turned it over to A. B. Burdick, a New York Book agent, who agreed to publish it provided Helper guaranteed him against financial loss. This Helper agreed to do and the book was published in June, 1857." Hugh T. Lefler, *Hinton Rowan Helper, Advocate of a "White America"* (Charlottesville, Va.: Historical Publishing Company, 1935), 19.

73. See above, pp. 40–43.

74. See below, pp. 205–207.

Vardry McBee, a wealthy South Carolina planter and merchant, was among the most public-spirited citizens of his time. He was particularly interested in building the economy of the South to a point where it would be in a stronger position in its relations with the North. To that end, he attended the railroad convention in Columbia in 1847. From there he went North to learn more about the railroad problem. While there he "was induced" to subscribe $10,000 to the Seaboard and Roanoke Railroad and some $20,000 to the Charleston, Louisville, and Cincinnati Railroad.[75] It was a somewhat uninitiated southerner who believed that his considerable investment with northern promoters would bring immediate benefits to those who had discussed their problems at the Columbia convention.

The investments that southerners made in northern and western lands suggest that their interest was more in making a wise, if speculative, investment than in building the southern economy or in developing the areas where plantation slavery could prosper. Paul W. Gates has clearly illustrated the speculative bent of large numbers of affluent southerners. He points out that between 1833 and 1837 eleven southerners purchased more than 50,000 acres of land in the Springfield, Illinois, land district.[76] The Virginia firm of Easley and Willingham had acquired more than 350,000 acres of land in the Midwest by 1855.[77] Even Eli Shorter of Eufaula, Alabama, one of the most uncompromising of all southern fire-eaters, was a speculator in northern lands. An advocate of disunion in 1850, he declared in 1858 that if Kansas were not admitted under the Lecompton Constitution the sons of Alabama were well prepared to do battle to defend the rights of slavery and the South. Even so, he

75. De Bow's Review, XIII (September, 1852), 317–18.
76. Paul W. Gates, "Southern Investments in Northern Lands Before the Civil War," Journal of Southern History, V (May, 1939), 159–60.
77. Ibid., 161–62.

toured Iowa and Nebraska in 1855, 1856, 1857, and 1859, purchasing 3,320 acres in Iowa and 9,625 acres in Nebraska.[78]

It was left for James De Bow, the prime defender of the South's interests, to commit the ultimate apostasy. Over and over, he urged southerners not to go North for anything and to invest their funds in southern enterprises. "People of the South," he said in 1856, "stand by your Lares and Penates, and taught by dear experience, wander off no more after the strange gods, on whose altars your willing sacrifices have burned no sweet incense."[79] Four years later, De Bow married for a second time and spent the greater portion of his honeymoon in Philadelphia and New York. Arriving at the St. Nicholas Hotel[80] and finding no room left, "Mr. De Bow, with his *usual determination*," reported his wife, and resolving "not to be *turned away*," immediately arranged with the proprietor to have one of the parlors fixed up for him. He purchased for his bride a handsome opera glass, made a *faux pas* by presenting her with "an elegant sewing machine," and delighted her with the large trunk that he purchased for her in Philadelphia.[81] Presumably he filled the trunk with items purchased on the honeymoon trip.

De Bow had become quite prosperous as the circulation of the *Review* increased, as he made valuable business contacts, and as he invested his funds shrewdly. By 1860 he had $30,000 in bank, railroad, and other securities; 1,000 acres of land in Louisiana; 160 acres in Texas; a house and lot in Richmond; and

78. *Ibid.*, 175. Gates gives numerous other examples of southerners investing in northern lands. Note, especially, the large holdings by John Slidell of Louisiana in Iowa, p. 173, and investments by J. C. Breckinridge in Superior, Wisconsin, and St. Paul Minnesota, p. 179. For an account of the extensive land holdings in the North of John H. Randolph, wealthy Louisiana planter, see Paul Everett Postell, "John Hampden Randolph, A Louisiana Planter," *Louisiana Historical Quarterly*, XXV (January, 1942), 163.

79. "Southern Travel and Travelers," *De Bow's Review*, XXI (September, 1856), 323.

80. Described as "very good" in [William M. Bobo], *Glimpses of New York City, by a South Carolinian (Who Had Nothing Else to Do)* (Charleston: J. J. McCarter, 1852), 88.

81. Skipper, *J. D. B. De Bow*, 111.

some real-estate holdings in Washington, D.C.[82] These were
business activities that any good southerner, and especially De
Bow, should have regarded as commendable. But De Bow did
not stop there; and as if to hedge against possible losses in the
South or against any conceivable misfortune on the part of the
South, De Bow invested rather heavily in the North. He purchased about sixty lots in St. Paul, Minnesota, which he valued at
$250 to $300 each; a quarter of a section in Washington County,
Minnesota, worth about $2.50 per acre; two lots in Leavenworth
and land in Brown and Doniphan counties, Kansas; and half a
section in Iowa valued at $20.00 per acre.[83] As late as 1860 he
paid $79.00 in taxes on his St. Paul property, while in 1861 he
was continuing to pay taxes on his Iowa holdings.[84]

The conclusion was inescapable, even in the closing years of
the antebellum period, that the North and South had not approached a level of economic equality or extensive and healthy
interdependence. The imbalance in favor of the North persisted
throughout the period. Southerners did not follow the examples
that many of them saw in the North, namely the remarkable
initiative and industriousness of the Yankees. Indeed, too many
of them frowned on these qualities; others even denied that the
northerners were industrious, a reaction that drew a strong cen-
sure from William Gregg:

> We never look for thrift while we permit our immense timber
> forests, granite quaries and mines, to lie idle, and supply ourselves
> with hewn granite, pine boards, laths and shingles, etc. furnished by
> the *lazy* dogs at the North—oh, worse than this, we see our back
> country farmers, many of whom are too lazy to mend a broken gate,
> or repair the fences, to protect their crops from the neighbouring
> stock, actually supplied with their axe, hoe, and broom handles,
> pitch forks, rakes, etc. by the *indolent* mountaineers of New Hamp-
> shire and Massachusetts.[85]

82. *Ibid.*, 130.
83. *Ibid.*
84. I am indebted to Professor Ottis Skipper for his letter of January 30, 1974, in
which he informed me about De Bow's tax payments.
85. Gregg, *Essays on Domestic Industry*, 8.

Southerners even winked at northern business practices that clearly discriminated against them. Some northern insurance companies imposed a higher premium on southerners who remained in the South during the summer months. Presumably this was because the South was a risky place to be between June and September. Such rates, moreover, were a further incentive to southerners to spend the summer in the North. Some southerners were puzzled by the fact that such insurance policies permitted them to spend their winters in New England "where, perhaps, his chances of life would be diminished by one half!"[86] One might have thought that such positions taken by northern insurance companies would have annoyed if not insulted southerners, but there is no evidence that they reacted in such a manner. Surely, they continued to go north in the summers and surely the insurance companies had a thriving business with southerners.

It seems clear that whatever dissatisfaction southerners had with their economic position vis-à-vis the North's, they were accomplices in the very exploitation that they so vigorously denounced. Merchants went north by the hundreds and built up huge accounts with banks and wholesalers. Tourists went north by the scores of thousands and, by all accounts, spent lavishly, even recklessly. Helper and Gregg assailed the southern merchants, while De Bow and Turner denounced the southern tourists.[87] Meanwhile, the southern conventions condemned virtually all southerners who had *any* business dealings with the North.[88] But the traffic continued; and in 1860 Thomas P. Kettell concluded that the trade balance in favor of the North was in excess of $200,000,000.[89] It should be remembered that Kettell

86. *De Bow's Review*, VI (September, 1848), 226.
87. See above, pp. 40–43.
88. See the resolutions before the conventions of 1850 and 1856 in *De Bow's Review*, IX (July, 1850), 123, and XX (March, 1856), 351. For a more extensive discussion of the conventions and their work, see Herbert Wender, *Southern Commercial Conventions, 1837–1839* (Baltimore: Johns Hopkins Press, 1930).
89. Thomas Prentice Kettell, *Southern Wealth and Northern Profits, As Exhibited in*

was writing in the hope that he would persuade northerners that their economic interest in the South and in southerners who traveled to the North was so great that the North should not countenance any possibility of separation.

Much of the claim that southerners were turning away from the North in the 1850s was wishful thinking. In 1856 De Bow said that "incensed by abuse which is heaped upon them, insulted by the creeds and platforms of powerful parties, outraged by attacks upon their individual property, all coming from the North, the southern people are awakening at last from their dreams of security and repose, and from their fixed confidence in the conservative classes of that section of the Union."[90] After John Brown's raid, one group was so certain of the determination of southerners to remain aloof from those in the North who were their real enemies that it organized the Southern Mercantile and Business Agency "to aid the indignant Southern trader in his quest for information about Northern merchants" so that they could trade "exclusively with those who are friendly to the South and her institutions."[91]

Southern businessmen were as unwilling to sever all connections with the North as were the thousands of southern travelers who were still visiting the North as late as the summer of 1860. Thus, they would deal only with those who were demonstrably friendly to the South and her institutions. That qualification gave them ample room to maneuver, since vast numbers of northern businessmen were at least not unfriendly to the South, and considerable numbers of them were, indeed, quite cordial. Many northern merchants invited southern spokesmen to visit them and explain to them the position of the South.[92] Others appealed for southern business by advertising in such journals as

Statistical Facts and Official Figures (New York: George W. and John A. Wood, 1860), 75.
90. "Southern Travel and Travelers," 323.
91. Foner, Business and Slavery, 160.
92. See below, pp. 215–16, 224–30.

De Bow's Review, thus benefiting from its stated policy of accepting advertisements only from northern firms that were known to be friendly to the South. Still others flattered southern merchants and politicians by lavish entertainment whenever they would accept it.[93]

It has been pointed out that by 1860 southern trade with the North had already begun to decline.[94] But even if orders from southern merchants were on the decline, northern businessmen had already established mechanisms by which southern business needs could be monitored and even stimulated when desirable. Many New York and Boston businessmen visited the South regularly and maintained valuable contacts there. Some took another important step and maintained correspondents in the South or established branches there. By 1850 Brown Brothers and Company, the great New York merchant bankers, had correspondents or offices in Charleston, Savannah, Mobile, and New Orleans.[95] Henry and Daniel Parish, who owned "the most successful dry goods firm" in New York, did a remarkable job of cultivating southern merchants by doing all or most of the purchasing for them and gradually becoming part-owners of several businesses in Charleston, Mobile, New Orleans, and Columbus, Georgia.[96] Perhaps a few southern merchants even had Yankee partners who knew "all those places where 'old goods are sold for Southern and Western trade'—all the large auction establish-

93. In 1858 a group of New York businessmen, endorsing the general principles that James H. Hammond set forth, invited him to be their guest of honor at a dinner whenever it would suit his convenience. Hammond declined, as indeed he declined "several other invitations for dinner this winter in the North." His health was not robust, and his work in the United States Senate was extremely demanding. Merritt, *James Henry Hammond*, 126. When Alabama Congressman Henry Hilliard visited Boston in 1849, Nathan Aplleton, the leading merchant of the city, invited him to be his guest during his stay. Henry W. Hilliard, *Politics and Pen Pictures, at Home and Abroad* (New York: Putnam's, 1892), 201.

94. Foner, *Business and Slavery*, 183–84.

95. John Crosby Brown, *A Hundred Years of Merchant Banking: A History of Brown Brothers and Company, Brown, Shipley, and Company, and the Allied Firms* (New York: privately printed, 1909), 262–64, 267–69.

96. Walter Barrett, *Old Merchants of New York City* (5 vols.; New York: Carleton, 1865), III, 139.

ments, all the second-hand dealers, and the pleasant den of My Uncle of the Three Balls."[97]

Southerners could lament the hard fact that they enjoyed few economic advantages in their relationship with the North. They could wring their hands over the inability or the unwillingness of southerners to strike out on a more independent course. They could pass strong resolutions in their conventions or remonstrate against those whose tastes and desires for northern goods seemed to be beyond their control. None of these positions could, in themselves, change the situation. Even if southerners had been more resourceful, more energetic, and more resolute, they could hardly have achieved a position of economic parity with the North. Their assumptions about their own economy and society clearly made it impossible for them to go beyond a certain point in making changes or adjustments. Under the circumstances they could not achieve more than a status of economic dependency.

97. Hundley, *Social Relations in Our Southern States*, 106.

An Album
of Southern
Travel

FOR NEW YORK.

UNION LINE OF PACKETS,

TO SAIL EVERY TEN DAYS DURING THE SEASON.

This Line is composed of the following Ships:

Ship CREOLE, new . . . . C. PIERCE, Master.
" ATLANTIC, " . . . . C. G. WORTH, "
" INDIANA, " . . . . H. T. COFFIN, "
" UNION, " . . . . JAMES DAVIS, "
" MEDIATOR, " . . . . W. R. BELL, "
" OSWEGO, " . . . . W. WILLIAMS, "
" HUDSON, " . . . . J G. WHITE, "
" FARWEST, " . . . . J. S. BENNETT, "

These ships are all of the first class, built in New York expressly for the trade, of light draught of water, and invariably cross the Bar without detention. They are commanded by Captains experienced in the trade, who will exert themselves to accommodate. Shippers may rely upon the utmost despatch in the discharge of their cargoes, and that the ships will sail punctually, as advertised.

Neither the owners nor Captains of these ships will be responsible for jewelry, bullion, precious stones, silver or plated ware, or for any letters, packages or parcels sent by or put on board them, unless regular bills lading are taken for the same, and the value thereon expressed.

For Freight or Passage, apply to

JOHN O. WOODRUFF & CO.,

31 Natchez Street,

OR TO

W. T. FROST,

68 South Street, New York.

"Business geting very Dull Owing to so many many persons having gone to the North." William Ransom Hogan and Edwin Adams Davis, *William Johnson's Natchez: The Ante-Bellum Diary of a Free Negro*, entry for June 11, 1836. *Photograph from* Cohen's New Orleans Directory *for 1855*.

"Don't attempt to 'do' the [Niagara] Falls in a day or even two days. Take a week, two weeks. There are thousands of things to interest and charm you. The scenery is grand beyond description, the climate truly Elysian. The wonder is that Southerners do not spend the entire summer at the Falls. Expect to be much humbugged and swindled by the exhibitors of sights and the sellers of trash." Dr. G. W. Bagby of Richmond, Virginia, November, 1854.

"Perhaps I may never look upon them again; but the impression made upon my mind, a Niagara of years can only wear away. It is a pleasure to recollect them. The sight of so much sublimity and so much terror, recurs to the fancy till it become familiar; and as the fatigue and annoyance of travel fades from memory, the imagination warms it into a poetic feeling, and we dwell upon it with delight. One of our party remarked, as our cars moved off, that Niagara Falls was the greatest 'watering place' upon earth!" A southerner writing "Two Days at Niagara," 1845. *Photograph courtesy of the New-York Historical Society, New York City.*

"I . . . visited lake George which is said to be thirty six miles in length and from ¾ to five miles in breadth having about three hundred and sixty five islands in it several of which are inhabited. On either side are mountains from five hundred to one thousand or more feet. At the head of the lake are the site and ruins of several old forts, built by the English and french while the United States were collonies of Great Brittian." Christopher Jenkins of Charleston, South Carolina, September 5, 1823. *Photograph courtesy of the New-York Historical Society, New York City.*

"The scenery in the celebrated White mountains is grand beyond description. This sublime scene consists of six or eight towering peaks, distinguished by the names of Washington, Franklin, Adams, Jefferson, Madison, Monroe and Pleasant. The highest of these peaks is Mount Washington, which is 6428 feet in height. The ascent to the summit of this Mount is attended with considerable fatigue; but the wild and sublime character of the scenery induces a stranger to climb upward and onward, till he gains the summit when all is richly repaid, and his fatigue apparently in a moment vanishes, by the view which is rendered uncommonly grand and picturesque, by the magnitude of the elevation, the extent and variety of the surrounding scenery, which is wild, picturesque and sublime on every hand." J. C. Myers of New Hope, Virginia, 1849. *Photograph courtesy of the New-York Historical Society, New York City.*

"I never was in so delightful a city [as Philadelphia]. Chestnut Street is worth all I ever saw before in the way of commercial elegance. You must see it. It really makes me sick to think of taking up my abode in Washington and were you not there I am not sure I should ever go back." James H. Hammond of South Carolina to his wife, 1836. *Photograph courtesy of the Free Library of Philadelphia.*

"Independence Hall is the only spot that has claimed any share of my affections. When I struck the old cracked bell that pealed the first warning to arms in defence of our rights as a free people, when I sat in the chair occupied by John Hancock . . . I felt my patriotism grow warmer and pulse beat quicker." Clement C. Clay, Madison County, Alabama, July 22, 1850. *Photograph from an engraving in Frank M. Etting*, An Historical Account of the Old State House of Pennsylvania.

"On Monday the Lectures [at the Medical College of the University of Pennsylvania] commenced and I have been busy ever since. It is enough to kill a horse almost to get 8 hours study every day upon hard benches. I feel very much like resting at night but there is no rest for the wicked—or righteous here, all fare alike. I have no time to think about the girls scarcely if I even felt disposed. You know that never was my disposition. It is one Anitomic-surgico-physicochemical Sing Song from morning to night, if Job himself was here his patience would be wearied. . . ." Neil McNair, of Coper Hill, Robeson County, North Carolina, November, 1838. *Photograph courtesy of the Library of the College of Physicians of Philadelphia.*

"I hope the gentleman [Rev. Abram Pryne of McGrawville, New York] has recovered his composure after the discussion of yesterday evening. And if the joints of his armor crack under the power of truth taught, it shall not be my fault; nor his; but the fault of the cause he advocates. . . . Last evening I was interrupted by repeated cries of 'time expired' and not even allowed to conclude my entire address. This annoyance came from ruffians and insolent free negroes." Rev. William G. Brownlow of Knoxville, Tennessee, in a five-day debate with Rev. Abram Pryne, at Philadelphia, September, 1858. *Photograph from W. G. Brownlow*, Sketches of the Rise, Progress, and Decline of Secession.

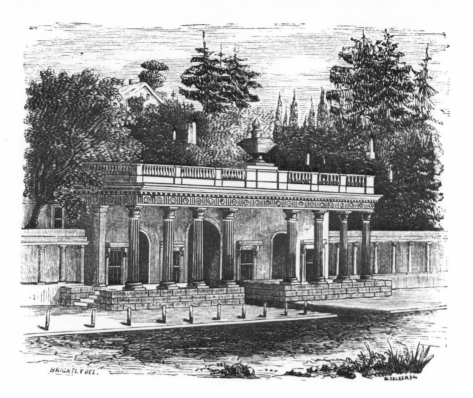

"On Monday the 17th, Dr. D—— and myself went to visit the Laurel Hill Cemetery [in Philadelphia], under the auspices of its founder, Mr. Smith. It is about four miles north of the State House, and consists of thirty-five acres on the banks of the Schuylkill, where they are very abrupt and picturesque. The plan is but partially executed as yet, but enough is already added by art to what had been previously done by nature, to show that it will take the lead among all our decorated repositories for the dead, and prove a profitable speculation for its proprietors. Lots not more than sufficient for single families permanently, sell from five or six hundred dollars, to perhaps twice as much, according to situation." From a Virginian's diary, "Tour to the Northern Lakes," 1837. *Photograph from R. A. Smith*, Smith's Illustrated Guide To and Through Laurel Hill Cemetery.

"But there were occasions when a pressure upon the time of Mrs. Rich [the Washington seamstress] necessitated the seeking of other assistance, and a hasty journey was made to Mlle. Rountree, of Philadelphia, or even to New York, where the fashionable dressmakers were capable of marvellous expedition in filling one's order completely, even to the furnishing of handkerchiefs and hosiery and slippers to suit a special gown." *Photograph from Mrs. Clement C. Clay, of Alabama*, A Belle of the Fifties.

"We are comfortably situated at the City Hotel in Broadway. After we had selected our rooms, I sallied out into that gay and brilliant promenade which intersects the city from north-east and south-west. You may there see, on a fine sun-shiny afternoon, all the fashion and beauty of this great city; the neat, tasteful Parisian costume, in close contrast with the more sober guise of London. There you may hear intermingled the language of the Gaul, the German, and the modern Roman. To the right and left you see the spires of various Christian temples; and smiling faces, and happy hearts will greet you at every step." Victor Chevillere, *The Kentuckian in New York*, 1834. *From the etching by Thomas Hornor, I. N. Phelps Stokes Collection, Prints Division, New York Public Library, Astor, Lenox and Tilden Foundations.*

"We are now staying at that famous new hotel on Broadway [the Astor House] that we all have heard so much about. . . . It occupies nearly a whole square, is elegantly furnished, and the living is delightful. All of us are very much at our ease, notwithstanding we are on Broadway." Mrs. James Green Carson of Natchez, Mississippi, June 12, 1836. *Photograph courtesy of the New-York Historical Society, New York City.*

"On the 15th July, 1853 the Crystal Palace was opened to public inspection, although it will be a month yet before all the articles for exhibition will be unpacked and arranged. . . . The palace itself is the most beautiful building on this side of the Atlantic. The effect is most imposing. You see no iron about it at all. It is painted and gilded all over. . . . Inside it is more enchanting still, for there the gilding and painted and stained glass show to more advantage." James T. Harrison of Columbus, Mississippi, July 17, 1853. *Photograph courtesy of the New-York Historical Society, New York City.*

"The Crystal Palace must characterize New York. What a wilderness of objects! Statues and statuettes, silks and satins, china and glass, furniture of all descriptions, and for all uses. What bright colors! What never ending glitter! What crowds of people! What questions they ask, and how strange their criticisms. Where shall the eye rest. Here is a bust of exceeding beauty. How perfect the classic outline of the face, and what serenity and sweetness in its expression!" "Cecilia," of Virginia, on a visit to New York in 1853. *Photograph courtesy of the New-York Historical Society, New York City.*

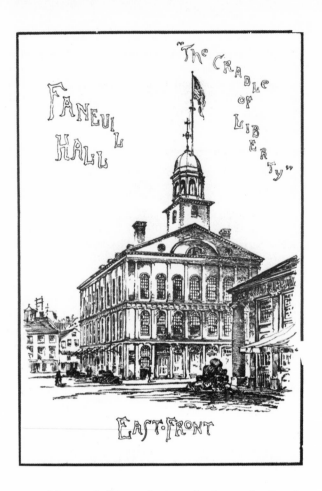

"There are separate parts of the city [of Boston] where fire has made inroads, and which have been subsequently remodelled after more tasteful designs.... The beautiful street containing old Faneuil Hall, and that noble structure, Faneuil Hall Market, extending from Washington Street to the harbor, the buildings embellished with piers and fronts of costly Quincy granite, belongs to these improvements." A Virginian's comments on a visit to Boston in 1836. *Photograph from Edward G. Porter*, Rambles in Old Boston.

"Your letter . . . reached me just before I left for Boston to lecture the Yankees, and found me much engaged in preparation for that work, and after ten days' absence I have been much bothered in getting it out of the press. It has attracted a good deal of attention, and therefore it is necessary at least to have it printed decently and correctly." Robert Toombs to Thomas W. Thomas, February 9, 1856. *Photograph from Ulrich Bonnell Phillips*, The Life of Robert Toombs.

"Harvard College, with its venerable halls, its rare cabinet of curiosities, its library of half a hundred thousand volumes ... the favored seat of the muses—a most renowned University, the second century of whose flourishing existence has recently been celebrated and chaunted in strains sweet and silvery as those of Wordsworth by a classical bard of our own day." Comments on a visit to New England in the *Southern Literary Messenger*, November, 1836. *Photograph from Hamilton Vaughan Bail*, Views of Harvard: A Pictorial Record to 1860.

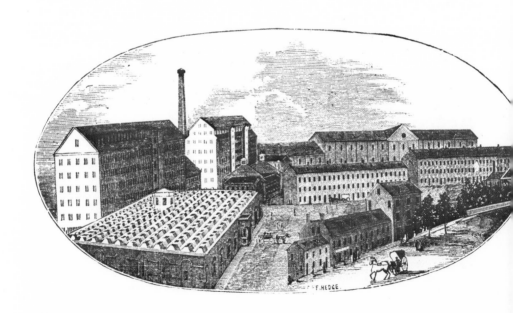

"When we first arrived [in Saratoga] we put up at Union Hall, a very respectable house, but the one where all the religious and sick people put up. . . . And as I did not come here to listen to lectures and prayers I proposed that we should move to Congress Hall which is much the gayest and most fashionable house in the place—the first night we came to this house there was a large Ball which was a considerable change in the scene." Eliza Thompson, Bertie County, North Carolina, August 1834. *Photograph from* Saratoga Illustrated: The Visitor's Guide to Saratoga Springs.

"Next morning I rose early, and started for Lowell in a fine carriage, with three gentlemen who had agreed to accompany me. I had heard so much of this place that I longed to see it; not because I had heard of the 'mile of gals;' no, I left that for the gallantry of the pres., who is admitted, on that score to be abler than myself; but I wanted to see the power of machinery, wielded by the keenest calculations of human skill; I wanted to see how it was that these northerners could buy our cotton, and carry it home, manufacture it, bring it back, and sell it for half nothing; and, in the mean time, be well to live, and make money besides. . . . I regret that more of our southern and western men do not go there, as it would help much to do away with their prejudices against these manufactories." Davy Crockett, 1834. *Photograph from Charles Cowley*, Illustrated History of Lowell.

1866. MOBILE AND OHIO RAILROAD. 1866.

This Road is laid with a heavy Fish Bar Rail, in every respect equal to a Continuous Rail, which prevents the rough jarring, unpleasant motion and noise experienced upon other Roads.

9.30 A.M. THROUGH TRAIN

LEAVES MOBILE DEPOT,

Corner of ROYAL & LIPSCOMB STS.,

DAILY, INCLUDING SUNDAYS, and makes close connections at Cairo with the Illinois Central Railroad for all points North, East, and West.

Two through Express Trains leave Cairo daily, and Three from Cincinnati and Chicago, so that missing a connection only involves a delay of a few hours.

THIS IS THE ONLY ROUTE THAT HAS

NEW AND ELEGANT SLEEPING CARS ON ALL NIGHT TRAINS.

Passengers have the privilege of stopping at the principal Cities of the West.

Through Tickets on sale at the Depot, by the principal Lines, to the following points:

		ALTON.............$36.10		JACKSONVILLE.....$40.70	
10 routes to		BALTIMORE..........53.55		KEOKUK............41.10	
9 1	"	BOSTON.............67.25		LA CROSSE..........54.60	
9	"	BUFFALO............56.60		LAFAYETTE..........41.95	
		BURLINGTON........45.60		LA SALLE...........40.85	
3	"	CINCINNATI.........42.60		MILWAUKEE.........46.60	
2	"	COLUMBUS..........46.60		MADISON............48.70	
6	"	CLEVELAND 51.10	30 routes to	NEW YORK 60.50	
		CHICAGO 43.60	9	"	NIAGARA............56.60
6	"	DUNKIRK............55.40	2	"	MEMPHIS............24.50
2	"	DAYTON 44.75	10	"	PHILADELPHIA......57.15
		DETROIT............51.75	7	"	PITTSBURG..........51.00
		DUNLEITH..........46.80		PRAIRIE DU CHIEN..52.60	
6	"	ERIE................54.10		QUEBEC.............67.60	
		INDIANAPOLIS.......41.60		ROCK ISLAND.......44.90	
		EVANSVILLE.........37.60		ST. LOUIS............34.60	
		FORT WAYNE........46.35		TERRE HAUTE.......49.45	
		GALENA 45.80		VINCENNES 37.10	
		GALESBURG 43.95	2	"	WHEELING 51.60
7	"	HARRISBURG........53.50	4	"	WASHINGTON 54.65

AND ALL OTHER IMPORTANT POINTS.

SLEEPING CAR TICKETS

FOR SALE AT THE TICKET OFFICE, MOBILE DEPOT.

Passengers for Baltimore, Philadelphia, New York, and Boston, will please decide which route they will take from Cairo before applying for Tickets.

"It is a noticeable fact in the travel over the railroads at this time that there are many more people going North than South. The trains are generally light from the North, while those from the South frequently bear very fair loads." Savannah *Daily Republican*, January 3, 1866. *Photograph from* Business Directory of the Principal Southern Cities, 1866.

IV

Black
Over
White ?

In 1860 there were approximately 7 million white people and 3,800,000 slaves in the South. Since there were only 384,000 slaveholders, 200,000 of whom had five slaves or less, two conclusions seem inescapable. One is that the number of large slaveholders was rather small; and the other is that at least three-fourths of the white population had neither slaves nor any immediate economic interest in the institution of slavery. The means—indeed, the affluence—required to make regular sojourns to the North almost invariably placed such travelers in the slaveholding class. And, of course, virtually all southerners "in good standing," slaveholders or not, were committed to the institution of slavery and were usually ardent defenders of it.[1] They generally accepted the proslavery argument that slavery was the normal, natural condition for Negroes and that, conversely, it was both unnatural and dangerous for blacks to live in a state of freedom.

Most southerners who went north were understandably interested in observing the condition of blacks, virtually all of whom were free by 1820. The southerners had undoubtedly seen free blacks in the South, especially if they had visited or

1. Some southerners were opposed to slavery and spoke out against it. Most of these, however, such as James G. Birney and the Grimké sisters, found it necessary to leave the South permanently. See Carl N. Degler, *The Other South: Southern Dissenters in the Nineteenth Century* (New York: Harper and Row, 1974), 13–46; and Betty Fladeland, *James Gillespie Birney: Slaveholder to Abolitonist* (Ithaca: Cornell University Press, 1955).

lived in Charleston, New Orleans, or other cities of any size. But
free Negroes in the South lived in a society dominated by slavery
and, indeed, were at the mercy of the white community—
especially the slaveholders—for any limited freedom that they
happened to enjoy. Nowhere in the South, after 1835, did they
exercise any of the privileges or rights of citizens; and their
enjoyment of freedom or even existence was, indeed, precari-
ous.[2] In the North the picture was different, or it was presumed to
be different. And southern whites wanted to see if northern
Negroes fared better or worse than free Negroes in the South.
Indeed, since they argued that slaves were happier and had more
security than southern free Negroes, they were really interested
in seeing if Negroes in the North fared better or worse than
slaves. They had some ideas on the subject, even before they
went; but they wanted to examine the situation firsthand, even if
merely to confirm their presuppositions.

It is difficult to ascertain the extent to which southerners took
any of their slaves with them when they went north. Those who
went on foot tours most assuredly did not. Men traveling on
business would not really have had any requirements beyond
those that could be met by hotel servants. Young men on holiday
or at the university, except perhaps the more fastidious, foppish
ones, would not need personal servants. Some of the wealthier
women, traveling alone, wanted their own maids, not merely for
service but for companionship as well. Large families found it
desirable to take along one or two servants, especially if they
rented or owned a house and remained in the North during most
of the summer months.

In their diaries, correspondence, and published accounts of
their travels, southerners made little or no mention of taking
slaves with them; and one is compelled to rely almost entirely on
fictional accounts or on litigation arising out of the presence of

2. Ira Berlin, *Slaves Without Masters: The Free Negro in the Antebellum South*
(New York: Pantheon Books, 1974).

slaves in the North. To be sure, Daniel R. Hundley referred to the "Cotton Snob" who visited watering places in the North "with liveried blacks galloping after him, looking as consequential and full of their own importance as though they followed the triumphal chariot of an emperor."[3] In his novel, *The Kentuckian in New York*, Alexander Caruthers describes Cato, the slave of the aristocratic young South Carolinian, Victor Chevillere, as a "tall old Negro, with a face so black as to form a perfect contrast to his white hair and brilliant teeth." In the trip to New York with Chevillere, Cato is the dutiful servant who performs all kinds of services for his young master: "The day being Sunday, I sent old Cato this morning to arouse Lamar quite early." When Chevillere went for a drive with his lady friend, Frances St. Clair, Cato was there: "We dismounted, while Cato held the horses in his most pompous style, seeming to have a shrewd suspicion that his best behavior at this house would not be entirely unacceptable to us." Cato was always the reliable one: "Accordingly, on the next morning, we were again blessed with a propitious day, and having risen early, and forewarned Cato of our intentions (which is always sufficient, you know) our equipage was ready, and we were soon at the door."[4]

When Judge Ebenezer Starnes of Pineville, Georgia, visited England in 1851 with his slave Billy Buck, they passed through New York en route. Starnes had supreme confidence in Buck and apparently gave him considerable freedom of movement during the trip. Indeed, in London Buck visited the Crystal Palace Exposition before Starnes did, since the Judge was indisposed during the first week they were in London. Buck returned full of excitement from his first foray into the city. He said that he never expected to see such an enormous city. In reviewing his travels with his master, he said that he thought Pineville was "some

3. Daniel R. Hundley, *Social Relations in Our Southern States* (New York: Henry B. Price, 1860), 173.
4. William Alexander Caruthers, *A Kentuckian in New York* (2 vols.; New York: Harper and Brothers, 1834), I, 177, II, 25, 33.

punkins until he saw Augusta," and it took "the shine out of it."
Then he saw New York, and Augusta was nowhere near it. But,
he observed, you could take Pineville, Augusta, and New York
and "wrap 'um all up together, and put 'um all into one of the
pockets of this big town." Judge Starnes proposed that if the
public thought well of "these letters from Old England, I may
give them, one of these days, the benefit of similar missives (and
of a visit by Billy Buck and myself) to New England."[5] Unfortunately, the volume never materialized. Perhaps they never made
the trip.

There could have been many reasons why Judge Starnes did
not visit New England with Billy Buck. The slave might have run
away, though the Judge argued—and had Buck declare while in
London—that he would never run away. A more likely reason is
that it became more dangerous to take slaves into the North
during the 1850s, because of the affirmative actions that both
black and white abolitionists took in behalf of freedom for the
slaves. In 1851 a writer in the *Southern Literary Messenger* took
notice of this change:

> Time was when this yearly migration [to the North] so far as it was
> connected with the seekers of pleasures at the watering places, was
> done, for the most part, in private vehicles. We can recollect the day,
> perfectly well, when the proprietor of Congress Hall [at Saratoga
> Springs] strained his eyes wistfully at evening down the long vista of
> the Albany Road for the four-in-hand turn-out of the Carolina gentle-
> man, and when the rumbling of the wheels of one of these equip-
> ages created a sensation through every corridor of the building. . . . At
> that time the Southern gentleman might take with him his dark
> body-servant Sam, without fear of having him stolen by the philan-
> thropists of the North, and Caesar, the carriage driver, might handle
> ribbons unassailed by any pious attempts to dethrone him from his
> exalted station. The conservative, looking back at this happy period
> and contrasting it with the present condition of affairs, will perhaps
> say, in the true spirit of the *laudator temporis acti*, that the old time
> was decidedly the better.

5. Ebenezer Starnes, *The Slaveholder Abroad: Or, Billy Buck's Visit, with His
Master, to England* (Philadelphia: J. B. Lippincott and Company, 1860), 22, 24.

With the coming of the railroad in the nonslaveholding states, the writer observed, "have also been brought forward more enlarged views of the rights of man, by reason of which the old family servants of the South are invariably stolen, should the Southern gentlemen be imprudent enough to take them along, so that they must be left at home if a Northern watering place is the point of destination."[6] A recent writer, looking back at antebellum Saratoga, reached a similar conclusion. The passage of the personal liberty laws, and the excitement attending the passage of the Fugitive Slave Act of 1850 "made it difficult for Southerners to come North now with their huge retinues of colored servants. Soon many of them ceased coming. They went instead to the small watering places on the Gulf of Mexico, to the springs of Virginia or to Tryon in North Carolina."[7] Even if the retinues were never huge and even if the southerners continued to come, their apprehensions and, indeed, discomfort in the North increased during the fifties.

No one was more uneasy about these trends than the northern businessmen—merchants, bankers, hotel owners, and others. They attempted to make amends by giving special attention to southern visitors, entertaining them, and inviting the leaders to

6. "Domestic Tourism," *Southern Literary Messenger*, XVII (June, 1851), 376. Hiram Fuller, the owner of the *Daily Mirror* in New York relished assuming the role of a southern girl, Belle Brittan, and writing of her experiences. On the subject of taking slaves north, "she" remarks: "It is in consequence of the conduct of these THIEVES [abolitionists] that comparatively few of our people are found at the Northern watering places this year. Our colored nurses and maids, and boys and coachmen, who have taken care of us and waited upon us from infancy, are indispensable to our comforts abroad, as well as at home; for I cannot bear to be washed and dressed and waited upon by white folks. It doesn't seem natural or right. But we dare not bring our best servants with us, because however much they may be attached to us personally, yet these lying abolitonists paint Free Niggerism in such false, yet alluring colors, that the strongest minds of our inexperienced slaves become discontented, even if they did not leave us." [Hiram Fuller], *Belle Brittan On a Tour, At Newport and Here and There* (New York: Derby and Jackson, 1858), 181.
7. Hugh Bradley, *Such Was Saratoga* (New York: Doubleday, Doran and Company, 1940), 131. See also Lawrence F. Brewster, *Summer Migrations and Resorts of South Carolina Low-Country Planters* (Durham: Duke University Press, 1947), 102–103; and Thomas D. Morris, *Free Men All: The Personal Liberty Laws of the North, 1780–1861* (Baltimore: Johns Hopkins Press, 1974).

speak in the North. And as abolitionism stepped up its activities, they became more anxious. In a moment of sheer exasperation in 1855, the editor of the New York *Evening Mirror* declared, "The Northern Abolitionists who steal the nurses, body servants, and coachmen from Southern families, are cheating our hotels and merchants of Southern custom, and our watering place society of the beaux and belles who were wont to grace it. We learn that all the popular summer resorts south of Mason and Dixon's line, are full this summer to overflowing. Such is the effect of fanaticism."[8]

All during the nineteenth century, it was a risky business for southerners to bring their slaves north with them. The antislavery sentiment that brought about emancipation in the northern states nurtured an intolerance of slavery even when bondsmen accompanied their masters on a temporary sojourn.[9] Whether, under such circumstances, a southerner was able to retain his slave depended on a number of factors. Among them were the intensity of the antislavery feeling in a given place, the presence of persons willing and able to challenge the owner, the status of the law, the attitude of the courts in cases that were litigated, and the attitude of the slave. If antislavery sentiment was not really strong and the slave would not cooperate, it would be difficult, perhaps impossible, for the most ardent abolitionists to secure the slave's freedom. One doubts, moreover, that there were many Billy Bucks among the slaves who served their southern masters in the North. If, on the other hand, a slave sought his freedom and the court took the attitude that the state law had abolished all forms of slavery there, the slave's chances for freedom were excellent.

The uncertainty of the outcome of the litigation for a slave's freedom is well illustrated in two cases arising in Pennsylvania

8. Quoted in Avery O. Craven, *The Coming of the Civil War* (Chicago: University of Chicago Press, 1957), 297.

9. For a discussion of the zeal with which many northerners sought to stamp out slavery altogether in the early years of the nineteenth century, see Arthur Zilversmit, *The First Emancipation: The Abolition of Slavery in the North* (Chicago: University of Chicago Press, 1967).

and involving South Carolina members of the United States House of Representatives. From the time he was elected to Congress in 1794 Pierce Butler, a South Carolina planter, maintained a home in Pennsylvania. He served in Congress from 1794 to 1805, except for two years when he was in the state legislature. His slave Ben traveled to Pennsylvania with him and to South Carolina for annual visits to the plantation. On one occasion when they were in Pennsylvania the slave secured a writ of habeas corpus and was discharged by the court. Butler then sued, claiming exemption on the grounds that he was (1) a member of Congress and (2) a mere sojourner in Pennsylvania. The court denied his claim and insisted that for two years he lost the privilege conferred on him under the exception provided in the emancipation act of 1780.[10] Butler was, therefore, a resident; and since residents could not hold slaves, the court granted Ben his freedom.[11]

Some years later, Langdon Cheves of South Carolina was a member of Congress. After Congress adjourned in 1813, Cheves went to Pennsylvania and took his slave Lewis with him. He rented a house in Philadelphia and remained there until December, when he returned to Washington. Meanwhile, Lewis had run away; upon his capture, he claimed that under Pennsylvania law he was free. The court disagreed and insisted that Cheves, by living in Pennsylvania, had not lost his right to his slave. In an opinion that clearly reflected his sympathy with the southern slaveholder, Judge William Tilghman said:

> We all know that our southern brethren are very jealous of their rights on the subject of slavery, and that their union with the other states could never have been cemented, without yielding to their demands on this point. . . . I am therefore of the opinion that the

10. For a discussion of the Act of 1780, see *ibid.*, 128–31, and Edward Raymond Turner, *Slavery in Pennsylvania* (Baltimore: Lord Baltimore Press, 1911), 78–79.

11. *Butler* v. *Hopper*, 4 Federal Cases 904, quoted in Helen T. Catterall (ed.), *Judicial Cases Concerning American Slavery and the Negro* (5 vols.; Washington: Carnegie Institution, 1926–1937), IV, 267.

domestic slaves of members of Congress who are attending the
family . . . even during its recess, gain no title to freedom, although
they remain in the state more than six months, whether the seat of
Congress be in Pennsylvania or elsewhere.[12]

Another Pennsylvania judge was of the opinion in 1821 that
exemptions were not confined to members of Congress. He
observed that southerners had for many years been in the habit of
visiting Pennsylvania, "attended with their domestic slaves,
either for pleasure, health, or business," a fact that was well
known to the framers of the state's act for the abolition of slavery.
Year after year, he observed, they passed the summer months in
the state, "their continuance scarcely ever amounting to six
months," the time required for residence. He admitted that if
these successive sojournings were added up it would, indeed,
amount to a prohibition, but would then be "a denial of the rights
of hospitality." Since York and Bedford Springs were frequented
"principally, and in great numbers," by southerners attended by
their slaves, the judge was not inclined to deny them the rights to
which they had become accustomed.[13]

In subsequent years it became increasingly difficult for southerners to enjoy the services of their slaves while traveling or
residing temporarily in the North. One year after the Pennsylvania judge had expressed sympathy and understanding in the
case of masters who brought their slaves to York and Bedford
Springs, another judge in the same state would not concede any
extenuating circumstances. A Charleston slaveowner rented a
house in Philadelphia in February, 1822, for three months. He
furnished it, brought a slave to serve as a domestic, and lived
there for more than ten months. The slave refused to return to
South Carolina, and the owner sought to have her returned to
him as a fugitive. The court declared that the slave was not a
fugitive but was free. The owner, in remaining longer than six

12. Commonwealth, *ex rel.* negro *Lewis* v. *Holloway*, 6 Binney 213, *ibid.*, IV, 272.
13. *Butler* v. *Delaplaine*, 7S and R, 378, *ibid.*, IV, 279.

months, had become a resident and had thereby lost all claim to the slave.[14]

Pennsylvania was not alone in reflecting an increasing antislavery sentiment in its judicial opinions regarding slaves of southerners in the North. A Georgia master took his slave, Nancy Jackson, to Connecticut where he began to spend a portion of each year, beginning in 1835. The owner left his slave there during the months when he was in Georgia. Some years later she sued for her freedom. The court held that she must be discharged, for she was in fact a free person. It was clearly illegal for a master to hold a person as a slave in Connecticut while he came and went over a period of several years. From the point of view of the court, it was clearly an illegal attempt to maintain slavery in the free state of Connecticut.[15]

Massachusetts was even more unequivocal in its opposition to southerners bringing slaves into the state. Two of its most notable cases involved slave children, and in both of them the abolitionists clearly had a hand. In 1833 Mary Slater, the wife of a Louisiana planter, visited her father in Boston and brought with her a six-year-old slave child, whose mother remained in Louisiana. During a period of several days when the mistress left Boston to visit friends, she placed the child in the care of her father. When certain antislavery elements learned of this, they went to court and secured an order to have the child seized. When Mrs. Slater objected, the court declared that under Massachusetts law, the child was free. The law of the comity of nations did not apply, the judge insisted, for then all slaveholders could come to Massachusetts and bring their slaves with them.[16] A few years later an Arkansas slaveholder brought her eight-year-old slave to Massachusetts; and after a visit she intended to

---

14. *Ex Parte* Simmons, 22 Federal Cases, 151, *ibid.*, IV, 279–80.
15. *Nancy Jackson* v. *Bulloch*, 12 Connecticut 38, *ibid.*, IV, 433–35.
16. *Commonwealth* v. *Aves*, 18 Pickering 193, *ibid.*, IV, 506–507. See also Leonard W. Levy, *The Law of the Commonwealth and Chief Justice Shaw* (New York: Harper and Row, 1967), 62–63.

take him back to Arkansas and hold him as a slave. The court said that she had no right to bring him there in the first place and ordered that he be freed and placed in the hands of guardians.[17]

Toward the end of the period, northern states would not tolerate even the transit of slaves across their borders when the masters were en route elsewhere. In 1855 a Philadelphia case attracted considerable attention because of the prominence of the slaveholder and because of the role of free Negroes in Philadelphia in securing the freedom of this man's slaves. J. H. Wheeler of North Carolina, who had been appointed United States Minister to Nicaragua, was en route there to take up his post. In his party, when he passed through Philadelphia, were three slaves, a woman and her two sons, ages twelve and seven. After they went on board ship, several free Negroes went aboard and persuaded the slaves that they were not obligated to go with Wheeler because they were on free soil. After a heated argument with Wheeler the free Negroes took the slaves away. A policeman refused Wheeler's entreaties to intervene, saying that "he was not a slave-catcher." The free Negro leader, Passmore Williamson, who had advised his followers to take the slaves away but had not participated in the abduction, was held in contempt of court for refusing to answer the court's request for information. This was little consolation to Wheeler, who suffered a second outrage when the woman slave, now residing as a free person in Massachusetts, asked the court to discharge Williamson on the ground that she had gone ashore voluntarily, determined to have her freedom.[18]

The decision in a New York case was even more clear-cut and explicit. In 1852 a Virginia woman, Juliet Lemmon, went to New York with eight slaves to secure passage to Texas. During Mrs. Lemmon's sojourn in New York, Louis Napoleon, described in the proceedings as a "colored citizen" of New York, applied for a

17. *Commonwealth* v. *Mary B. Taylor*, 3 Metcalf 72, quoted in Catterall (ed.), *Judicial Cases*, IV, 509.
18. U.S. *ex rel. Wheeler* v. *Williamson*, 28 Federal Cases, 682, *ibid.*, IV, 311–13.

writ of habeas corpus to bring the slaves before the court for their release on the ground that they were being held illegally. The judge granted the writ and discharged the slaves. Merchants and other business groups in New York were furious and showed their sympathy for the owner by raising $5,280 in less than a week to compensate the Lemmons for their loss.[19] Lemmon, the husband, came forward and appealed the case, arguing that his wife was merely in New York to secure passage to Texas and surely could not be divested of her possessions during a brief layover. In a decision handed down in March, 1860, the court emphatically disagreed. The judge said that New York law forbade slaves to be brought into New York "for any pretence whatsoever, and every slave person brought in shall be free."[20]

In the 1850s only the most imprudent southern visitors would bring their slaves into the North. The courts had made it painfully clear that they would countenance no property in slaves. Abolitionists, moreover, confirmed the South's worst fears—not only in condemning slavery and slaveholders, but in stealing slaves away from what they were pleased to call the "slave stealers." Worst of all, perhaps, was the boldness and "impudence" of militant free blacks who were willing to take any action necessary to bring their brethren into the ranks of free people. It was enough to cause sojourning slaveholders to leave their chattel at home. It was almost enough to cause the masters to resist the temptation of going north themselves.

Understandably, very few southern blacks traveled in the North on their own. Whether a slave or a free person, there was the possibility that, as in the South, a black person would be

19. Philip S. Foner, *Business and Slavery: The New York Merchants and the Irrepressible Conflict* (Chapel Hill: University of North Carolina Press, 1941), 62.

20. *Lemmon v. The People*, 20 N.Y. 562, quoted in Catterall (ed.), *Judicial Cases*, IV, 405–406. The one exception in this late period regarding slaves in transit was made by a California judge in 1858. He said that he was lenient in returning the slave to the owner because that was the first such case to come before the court. The judge declared that in future cases, he would enforce the rules strictly, which meant that under normal circumstances transit of slaves would be denied to slaveholders. *Ex Parte* Archy, 9 California 147, *ibid.*, V, 332–34.

under suspicion of being a fugitive. If he was attending a northern school or college he enjoyed the protection of his sponsor, not infrequently a white parent.[21] There were instances, perhaps rather rare, when masters trusted their slaves so completely that they permitted them to hire themselves out in a job that occasionally took them into the North. In the Great Dismal Swamp, Olmsted heard of a case where the master permitted his slave to go to New York as a cook on a lumber schooner. The slave returned, but shortly after that he purchased his freedom and went to Liberia.[22] Although most slaves who went to the North or were taken there to be emancipated remained there, one can find examples of manumitted slaves who returned to the South. William Johnson, the Natchez free Negro diarist, noted on July 16, 1847, that "Dr. Winston returned from Cincinnati this morning in Good Health." Winston was not a physician but a slave who had gone to Cincinnati for the express purpose of being manumitted.[23]

If, indeed, it was unsafe for a southern white to take his slaves north with him, he had two options by which he could avail himself of the services of blacks. He could take his slave and instruct him that when in the North he was to inform all inquisitive persons that he was free; or he could hire a slave who was virtually free and would, because of his experiences, have no difficulty conducting himself as a free person. Colonel Andrew Jackson Polk of Maury County, Tennessee, took both options;

21. See above, pp. 61–62, 276.
22. Frederick Law Olmsted, *The Cotton Kingdom*, edited with an introduction by Arthur M. Schlesinger (New York: Alfred A. Knopf, 1953), 116. See also page 321, where a slave tells Olmsted of his own travels to Philadelphia and New Jersey. A Kentucky master was not so fortunate. The slave was apparently a favorite and was regarded as thoroughly reliable. Indeed, his master had promised him his freedom upon payment of $400. Meanwhile, the master sent the slave into Ohio on an errand. The slave refused to return, and the Ohio court declared him to be free. *Anderson* v. *Poindexter* et al., 6 Ohio St. 622, in Catterall (ed.), *Judicial Cases*, V, 18–20.
23. William R. Hogan and Edwin A. Davis (eds.), *William Johnson's Natchez: The Ante-Bellum Diary of a Free Negro* (Baton Rouge: Louisiana State University Press, 1951), 576. In 1850 Winston went north again, this time with James Cox, a leading white citizen of Natchez. *Ibid.*, 723.

and in his autobiography his Negro companion, James P. Thomas, has given a vivid account of their experiences. In 1848 Polk went to Nashville, where Thomas was living and said that he was going to New York shortly and that Thomas should be ready to go with him. Thomas, who was technically a slave, told Polk that he had just purchased a business and did not think that he could go; whereupon, Polk said, "Don't tell me about your business. I'll buy it and shut it up." He offered to pay him liberally and told him to be ready the following Tuesday, to which Thomas finally agreed.

They traveled by stage to Louisville, then by packet to Cincinnati, then overland to Buffalo and the Falls and then to Albany and down the Hudson River to New York. On the steamer, several passengers asked Thomas many questions regarding Polk. Was Mr. Polk of the same politics as the President? No. How many slaves does he own? About three hundred. Do you belong to him? No. "Some believed it and some would not." Obviously, Polk relished the public curiosity over his relationship with Thomas. When, for example, Polk decided to take a rest while on the steamer, he gave to Thomas, in the presence of many passengers, his valuables for safekeeping: his gold headed cane, his gold watch, and a "well filled pocket book." Thomas said that he had nothing to do but rest on the head of the cane and answer curious people's questions until they neared New York. "An elegant fob was attached to the watch which caused many to ask, 'What time is it?'"

At the Astor House where they registered, Polk called the clerks' attention to Thomas and told them to make certain that he was made comfortable. Thomas was one of seven or eight gentlemen's servants, including Daniel Webster's man servant; they took their meals together and discussed the various activities of their employers. Thomas seldom saw Polk and was, therefore, free to visit Barnum's, various museums, and other places of interest. Whenever he ate outside the hotel, Polk would ask about his funds. When Thomas would inform him that he had some left, Polk would hand him a ten dollar bill and say, "Put this to it." One of his orders was, "You dress well. Don't let those fellows down you."

When Thomas was moving about New York and Philadelphia on his own, he had the experience of seeing how the North treated free blacks. After he purchased a ticket and took his seat for a performance of Campbell's Minstrels, an usher called him out and told him that "some of our people are not satisfied with you here and I will have to return you your money." He attempted a short apology, but Thomas took the money and left. "I felt as though I would like to meet another man who would have the affrontry to advise me to run away to live in New York," he said. In Philadelphia he boarded an omnibus to go to Fairmont, "with one old fellow in the Bus. He came near tearing the door off getting out. Other passengers looked in without entering. I didn't know what the trouble was until the driver called me up on the seat with him. He said, 'I don't care but I might lose my job.'" After a further sojourn in Washington, Richmond, and Raleigh, this virtually free Negro seemed pleased to return to Tennessee and his business interests.

In 1851, Andrew Jackson Polk was ready for another northern adventure, and so was James Thomas. This time Polk was accompanied by his wife, two children, and a nurse, Kitty, as well as Thomas. In New York, they took apartments at the Irving House. Polk informed the clerk that he had two servants "and any order from them must be honored." There were many other southerners at the hotel, including Dr. and Mrs. Percy of Nashville who brought a maid, "a tall handsome girl, a quadroon." Thomas seemed quite pleased to show her around the city, but he was not prepared for all the stares from other pedestrians who were interested in the young woman's dress "of light material, gauzy in appearance," or her "pretty little sun bonnet lined with a pink color," or her color and features. Thomas' discomfort was more than compensated by the pleasure of her company.

After four or five weeks in New York, the party went to Saratoga, which, in the eyes of Thomas, must have been "a charming place before fashion and folly got in." There were large numbers of Bostonians, "who seemed to go together," New Yorkers who "appeared to mingle more freely," and Philadelphians, who "formed their clique." The many southerners who "seemed easy and comfortable and dared to talk above a whisper, were all well behaved."

After Saratoga they visited Boston and stayed a week at the Revere House. Now that they were in the land of the abolitonists, Polk became apprehensive for the safety of his maid, to whom he gave firm instructions. "Kitty," he said, "you are not to call me master while we are in Boston." When she asked how she should address him, he replied, "Call me Mr. Polk. You are just as free here as I am. If you were to go out on the street I couldn't touch you and if those people knew you belong to me they would come and carry you off and you would never see Isaac again." This troubled Kitty, who complained to Thomas that she had never told a lie in her life. Thomas assured her that she was indeed free in Boston, as Polk had indicated. Kitty concluded that she would prefer to get along in Boston without any trouble in order to be able to return to Tennessee to her family and friends.

The test was not long in coming. A few days later, when Kitty took the Polk child out for a walk, she saw a well-dressed lady and gentleman watching her closely. Finally they walked up to her, and the man asked to whom the baby belonged. When Kitty replied that it was Mr. Polk's, the man then asked, "Do you belong to him?" She stammered out, "No Sir."

"Then you are free?"

"Yes Sir."

"How long have you been free?"

Kitty then happened to think "how long it had been since

the Lord freed my soul from sin and I said 'fourteen years.'"

The man then said, "If I knew you wasn't free you shouldn't stay here." Then, they left her, whereupon Kitty repaired to her room and remained there until the Polks came home from their drive. Perhaps it was a relief not only for Kitty but for the Polks as well to quit Boston for Newport, where they remained until the season closed.

Thomas recorded other noteworthy experiences. In New York he encounted a bright mulatto from Natchez, a Mr. Cary, who played the flute elegantly. At the theater, Thomas saw a celebrated actress in the role of the queen in *Henry VIII*. In Rochester, Mrs. Polk's hairdresser wanted to take the children to see Frederick Douglass, whom she knew. Polk refused, saying that he did not want to be the subject of an article in Douglass' newspaper. Perhaps the trip provided some stresses and strains for each of the travelers; but for a southern Negro it was a rare opportunity to see the world.[24]

In Louisiana Andrew Durnford was a free Negro planter and slaveholder, who had interesting contacts among white Louisiana planters, including the wealthy John McDonogh, as well as in the North. In 1835 Durnford journeyed to Philadelphia to sell his sugar crop and to discuss with certain persons there the establishment of a colony in Liberia. He had a long and rewarding visit with Elliott Cresson, an abolitionist and colonizationist. Durnford wrote McDonogh that Cresson was "all smartness, activity, gayity, a perfect gentleman," who took him on a sightseeing trip around the city. After concluding his business there, Durnford proceeded to Richmond, where he purchased several

24. The reference was, perhaps, to William McCary of Natchez, the son of William Johnson's closest friend. In 1849 young McCary went to Cincinnati to work. *Ibid.*, 669. I am indebted to Professor Loren Schweninger of the University of North Carolina, Greensboro, for sharing with me the unpublished autobiography of James Thomas, which he is editing. The accounts of Thomas' trips to the North are from scattered portions of the manuscript, which is in the Moorland-Spingarn Research Center at Howard University.

slaves despite the fact that prices were very high, thanks to the spoiling of the market by Alabamians.[25]

As southerners observed free blacks in the North, they reported little that impressed them favorably.[26] Perhaps they did not see much that they regarded as favorable, or perhaps they were not inclined to publish articles or to write their friends and relatives about conditions among free blacks that could suggest the desirability of their being free. It is not without significance that some of the most favorable comments were made by a Virginia planter—not in the southern press or to other southerners, but to Frederick Law Olmsted from New York; and it was Olmsted who wrote about them. In a northern city the Virginia planter had met a former slave fifteen years after he had run away from his master. He was engaged in a "profitable and increasing business," had acquired more than ten thousand dollars worth of property and was living "a great deal more comfortably and wisely than ever his old master had done." The Virginian also recalled encountering in Philadelphia a former Virginia slave woman who lived in a "handsome three-story building, furnished really with elegance," and who owned three other houses that she rented. She was anxious that her children be well educated, and she was "employing the best instructors for them which she could procure in Philadelphia."[27]

Perhaps the most favorable and comprehensive picture of life among northern free Negroes by a southerner was given by Joseph W. Wilson. Although virtually nothing is known of the author, his descriptions of life among the higher classes of "col-

25. David O. Whitten, "Slave Buying in 1835 Virginia as Revealed by Letters of a Louisiana Negro Sugar Planter," *Louisiana History*, XI (Summer, 1970), 233–35.

26. One incident in Philadelphia impressed Paul Hamilton Hayne in 1854. When he re-visited a favorite restaurant, Parkinson's, that year "the black waiter to whom I had given a sundry 'half-pence' last summer rushed up and shook my hand with a heartiness, which (considering he knew that I was a slaveholder) spoke loudly in favor of his good sense." Paul H. Hayne to Mary Michel Hayne, August 25, 1854, in Paul Hamilton Hayne Papers, Duke University, Durham.

27. Olmsted, *Cotton Kingdom*, 73.

ored society" in Philadelphia in 1841 are marked by a fairness in
approach and a clarity of style that commend his work to students
of the subject. Wilson said that the Negro population ranged from
those who enjoyed "all the social blessings of this life" to those
who "are to be found in the lowest depths of human degradation,
misery, and want." He was impressed with the fact that they had
"their own churches, school-houses, institutions of benevolence, and others for the promotion of literature; and if I cannot
include scientific pursuits, it is because the avenues leading
to and upholding these, have been closed against them."

Among the institutions and aspects of Negro life in Philadelphia that Wilson described were the churches—primarily
Methodist, Presbyterian, Baptist, and Episcopalian. Mutual relief societies were more numerous than those of any other organized group, while some were devoted exclusively to outdoor
benevolence, chiefly among the women. Adults were generally
not well educated, but "having often had the occasion to feel the
necessity of a good education themselves, they have thereby
been led to spare no exertion for securing the same for their
children." Consequently, the young people were enjoying many
of the advantages that had been denied their parents. Despite
the restrictions and discouragements "at almost every step in the
pursuit of knowledge," Wilson was willing to assert that "most of
them have equalled, and many far surpassed, the best opportunities afforded them."

There were divisions and differences among Philadelphia's
free Negro population; and Wilson did not fail to notice them.
There was a tendency, he said, "untiring and ever constant, to
detract the one from the merits of the other." The result was that
suspicion and distrust "very naturally usurp the place of confidence." Those born in Philadelphia, moreover, exhibited some
hostile attitudes toward those who had come there from the
South, but these attitudes were gradually overcome as "southerners" continued to live among them.

The high level of social and cultural interests greatly impressed Wilson. Most of the young ladies were competent to perform on the piano, guitar, "or some other appropriate musical instrument." The conversation among them was "varied, interesting and instructive," and the topics were discussed in a "mild, dignified and becoming manner, in which the ladies mostly take part and contribute their full quota." Small wonder that Wilson could conclude:

> If prejudiced persons were to be governed more by positive knowledge . . . than they are by rash, hasty, groundless conclusions, very different views than at present generally obtain, would soon be formed, respecting the degree of refinement and cultivation to be found among the higher classes of colored society. The ease and grace of manner with which they are capable of bearing themselves in company . . . render their society agreeable and interesting to the most fastidious in such matters; and speak loudly against the injustice that is done them, in refusing to accord them any knowledge, possession or practice of those qualities or accomplishments.[28]

Few if any southerners would go to the trouble of studying northern Negroes as carefully as Wilson did; and the observations of most of them merely confirmed the views they already had. To most of them blacks were not as invisible as they would be to Josiah Nott, the Alabama physician and ethnologist. When he moved to New York in 1867 he found the city to be "without morals, without political scruples, without religion and without niggers."[29] Indeed, southern travelers saw more of blacks than they wanted to. A group of southerners from Virginia, on a Lake Ontario steamer, were mortified to discover a Negro in the dining room as a guest—and at the table to which they were assigned! They informed the captain that they could not sit at the

28. [Joseph W. Wilson], *Sketches of the Higher Classes of Colored Society in Philadelphia, By a Southerner* (Philadelphia: Merrihew and Thompson, 1841), 14, 16, 25–27, 39, 47–48, 58–60. See also Leon Litwack, *North of Slavery: The Negro in the Free States* (Chicago: University of Chicago Press, 1961), 181–82, 296–97.

29. Quoted in William R. Stanton, *The Leopard's Spots: Scientific Attitudes Toward Race in America* (Chicago: University of Chicago Press, 1959), 187.

table with a black man. The captain told them that they need
not leave, for he would order the Negro away. The Negro,
highly educated and well known in Ontario, where he lived,
would not leave, insisting that he had as much right to sit there
as the best of them. The captain then took him by the collar and
threatened force, against which the other passengers "loudly
remonstrated." At that point the young Negro rose and left the
table, after which the Virginians dined in peace. When the boat
arrived at Kingston the captain was apprehended on a warrant
for assault "and had to pay a heavy fine for his officiousness."[30]

Race mixing—by which southerners meant having any contact, however remote and impersonal, with a Negro who was
not in a servile position—was abhorrent to southern whites
wherever they found it. One South Carolinian, attending a
London concert by Jenny Lind, heard little of the music because his seat in the theater "was in juxtaposition to that of a
burly black negro."[31] Those visiting in the North were just as
miserable when placed in a similar situation. The sense of social equality that southerners ascribed to northern blacks was
responsible for their "impudence and want of politeness."
James Harrison, the Mississippi planter, had seen free Negroes
"refuse to exchange seats (much less give them up) to accommodate a party of ladies who desired to get together as one
company."[32] R. G. Morris, addressing the Richmond convention in 1856 claimed that southerners were no longer frequenting Saratoga and Cape May in large numbers because of the
treatment "they have received from the free negroes" in the last
few years. It had been reported, he said, that "some of these
fashionables were grossly insulted, and even beaten, by the

30. Alexander MacKay, *The Western World: Or Travels in the United States in
1846–47* (2 vols.; Philadelphia: Lea and Blanchard, 1849), I, 103–104.
31. David W. Aiken, "Autobiography," 1848, in the University of North Carolina,
Chapel Hill.
32. James T. Harrison to his wife, August 15, 1853, in James T. Harrison Papers,
University of North Carolina, Chapel Hill.

darkies."[33] Even if they were not beaten, the chances that one's wife or daughter might be seated in a car "next to a runaway negro" were enough, one writer claimed, to cool the ardor of southerners for visiting the northern watering places.[34]

William Bobo of South Carolina saw more race mixing in New York City than he wanted to see. Five Points was the center of Negro life and, consequently, from Bobo's point of view, the place where there was the greatest amount of race mixing and, of course, depravity. "The population of the Points is about equally divided between whites and blacks. The blacks however are, for the most part, the rulers; they own and keep a majority of the drinking and dance-houses." For example, there was the ball at Pete Williams', where males and females, "black, yellow and white," were seated or swaggering about the room. Pete, who was the Negro owner, was dealing out whisky, tobacco, beer, and "segars." Then, the music began "and away they whirl in a most disgusting and revolting manner. . . . Let us get out," he concluded; "my senses refuse to behold longer such scenes."[35] Apparently he did not have enough! Later, he visited Church Street, the "Negro street where Dutch and negroes stand on the same platform. . . . Did you ever see such a mixture of negroes and whites all on an equality?" He then described race mixing in card games, drinking parties, and the like at the Negro hotel, the St. Charles Exchange. After remaining somewhat longer than such a very sensitive person would be expected to, Bobo said, "We will now leave them and proceed on our way; you have had enough of this hole for one time."[36]

Even when the contact between blacks and whites in the

33. "Southern Educational and Industrial Development," *De Bow's Review*, XX (May, 1856), 625.
34. "Domestic Tourism," 376.
35. [William M. Bobo], *Glimpses of New York City by a South Carolinian (Who Had Nothing Else to Do)* (Charleston: J. J. McCarter, 1852), 95.
36. *Ibid.*, 125–29.

North was on a higher plane, it was deplored by southern observers. J. C. Myers expressed quiet outrage over the fact that in
a New England church, four or five white members were acci-
dentally bypassed at communion before the minister began to
serve the black members. From Myers' point of view, it simply
should not have happened.[37] In the 1858 Philadelphia debate
between William Brownlow of Tennessee and Abram Pryne of
McGrawville, New York, there were blacks as well as whites in
the audience. When Brownlow was interrupted with cries of
"time expired," he insisted that the "annoyance came from
ruffians and insolent free negroes."[38]

It was the generally degraded condition of northern blacks on
which southerners were most pleased to comment. "All the
social advantages, all the respectable employments, all the
honors, and even the *pleasures* of life are denied free negroes of
the North, by pious Abolitionists full of sympathy for the
downtrodden African," Parson Brownlow told his Philadelphia
audience in 1858.[39] Daniel R. Hundley seemed actually delighted to hear Henry Ward Beecher describe the condition
of free Negroes more graphically and authoritatively than
any southerner could have done: "They are refused the common rights of citizenship which the whites enjoy. . . . They are
snuffed at even in the House of God, or tolerated with ill-dis-
guised disgust. . . . *We heap upon them moral obloquy more
atrocious than that which the master heaps upon the slave.*"[40]
Even Major Jones of Pineville, Georgia, remarked on the wretchedness of free Negroes when he visited Philadelphia: "Thar they
was, covered with rags and dirt, livin' in houses and cellers,
without hardly any furniture; and sums of 'em without dores or

37. J. C. Myers, *Sketches on a Tour through the Northern and Eastern States, the
Canadas and Nova Scotia* (Harrisonburg, Va.: J. H. Wartmann and Brothers, 1849), 382.

38. *Ought American Slavery to be Perpetuated? A Debate between Rev. W. G.
Brownlow and Rev. A. Pryne, Held at Philadelphia, September, 1858* (Philadelphia:
J. B. Lippincott, 1858), 140–41. For a full discussion of the debate, see below.

39. *Ibid.*, 44.

40. Hundley, *Social Relations in Our Southern States*, 300–301. Italics in the
original.

winders. Pore, miserable, sickly-looking creaters! It was enuff to make a abolitionist's hart ake."[41] One wonders if the heart of Jones or Hundley or Brownlow really ached as they concluded that the slave in the South did not suffer any of the hardships that free Negroes suffered in the North.

To southerners the most dramatic evidence of free Negro degradation in the North was that some were considering returning to the South and some had actually returned. What better testimony could there be than the declaration by a black person that conditions in the North were unbearable? And what a display of honesty and intelligence when they did make such a declaration! In 1828 a southern visitor to New York was served "by an intelligent young man of colour" who indicated that he was seriously considering returning south to his master who had taken him and his wife north to manumit them. He had rejected the idea of going to Liberia, because the reports from there were that it was "the most miserable place in the world. I had rather remain here." When the white man then pointed out that if he returned to the South he could not know into whose hands he might fall in the event of his master's death, he replied that he would prefer to take that chance than to remain where he was.[42]

Whenever blacks took the fateful step of returning south, whites made the most of it in every possible way. At White Sulphur Springs, Edmund Ruffin met a mulatto free Negro, Joseph Mackintosh, who had traveled through the North and gone on to Liberia to live. He also found it a "miserable place" and would not consider living there or in the North. At the Springs many whites visited Mackintosh to listen to his account of his unpleasant adventures.[43] When a former slave went to

41. William T. Thompson, *Major Jones's Sketches of Travel*, in Warren S. Tryon (ed.), *A Mirror for Americans: Life and Manners in the United States, 1790–1870, As Recorded by American Travelers* (3 vols.; Chicago: University of Chicago Press, 1952), I, 203.
42. *Southern Review*, I (February, 1828), 224.
43. William Kauffman Scarborough (ed.) *The Diary of Edmund Ruffin* (3 vols. projected; Baton Rouge: Louisiana State University Press, 1972), I, 332–34.

Cincinnati to live, his difficulties were numerous; and when there were no work opportunities, he was accused of stealing. In his plea of guilty, he made a statement that the southern press printed with obvious relish. "Since I came here," he said, "I have been kicked about and abused by all classes of white men; can't get work from no one; and to borrow money . . . that is out of the question." He concluded by saying that as soon as he served his time on the chain gang he would return south and become a slave. Apparently the South was in short supply of similar stories. The Greensborough *Patriot* printed the same story in 1854 and 1859.[44]

Perhaps no experience was more exasperating or more embarrassing to southerners than the pursuit of their fugitive slaves. If improved means of transportation—better stages, packets and steamships, and railroads—made the trips of southerners to the North easier, the same was true for fugitive slaves. In the border states resourceful slaves, with or without forged passes, could purchase stage and rail tickets and be on their way to freedom before advertisements appeared announcing their escape.[45] Farther south slaves could use the master's horses for the getaway or they could secure the cooperation of other blacks—and even whites, sometimes—and make it to the North. Even if, as Larry Gara has argued, there was no "deep-laid scheme" or any widespread and effective mechanism to "run" slaves from south to north, a sufficient number escaped to convince the owners that a conspiracy existed and that northerners were responsible.[46]

44. Greensboro *Patriot*, December 2, 1854, and November 11, 1859.
45. In 1841 a Kentucky court said that the increase and improvement of stage lines was "increasing the evil of slaves running away." In the case before it, the court held the stage liable for selling a slave a ticket and ordered the company to compensate the owner for his loss. *Johnson* v. *Bryan*, 1 B. Mon. 226, in Catterall (ed.), *Judicial Cases*, I, 356. This was merely one of many cases, in a number of states, in which a transport company was held liable for the cost of a slave who escaped on a public carrier while posing as a free man.
46. Larry Gara, *The Liberty Line: The Legend of the Underground Railroad* (Lexington: University of Kentucky Press, 1961); see, especially, Chapter 4. See also Charles S. Sydnor, "Pursuing Fugitive Slaves," *South Atlantic Quarterly*, XXVIII (April, 1929), 155–56.

Undoubtedly, the vast majority of northerners conceded the right of southerners to pursue and recover their fugitives without any interference. Since the state personal-liberty laws of the 1840s indicated that states should not lend their facilities and personnel to aid in the recovery of fugitives, the recoveries were regarded as acts of hostility and, indeed, an invitation to northerners to support the fugitives. Meanwhile, federal laws—the act of 1793 and the more stringent act of 1850—seemed sufficient to extend to slaveholders the protection they required. Businessmen in the North thought that it was sheer madness for any northerners to defy the fugitive slave laws or interfere with their enforcement. Even if slavery was a great evil, one of them said, "the business of the North, as well as the South, has become adjusted to it."[47] Many northern ministers likewise supported the fugitive slave laws. "When a slave asks me to stand between him and his master," said Reverend W. M. Rogers in Boston, "What does he ask? He asks me to *murder a nation's life*; and I will not do it because I have a conscience—because there is a God."[48] Small wonder that the abolitionist Samuel J. May declared that the conduct of the clergy and churches was the "most serious obstacle to the progress of the antislavery cause."[49]

Neither the clergy nor businessmen, however sympathetic they might be, could return fugitive slaves to their owners. And it was the humiliating experience of going north and seeking them out that rankled even the mildest of masters. Even when they were treated well, it was little consolation. Late in 1850 a slave belonging to Richard Riddick of Pantego, Beaufort County, North Carolina, escaped, and it was believed that he went to Boston. Riddick went there in an effort to secure his return. He described his slave to the deputy United States marshal, who was certain that he had seen a person of that description working

47. Samuel Joseph May, *Some Recollections of Our Antislavery Conflict* (Boston: Fields, Osgood and Company, 1869), 127. See also Foner, *Business and Slavery*, 26.
48. Stanley W. Campbell, *The Slave Catchers: Enforcement of the Fugitive Slave Law, 1850–1860* (Chapel Hill: University of North Carolina Press, 1968), 70.
49. May, *Recollections of Our Antislavery Conflict*, 329.

in a factory. When Riddick went to the factory to identify his slave, he was not certain. "I was afraid the wrong one might be taken," he later wrote the United States marshal at Boston, "for I then thought there might be many at work there." He was convinced that the people in Boston had done all they could.[50]

Some Georgians seeking a fugitive slave were even more pleased with the treatment they received in Boston. When the agents of James Potter went to Boston in a successful effort to recover Thomas Sims, Potter's slave, they were so pleased with their treatment that they published in the Savannah *Republican* an open letter to the citizens of Boston. "We were most hospitably received," they declared, "and were surrounded during our stay there by hundreds of gentlemen who aided us by every means in their power. The merchants of the city in particular were conspicuous in their efforts to serve us. . . . Everything we saw and heard in Boston had left in our minds the strong and enduring impression that the respectable citizens of that place are a law abiding people—determined to see the laws executed and determined to do justice to the South."[51]

A few pleasant or favorable experiences of southerners who sought to recover fugitive slaves were insufficient to ease the anxieties of southerners or convince them that they would receive fair treatment in the North. Southerners themselves were caught in the web of propaganda spun by abolitionists who called them man-stealers and who vowed defiance of the federal laws in their protection of fugitives. And if southerners were man-stealers, abolitionists demonstrated that they could rescue such men. Their sensational rescues of Shadrack in Boston (1851), Jerry in Syracuse (1851), and Glover in Milwaukee (1854) greatly heightened the sense of frustration that southerners felt.[52]

50. Richard H. Riddick to Charles Devens, February 17, 1851, in Richard H. Riddick Papers, Duke University, Durham.

51. Quoted in Campbell, *Slave Catchers*, 120–21.

52. For detailed discussion of these and other rescues, *ibid.*, 148–69. See also Jacob R. Shipherd (comp.), *History of the Oberlin-Wellington Rescue* (Boston: John P. Jewett and Company, 1859).

They knew, moreover, that blacks in the North were doing what they could to protect fugitives. They had organized the New York Committee on Vigilance (1835), the New England Freedom Association (1845), and the Chicago Police Association (1850) for the express purpose of preventing the return of escaped slaves to bondage.[53] The utter desperation of blacks was best expressed by Frederick Douglass, who said, "The only way to make the Fugitive Slave Law a dead letter is to make half a dozen or more dead kidnappers."[54]

Whether they were pursuing their own fugitives or merely traveling in the North, southerners encountered many situations that suggested not only a hostility to slavery but what they felt was a callous disregard for the law as well. In 1837 a Virginian encountered two Negro men on a steamer on Lake Erie. One said that he had been emancipated by his master in Richmond. The other admitted that he had run away, "but refused to say from whom," of course.[55] Most southerners discovered that the pursuit of their slaves was a real trial. If they were successful in tracing their chattel, there was the great likelihood that someone would warn the fugitives. After pursuing two of his slaves from Virginia to Pennsylvania in 1845, the owner then discovered that they had been warned and had fled. A local citizen was fined five hundred dollars for harboring fugitives, but there was nothing to compensate the owner for his loss.[56]

Riots or near-riots occasioned by the pursuit of fugitive slaves were not uncommon and must have given owners a distinctly unfavorable impression of the North. In 1847 a slave family, mother, father, and three sons, absconded from their owner in Boone County, Kentucky. For more than one month the owner and several friends pursued them without success. Two years

---

53. Gara, *Liberty Line*, 101–102.
54. Rochester (N.Y.) *Frederick Douglass' Paper*, August 20, 1852.
55. "Tour to the Northern Lakes," *Southern Literary Messenger*, III (November, 1837), 687.
56. *Van Metre v. Mitchell*, 28 Federal Cases 1036, in Catterall (ed.), *Judicial Cases*, IV, 305.

later the owner learned that the fugitives were living in Cass County, Michigan, whereupon he set out, with several others, to recapture them. When he found them and told them he had come to take them back, the two younger boys and their mother seemed willing to return. The oldest one, who had married, was unwilling to go unless his wife went with them. She declined, and her husband was tied up and taken. When the owner arrived in South Bend, a large crowd of more than one hundred blacks and whites, including the sheriff, intercepted the travelers. The sheriff required the owner to go into court to prove that the Negroes in his custody were his slaves. The judge set the blacks free, on the ground that they were in a free state; and the owner and his friends, with weapons drawn, demanded the release of the alleged slaves. The Negroes were placed in jail for safekeeping, after which they were discharged. The owner, however, was able to obtain a verdict of $2,850 in damages against the Michigan resident who had been harboring them.[57]

By any measure, the pursuit of fugitive slaves was not a rewarding experience, even when it was educational. First of all, it was expensive even if successful. The return of Thomas Sims to Georgia cost his owner more than $3,000. Although this was unusually high, because of lengthy litigation, any running away required hasty, unplanned trips by the owner or his agents if there was to be any chance of recovery.[58] Secondly, the pursuits were almost invariably unpleasant, and only a few owners were as cordially received as those who went to Boston in 1851. In many parts of the North, defiant and threatening free Negroes, heckling abolitionists, hostile sheriffs, and even unfriendly judges could make life miserable for slaveowners in search of their slaves, and frequently did. Finally, it was dangerous. Fugitive slaves, desperately seeking a better life, did not always

57. *Norris v. Newton*, 18 Federal Cases 322, *ibid.*, V, 35–36. See, also, the case of six slaves who escaped from Kentucky to Michigan in 1843 and whose return was prevented by free Negroes who deliberately created an incident during which the slaves escaped their owners and fled to Canada. *Ibid.*, V, 81–84.
58. Gara, *Liberty Line*, 141.

return quietly when captured by their owners. If their capture
led to a riot, it could, in turn, lead to tragedy, as it did in Christi-
ana, Pennsylvania, when a Maryland slaveholder was killed and
his son seriously wounded in 1851.[59] Such experiences inevitably helped to build up southern hostility toward the North.

It was the "heckling" abolitionists, with their self-righteous
contempt for slaveholders, that most aggravated southerners in
the North. And they welcomed assurances from other northerners that abolitionism was not representative of northern
thought. "*Abolition*, if not dead here, is in a state too desperately
feeble to give us an hour's uneasiness," a Virginian wrote from
New England in 1834. Of the many intelligent men with whom
he had talked, there was "but a single one who does not repro-
bate the views of Messrs. Tappan, Cox, Garrison and company as
suggestions of the wildest, most pernicious fanaticism." The
Virginian was convinced that at least nine-tenths of the votes and
"ninety-nine hundredths" of the intellect of the country favored
letting the South wholly alone. He insisted that Garrison and his
"will-o-the-wisp, the *Liberator*" were held in utter contempt. A
professor in Cambridge predicted that in two years abolitionism
would be as dead as antimasonry was then. "In a word," he
concluded, "the south may be assured, that on this point, New
England is sound, at least the three states [Massachusetts, Rhode
Island, and Connecticut] which I have visited."[60]

While abolitionism was not dying in New England in 1834, as
the Virginian wished to believe, it was not yet a threat to the
peace and stability of the South. And those southerners who
traveled in the North in the early antebellum years seemed more
interested in the wonders of northern civilization than in what
they would later describe as its deadly defects. Even so, abolitionism could bear watching; and some southern travelers were
inclined to do precisely that. If they expressed no great alarm

59. Campbell, *Slave Catchers*, 151–52.
60. "Letters from New England—1," *Southern Literary Messenger*, I (November,
1834), 87–89.

over the Tappans and the Garrisons, as some southerners were
doing back home, it was in part because on close inspection they
did not appear to be very formidable and in part because southern visitors got the distinct impression that the abolitionists were
just about as unpopular in the North as they were in the South.
"The abolitionists are few in number," wrote a southern student
at an eastern college in 1843, "and are universally held in that
contempt, which the wildness of their schemes justly draws
down upon them."[61] If the young southerner did not reflect
complacency, neither did he express indifference.

Toward the end of the 1840s, with the intensification of the
intersectional controversy, southern travelers became more sensitive about abolitionist sentiment and activities. In the previous
decade, for example, the controversy over the distribution of
abolitionist writings had culminated in the burning of such materials at the Charleston post office. Between 1836 and 1844 a "Gag
Rule" prevented the receiving of antislavery petitions in the
House of Representatives; and the fight over its repeal greatly
increased hard feelings between the North and South.[62] Thus,
when a Virginian was in Connecticut in the late spring of 1847,
he was interested in seeing how much abolitionist sentiment
there was in the village he was visiting. His landlord did what
was essential for the guest's comfort, but was "grudging of bland
words, and even of courteous answers to questions," he reported.
"Says there are more abolitionists in the neighborhood. Indeed a
fire-eating one is at my elbow while I jot down these notes: a

61. A Southron, "Vacation Scribblings; Or, Letters from a College Down East,"
Southern Literary Messenger, IX (July, 1843), 438. When a southern editor met a
number of delegates attending an abolition convention in Mount Vernon, Ohio, his
greatest concern was the numerous misrepresentations of southern slavery that he heard
and which he attempted to correct. B. B. Minor, "Slavery in the French Colonies,"
Southern Literary Messenger, X (May, 1844), 268.

62. For a discussion of these incidents, see W. Sherman Savage, *The Controversy
Over the Distribution of Abolition Literature, 1830–1860* (Washington: Association for
the Study of Negro Life and History, 1938), 66–81; and Henry H. Simms, *Emotion at
High Tide: Abolition as a Controversial Factor, 1830–1845* (Baltimore: Moore and
Company, 1960), 68–71, 93–117.

working-man he calls himself. His reasonings on the subject are above my comprehension."[63]

By 1849, the matter of abolitionism was of sufficient importance to justify an extensive discussion of the matter in *Sketches on a Tour Through the Northern and Eastern States*, which the author, J. C. Myers, thought would be helpful to subsequent travelers. He classified the abolitionists of New England in three groups: "the moderate, the ultra, and the fanatic." He was pleased to report that the majority belonged to the moderate group, "honest in their abolition opinions, acknowledging they have no right to meddle with the institutions of other states." The ultra abolitionists were those who bitterly denounced slavery in the South and the federal system that gave the South more representation than she was entitled to. They were quite ready to meddle with southern institutions "and to inflict on the South, such measures as . . . will have a tendency to favor . . . their ends." The fanatics were the most deluded, who, though few in numbers, "make up in part by their untiring energy in speaking, writing and laying deep and dangerous schemes." They were so perfectly mad on the subject of slavery, declared Myers, that their whole soul was filled with burning gall, and they were ever seeking an opportunity to "spit . . . venom on the South, for the purpose of withering down her institutions, even at the very hazard of shivering into fragments, our glorious Union."[64] From this point on, it would be well for southerners to study carefully those whom they encountered in the North.

The controversy over slavery and the debates in Congress that led to the Compromise of 1850 raised to the danger point the level of bitterness and recrimination in the charges and counter-charges between the North and South.[65] The inveterate traveler,

63. A Virginian, "One Day of a Foot Tour in Connecticut," *Southern Literary Messenger*, XIV (June, 1848), 386.
64. Myers, *Sketches on a Tour*, 378–84.
65. See Holman Hamilton, *Prologue to Conflict: The Crisis and the Compromise of 1850* (Lexington: University of Kentucky Press, 1964).

William Gilmore Simms, did not make his usual trip to the North in the summer of 1850. When he wrote his good friend James Lawson, to tell him that it was unlikely that he would be his guest that summer, Simms merely indicated that he had too much to do in Charleston.[66] In a piece in the *Southern Quarterly Review*, which he edited, Simms gave reasons why neither he nor any other self-respecting southerner should visit the North. He was moved to comment on the North in his review of two important works on the South, Charles Lanman's *Letters from the Alleghany Mountains* and William C. Richards' *Georgia Illustrated*. The significance of these works was almost lost as Simms launched into his diatribe against the North.

In the summer of 1849 there was an epidemic of cholera in several northern cities; and New York, with approximately five thousand dying from the dread disease, was the hardest hit.[67] Suggesting that there was no such thing as an unmixed evil in the world, Simms said, "The cholera, which devastated the cities of the North last summer, and the abolition mania,—which is destined to root them out, and raze them utterly from the face of the earth, if not seasonably arrested,—have proved, in some degree, highly serviceable, if not saving influences, for the people of the South." How many thousands of wandering idlers from the South had been denied their usual "inane indulgences" by the dread of pestilence, Simms asked. "And how many other thousands, capable of appreciating the charms of nature, and the delights of a glorious landscape, were, in like manner, compelled to forego the same progress, by the patriotic sentiment which revolts at the thought of spending time and money among a people whose daily labor seems to be addressed to the

66. William G. Simms to James Lawson, June 19, 1850, in Mary C. Simms Oliphant and T. C. Duncan Eaves (eds.), *The Letters of William Gilmore Simms* (5 vols.; Columbia: University of South Carolina Press, 1954), III, 49.

67. Charles Rosenberg, *The Cholera Years: The United States in 1832, 1849, and 1866* (Chicago: University of Chicago Press, 1962), 101–14. See also Allen Nevins (ed.), *The Diary of Philip Hone, 1828–1851* (2 vols.; New York: Dodd, Mead and Company, 1927), I, 870–75.

neighborly desire of defaming our character and destroying our institutions?"

Simms asserted that there was a race in the South that could best be described as "soft-heads," whose dignity required "foreign travel" for its proper maintenance. For such people, he said, it was absolutely necessary that they should go away each summer. "The habit required it, and the self-esteem if the tastes did not." He boasted that the cholera was confined to the North because "either the climate of the South was too pure, or the habits of the people too proper, to yield it to the requisite field for operation. Consequently, for once the "soft-heads" were compelled to remain at home. For thirty years they had been feeding the abolitionists who "rage in all places, fireside, street, exchange, hotel, and, not so much seeking to reform and teach, as to outrage and annoy." At last the "soft-heads" were beginning to feel somewhat uncomfortable "sitting cheek-by-jowl, at Saratoga, and other places of vulgar resort, and hearing themselves described as robbers and wretches by the very people whose thieving ancestors stole the negro with whom to swindle our forefathers."

Simms believed that because of the cholera *and* the intensification of abolitionism perhaps as many as twenty thousand southerners refrained from going north the previous summer. This was, he said, painful in the extreme, for the tour to West Point, Saratoga, Newport, and Niagara "was a sort of pilgrimage as necessary to the eternal happiness of our race of 'soft-heads' as ever was that made, once in a life, to Mecca, by the devout worshipper in the faith of Islam!"[68] In the following summer, Simms, and perhaps the twenty thousand other southerners who had remained at home in 1850, were back in their old haunts in the North.[69] Ironically, the ill-wind blew in the direction of

68. "Summer Travel in the South," *Southern Quarterly Review*, XVIII (September, 1850), 24–32.
69. See above, pp. 40–43.

Simms himself in 1854, when an epidemic of cholera broke out in Charleston and the *Southern Quarterly Review* for July had to be published in Columbia.[70]

By 1850, then, Simms had come to represent—at least in his utterances if not in his actions—the extreme southern reaction to northern abolitionism. But he did his fellow southerners an injustice by referring to them opprobriously as "soft-heads" because they, like Simms, frequented the North. Their presence in the North was no indication of their lack of awareness of abolition sentiment or any yielding to the antislavery argument. They had their own reasons for going to the North, as indeed Simms had. When David Aiken of South Carolina went to Cincinnati in 1850, he too was impressed with the abolitionist sentiment that was more widespread than he wanted to believe. And he had every opportunity to argue with those who held antislavery views, but he did not do so because he found the people "as ignorant of the institution South . . . as if a Great Desert lay between Cincinnati and the Kentucky shore."[71] A. F. Rightor of Louisiana listened carefully to the arguments he heard in the North, and he made distinctions among the views that northerners held, as he made among views held by southerners. In 1851 he heard Rufus Choate deliver a "noble and patriotic discourse" before the students at the Harvard Law School. Choate, though antislavery in his views, had been a supporter of the compromise measure of 1850 and had praised the role of Daniel Webster, who was denounced by many of his Massachusetts constituents.[72] Of Choate's address, Rightor said, "No man from the South, who had one particle of patriotism could object to any one word, or any one sentiment of the whole of his address." Rightor felt that the southern fire-eaters and the "higher law men" would both lose their influence, since they were primarily interested in

70. *Southern Quarterly Review*, XXII (July, 1854).
71. Aiken, "Autobiography."
72. For an account of Choate's career, see Claude M. Fuess, *Rufus Choate, The Wizard of the Law* (New York: Minton, Balch and Company, 1928).

riding into power "upon the storm of this black excitement."[73]

Among abolitionists who attracted the attention of southerners—perhaps as much for his showmanship as for the content of his sermons—Henry Ward Beecher was high on the list. Not only was he the brother of the author of *Uncle Tom's Cabin*, so fiercely reviled in the South, but he had built a reputation of his own as one of slavery's deadliest enemies. In 1853, John R. Thompson, the editor of the *Southern Literary Messenger*, was visiting in New York and went over to Brooklyn one Sunday to hear Beecher. Arriving just in time to hear the pastoral prayer, Thompson heard southerners being prayed for "as among those steeped in the guilt of slavery, as one of a numerous band of murderers and robbers." He was pleased, however, to hear Beecher offer a fervent supplication in his behalf.

At the beginning of his sermon, Beecher announced a text; but he soon strayed from it and "took a wide range over the entire field of polemics, and touched every topic of present interest in science, government and morals." He paced across the platform, "moving with an agility that would do credit to Francois Ravel." His gestures were proper, and his words were well chosen. He was beyond question the most forceful speaker that Thompson had ever heard. Beecher finally got around to slaveholders, whom he called "man-stealers, hypocrites, and everything that is vile and brutish and despicable." He then turned on the New York merchants who tolerated southerners through cowardly considerations of trade. He criticized the clergy that was more concerned about problems thousands of miles away than with the fact that some three millions of their own fellow human beings under their own government were deprived of the word of God. Thompson was not unduly shaken:

> We listened to all these things with becoming composure, bethinking ourselves of the ninth commandment now and then, but we could

73. A. F. Rightor to Andrew McCollam, July 25, 1851, in Andrew McCollam Papers, University of North Carolina, Chapel Hill.

not repress a feeling of sadness on coming out of the building amid the throng of well-dressed and intelligent-looking people who worshipped there, to think that, week after week, these people were being instructed as a religious duty, to despise their fellow-citizens—even their Christian brethren—of the Southern States, nor could we dismiss the painful apprehension that one of these days this instruction would work out its legitimate effect in fraternal strife. Should such disaster occur, the Rev. Henry Ward Beecher will be among those accountable for it.[74]

Some southerners were not as composed as Thompson when they heard northerners inveigh against the South and its institutions. Paul Hamilton Hayne, in Boston to see his book of poems through the press, was furious at what he heard and saw in that "very hot bed of abolitionism." Bostonians, he wrote his wife, were "absolutely rampant on that question." He heard a sermon in which the Presbyterian minister said that every slaveholder must be damned, "the nominal Christians who held that property, more inevitably than others. Such cant and fanaticism I never heard even from the amiable Theodore Parker." Hayne was certain that the time would come when the controversy over slavery would reach a point when the people of the South, "if they have manhood in them, will resist as Mr. Benton expresses it to 'the funeral.'" He had his doubts about his own South Carolina which was "too lamentably ignorant to appreciate her wrongs." To help his state prepare herself, he had spent several days preparing an elaborate article on the slavery question for the Charleston *News*.[75]

Abolitionism was gradually taking its toll, even on southerners who were inclined to tolerate it, if for no other reason than to justify their traveling in the North and observing the antislavery people at close range. One southern planter, no longer willing to excuse or explain away the foibles of abolitionism in 1857, did seek to explain what had happened to the movement *and* to

74. *Southern Literary Messenger*, XX (January, 1854), 60–61.
75. Paul H. Hayne to Mary Michel Hayne, October 27, 1854, in Paul Hamilton Hayne Papers.

himself over almost three decades. When he was attending a New England college in 1830, he went one evening, out of youthful curiosity, to a public meeting convened by a new group calling itself the Society for the Abolition of Slavery. Although the "wild glare of an unsettled brain marked the countenances of most of those who conducted the meeting," they disclaimed any intention to interfere directly with slavery in the states. Instead, they focused on its cruelties and immoralities in an effort to influence public opinion in the North, which would, in turn, press the South to "ameliorate and speedily extinguish the unholy institution." It seemed to the young southerner a perfectly harmless exercise from which most of the assembly went away "smiling and pitying the strange enthusiasts, who could embark on so hopeless an undertaking."

What had happened to the movement in the years between 1830 and 1857 and what he observed in the latter year was enough to turn him, who had opposed disunion in every shape and form, into an ardent disunionist. The movement that in 1830 had been the concern of only a few starry-eyed visionaries had become by 1857 the obsession of vast numbers of the most substantial elements in the area. Let a person "travel through New England, confer with her intelligent farmers and villagers, attend her hustings; talk with her soberfaced men of business, mercantile, manufacturing, professional, or educational; go into her churches; read her daily, weekly, and monthly periodicals, examine the shelves of her bookstores, and tell me what he had heard and seen *touching slavery*." Only those who are motivated by greedy and selfish interests and seek to exploit their southern customers will in any way express sympathy for the South. All the others will not only express hostility to the South and its institutions but will call for their merciless and utter destruction at the earliest possible moment.[76]

76. "South Side View of the Union, by a Southern Planter," *De Bow's Review*, XXIII (November, 1857), 462–64. In 1859, Benjamin L. C. Wailes of Natchez was thunderstruck by the attitude toward the South of the librarian of the American Philosophical

By the late fifties, then, many southerners who saw what was happening in the North were convinced that northerners were out to destroy the institution of slavery. What was worse, these fanatics advocated the kind of reform *in the South* that would clearly place blacks over whites. It mattered not that blacks occupied a degraded position in the North and that the abolitionists were doing little if anything to elevate them. It mattered not that the hopeless condition of blacks in the North was the best possible argument in support of slavery. It did not seem to matter that federal laws were clearly on the side of the slaveholders, for they had been reviled and condemned when they sought their fugitive slaves, and by none in the population more than the degraded free Negroes. Thus, it was the southerners' experience with the problem of race in the North—including fugitives, race mixing, racial degradation, and fanatical abolitionism—that contributed significantly to disunionist sentiment in the South.

Society. When Wailes called on him to enlist his aid in recruiting teachers for Jefferson College in Mississippi, the librarian took the opportunity of introducing the subject of slavery. Wailes found him "the most rabid, stark crazy man on the subject" that he had ever encountered and he was particularly surprised "to find such narrow fanatical views entertained by a man of his position." Charles S. Sydnor, *A Gentleman of the Old Natchez Region: Benjamin L. C. Wailes* (Durham: Duke University Press, 1935), 284. Regarding a different sentiment in the North see Howard C. Perkins, "The Defense of Slavery in the Northern Press on the Eve of the Civil War," *Journal of Southern History*, IX (November, 1943), 501–31.

V

A Far Cry
from
Eden

Whatever southerners saw in the North they found invariably interesting and frequently attractive and admirable. If they seldom expressed complete admiration for what they saw, perhaps it was because they felt, as did the editor of the *Southern Literary Messenger*, that admiration was "one of the most exhausting processes the mind can undergo."[1] At times, however, they did shed their restraints and become quite enthusiastic if not ecstatic. But even as they expressed admiration, they felt obliged to reaffirm their loyalty to the South, as if, somehow, admiration for the North bespoke a certain betrayal of their own section. Northern cities were the centers of incredible activity and excitement, but the rural South was more wholesome and healthy. Northern colleges and universities could boast certain advantages in equipment and personnel, but southern educational institutions were best suited for southerners. Northern factories reflected real Yankee ingenuity and efficiency, but the problems they created in human and labor relations had already been solved by the South's superior economic and social order. The wealth of the North was "fugitive and fictitious," said George Fitzhugh, while that of the South was "permanent and real."[2] Northerners themselves were enterprising and resourceful, but southerners, devoid of guile and deception, were more honest and honorable.

1. *Southern Literary Messenger*, XIX (August, 1853), 518. The editor made this remark after visiting the Crystal Palace Exposition in New York in the summer of 1853.
2. George Fitzhugh, "The Wealth of the North and South," *De Bow's Review*, XXIII (December, 1857), 592.

Thus, a grudging concession was coupled with a certain ambivalence as southerners viewed the North. If northern civilization was remarkable, it was also an enigma; and any self-respecting southern observer would have some very serious reservations about embracing it uncritically, if at all. And the most serious reservation was not regarding northern cities, northern colleges, or even northern industry, but in what southerners sensed to be a northern condescension toward them and a general disdain for their way of life. Southerners felt that northerners regarded them as crude country bumpkins, good for exploitation but in no way their cultural or social or business equals. What was especially galling to many southerners was that northerners were always grasping for their money and, at the same time, excoriating them for the way they made it. These reservations were not strong enough to restrain southerners from going north. As they went, however, they were resolved not to be "taken in" by everything that they saw and, at all times, to resist the notion that the South was hopelessly backward.

Southern resistance to all features of northern life that might possibly seduce them—the subtle as well as the obvious—was as fierce as it was, at times, childish. It could be seen in the comparisons that southerners constantly made between the North and the South that were, more often than not, invidious to the North. And these comparisons could easily reach the level of the absurd. In 1834 a Virginian, delayed in his trip from Pittsfield to Albany, explained that he had been caught in a thunder storm. It was "quite as magnificent as most that we have in Virginia"; but then he added, with an obvious touch of pride, "only our thunder and lightning are far superior."[3] A young Georgian, after graduating from Princeton and going on to study law at Litchfield, Connecticut, had some comments about the weather that were somewhat more incisive than those of the Virginian.

3. "Letters from New England—3," *Southern Literary Messenger*, I (January, 1835), 217.

"The air is more piercing here than it was generally at Princeton," he told his father, "but I have the consolation of seeing that I am not made of more chilly materials than the native New Englanders. I wish I were as well seasoned to Southern roasting as to Northern freezing."[4] Happily, most southerners were concerned with other matters than the weather; but whether their comments on the weather or on other matters were adverse or favorable, it was the comparison—implicit if not clearly stated—from which they seemed unable to escape.

Southerners felt especially well qualified to comment on the physical features of the northern countryside. Even if they lived in a southern town or city, they had some familiarity with the southern countryside, through their own plantations or other rural connections, that had sharpened their powers to observe any rural scene, North or South. Those who journeyed to the northern cities by ocean packet or river steamer had little opportunity en route to view the rural scenes of the North; and once there, all too few of them were sufficiently interested to make special excursions into the rural areas. Overland travelers, though doubtless fewer in number, had a much better opportunity to see the rural North; and they seldom failed to speak with authority about what they saw. A few intrepid souls made walking tours. Despite their difficulties with the terrain and the weather, they were able to see both the land and the people better than most.

It was the northern countryside of which southerners had the least criticism and with which comparisons seemed the least important. After all, northerners could hardly take credit for the virtues and beauty that nature had bestowed; and perhaps this fact alone moved southerners to make quite generous remarks about the scenery and to claim it for the entire country. Students from the South had a special feeling in that regard. While touring

4. W. C. Cumming to Thomas C. Cumming, April 1, 1807, in Alfred Cumming Letters, Duke University, Durham.

a portion of New England, after being "let loose from the prison-walls of a university," one of them said, "Give me to see the sublime and beautiful in nature—the rocks and torrents, forests and mountains, hills, vales, and grassy plains that are found in my own lovely land—give me to know and love my country, and I ask no more."[5] Another exclaimed, "But it *is* a glorious sight. . . . Nature and Art appear to have 'improved upon themselves' in spreading out before you the beauties of their own creation. O it makes me feel *proud of my native land*, and calls forth the tribute of a grateful heart to the Creator of all."[6]

If southern students were apt to regard northern scenery as a national resource, their elders—more prone to making comparisons—spoke no less admiringly of its beauty and attractiveness. A Virginia planter, having traversed Massachusetts and Connecticut "in jersey wagon and on foot, on highways and by-ways," had earned the right to speak on the subject and especially on what man had done to improve the scenery. "The country is more hilly, or rolling, as our farmers would say, than the lower half of Virginia; and the hills have, generally, a smaller base and a more gracefully swelling, dome-like top, than our hills. These rotundities, with their concomitant hollows, traversed by numberless stone fences, with here and there patches of woodland and detached white farm houses, half imbosomed in elms and fruit trees; while, perhaps, two or three villages, with steeples piercing the sky, are at once within the view, exhibit everywhere landscapes of a beauty unknown to eastern, or indeed to western Virginia."[7] This was New England scenery at its best, and it is clear that the traveler would be pleased if Virginians could give their own countryside a similar

5. J. Q. P., "Extracts from Gleanings on the Way," *Southern Literary Messenger*, IV (April, 1838), 249.

6. A Southron, "Vacation Scribblings; Or, Letters from a College Down East," *Southern Literary Messenger*, IX (July, 1843), 439.

7. "Letters from New England—1," *Southern Literary Messenger*, I (November, 1834), 84–85.

appearance by providing more stone fences, more white houses, and even more steeples "piercing the sky."

Travelers in the middle states had similar experiences, where one in New York was "struck with the never-ending variety of its lovely landscapes, at one time presenting the blue, bold majesty of the Catskills, at another, the undulating region of the Genessee."[8] "I had never imagined that anything half so grand and so picturesque awaited us," said another as he began his upriver jaunt from New York City. "The half had not been told. Besides the splendor of the scenery,—the tremendous hills and ravines on one side, and the gently levelling upland and lowland fields and meadows, full of fertility and the promise of rich harvests, on the other,—there were a thousand associations with the early history of our Republic, especially with that interesting period, when 'men's souls were tried,' which rendered it a continuous and uninterrupted scene of thrilling and exciting interest." He found Lebanon Springs quite attractive, despite the fact that its waters had "no very decided mineral or medicinal qualities." There were commodious bathing houses, which added to the pleasure of a visit. "But even in this respect," he concluded, "they cannot be compared with the warm and Hot Springs of Bath County in Virginia."[9]

Although the English and the Germans had exerted quite different influences on the history of Pennsylvania, one visitor rejoiced that neither group had done anything to mar the beauty of the countryside of the keystone state. The Schuylkill River flowed "in sublime grandeur" through the great transverse gorge at Reading. The mountains northwest of Reading afforded "picturesque and romantic scenery," and no traveler could fail to "remark the long and uniform parallel ridges with intervening valleys, like so many gigantic wrinkles and furrows," which

8. "Lake George," *Southern Literary Messenger*, IX (November, 1843), 697.
9. Viator, "Traits of a Summer Tourist," *Southern Literary Messenger*, II (October, 1836), 698, 699.

marked the geographical outline of that region. In still another area were the celebrated coal mines, with "some beautiful coal seams, which appeared very smooth and glittering." Finally, there were the many fertile, well-cultivated valleys in many parts of the state and the "glorious sunset on the islands and waters of the noble Susquehanna . . . the richest and loveliest scene" that one southern visitor had witnessed in his trip through Pennsylvania.[10]

If comparisons with the South were not more frequent, perhaps it was because southerners had not previously thought in terms of "their land versus ours," and had certainly taken for granted that which they now felt impelled to evaluate. It was not until the abolition agitation turned some of them toward southern resorts that they really began to explore the South, as one southerner put it in 1856, "and then they were startled to find themselves entering an almost enchanted region of which they had never before heard." It took one who was thoroughly familiar with both sections to make meaningful comparisons, but this southerner would not make them. And it was not that he felt unqualified to do so. He believed that he had rambled over more of the lake country and New England "than nine-tenths of the Northern pleasure-seekers who frequent the Springs." He had been to Niagara, fished in Lake George, "watched the sea break over the craggy promontory of Lake Nahant and loitered for days along the banks of the Hudson." But comparisons were both unnecessary and pointless. "Even were we disposed to concede, as we are not, that Nature has been more lavish of her beauties in the Northern States, we should still contend that one can better enjoy scenery in the South, for here one's meditations upon a prospect of unusual sublimity are not interrupted by the intrusion of a crowd of vulgar people just arrived in the last train, who

10. J. C. Myers, *Sketches on a Tour through the Northern and Eastern States, the Canadas and Nova Scotia* (Harrisonburg, Va.: J. H. Wartmann and Brothers, 1849), 452–59.

insist upon his hearing their own opinions of it."[11] Even where scenery was concerned, the sectionalists of the 1850s had replaced the nationalists of the 1830s.

As southerners confronted the urban scene in the North, they were on less sure ground than when they viewed the countryside. After all, there was nothing in the South to compare with Boston, New York, and Philadelphia; and any attempt to place southern urban centers, even New Orleans, in the same category with the great metropolitan centers of the North would merely point up the vast differences. When William A. Caruthers, in *The Kentuckian in New York*, had Beverley Randolph say that in both artificial and natural beauty Savannah was superior to the great northern cities, one had to understand that Caruthers himself had already decided to move to Savannah![12] Since the orientation of southerners was essentially rural, moreover, they had little preparation for a truly critical appreciation of urban life; and they were likely to view the northern city in a most elementary and unsophisticated way. Consequently, these very complex urban organisms tended to be huge or pretty or noisy or wicked or all of those things and more. It should be remembered that the great cities and watering places—with their own brand of urbanity—were the chief magnets for travelers from the South. Except for those who found fault with virtually everything, the visitors did not go to criticize but to enjoy. And while it is possible that they were pleased when they discovered some defects in the cities, they did not reproach themselves for having visited places that had their weak points.

Quite naturally, one of the first comments that the southern visitor made was on the physical appearance of the cities. Philadelphia impressed them with its orderly and regular plan and its clean streets. What Boston lacked in physical appearance,

11. "Domestic Tourism," *Southern Literary Messenger*, XVII (June, 1851), 378–79.
12. William Alexander Caruthers, *A Kentuckian in New York* (2 vols.; New York: Harper and Brothers, 1834), II, 136.

with its crooked streets and unpretentious houses, was more than balanced by its great public buildings and its memorable Commons. New York was a magnificent combination of the old and new, the irregular and haphazard shape of the older parts and the orderly layout of the newer uptown.[13] Nor did they remark merely on the "Big Three." Indeed, some of them found some of the smaller cities more worthy of praise. Cecelia described Hartford as a "pretty city," standing on the western bank of the Connecticut River. "The beautiful trees that shade its streets, its fine houses with their encircling shrubbery and flowers, its benevolent asylums, its college, and the Athenaeum with its library and gallery of paintings, are among the objects of interest to pleasure-seeking travellers."[14] New Jersey had its attractive cities, and one of the favorites was Newark, "well built with spacious streets and handsome houses, many of which are animated with fine, graceful streets."[15] There seemed to be a general consensus among southern visitors regarding the attractiveness of northern cities. As one of them said: "The beautiful architecture of the Northern cities, the spacious and shaded parks, the tasteful gardens, the excellent roads, the chaste amusements of the metropolis, the increased attention that is paid to the fine arts, and the high standards to which collegiate institutions have advanced the education of the rising race, are flattering evidences of the progress of civilization and refinement."[16]

The sheer size of the northern cities was another feature that impressed the visitors; and if they made no reference to population figures, they were constantly remarking on those things, such as the crowds, the bustle and the noise, that characterized

13. For some reactions to these appearances, see above.
14. Cecelia, "Memories of Home Travels," *Southern Literary Messenger*, XX (January, 1854), 30. See, also, comments about Cincinnati, "one of the handsomest towns in the United States," in H. Ruffner, "Notes on a Tour from Virginia to Tennessee," *Southern Literary Messenger*, V (February, 1839), 139.
15. Myers, *Sketches on a Tour*, 429.
16. *Southern Literary Journal*, III (November, 1836), 229.

large cities. When he arrived in New York in 1853, a Tennessee planter was "right glad to be amidst all the noise and bustle of omnibus's and carriages."[17] A visitor from Virginia was pleased to learn, when he reached New York, that half the town was "out of town." He was delighted with the news, but was unable to reconcile that bit of information with his three hours of trudging about the city in search of a room. He soon learned that by "out of town" was meant that "wandering, gossiping, gadding, sightseeing, lionizing, country-visiting portion of this great Babel, who make it a point to spend all 'the months that have no R,' at the crowded watering places of their own and neighboring states. But they have left the streets as noisy, as crowded, and as business-like as ever, and a stranger feels quizzed when told that they are empty."[18]

New York was, of course, the busiest and noisiest of all cities, and to some visitors it never achieved a moment of quiet, even at night. A Mobile woman, traveling with her husband who was indisposed most of the time, complained that "the noise of the streets . . . exceeds anything I ever knew. We can scarcely take any rest in consequence. People seem never to repose here. All night long the streets are resounding with the rattling of carriages over the stony streets."[19] And if Philadelphia and Boston were more sedate and dignified, they too were busy and the crowds were enormous. What puzzled one visitor was not the hustle and bustle of the big cities, but a similar activity in the smaller ones. Within a space of sixty miles he saw four Connecticut towns—Bridgeport, New Haven, Middletown, and Hartford—which, "though small, were all teeming with life and activity." Even in the villages between the towns everybody appeared to be busy. He was moved to ask, "What supports these towns? On what do

17. John Stewart Oxley to Tom Henry, October 1, 1853, in Gustavus A. Henry Papers, University of North Carolina, Chapel Hill.

18. Viator, "Traits of a Summer Tourist," 697.

19. Sarah Gayle Crawford Diary, August, 1853, in Gayle-Crawford Collection, University of North Carolina, Chapel Hill.

they subsist? Here are ships. What do they carry? What does this country produce to constitute the basis of their commerce? At home we had seen our wharves crowded with cotton and rice, and we knew that the ships came for them; but what does Connecticut produce to tempt the mariner across the ocean?"[20] This observation was made in the 1820s, and the traveler was just as puzzled thirty years later, for he had so little understanding of the composition and complexities of urban life.

Even if there were features of urban life that remained enigmatic, it was clear to many southern visitors that the city afforded opportunities that existed nowhere else. Only in a city such as New York could one see the "workings of commerce on a grand scale—docks crowded with ships bringing every description of foreign cargo, the thousands of merchantmen, the streets of banking houses, and the stock exchange." And "in the midst of an almost infinity of mercantile affairs that are going on in this market-house of the Union, he witnesses all the bitterness of political strifes, all the energy of partizanship, and the animosities of hatred." But this seemed inevitable because of the intense rivalry and activity that pervaded the society. All of this, said the writer, tended to expand the mind of one who studied the city, "bringing him into connection with and laying open to him the interior machinery of society,—the means by which an overgrown city operates on distant communities, and the influences it exerts whether for good or evil, on society at large."[21]

Urban life in the North, moreover, gave to southerners precisely those experiences that were all too rare at home if, indeed, they existed at all. If they wanted to fire their sense of patriotism, they could visit Independence Hall in Philadelphia or Faneuil Hall in Boston, "the Athens of the Republic," as a southern editor put it.[22] No similar monuments existed in any of the five slave

20. *Southern Quarterly Review*, XXVI (October, 1854), 433.
21. *Southern Literary Messenger*, VII (July, August, 1841), 557.
22. *Southern Literary Journal*, III (November, 1836), 331.

states that had been colonies. If they wanted to attend the theater or concerts or opera, they could find these a part of the regular cultural life of many northern cities, whereas they were infrequent attractions even in the most advanced southern communities. If they desired to combine business with pleasure and enjoy amenities that gave them a sense of refreshment and well-being, a sojourn in a northern city, preferably *the* northern city, was the best place to do it.[23]

But if the northern city was the "noisy, busy, great and animating emporium," with displays of magnificent opulence and splendid appearances, it was also the place where one saw the "squalid hut of poverty, of filth, of extreme misery and degradation."[24] And such sights, all too numerous, came easily to the attention of the southern travelers who were persuaded that urban misery and depravity were infinitely more unattractive than rural poverty. They believed, moreover, that there was less excuse for it in the northern city where there was so much wealth and where so much attention was given to the shortcomings of the South. "Anyone who walks the streets of New York with his eyes and ears open, sees and hears many strange and horrid things," said William Bobo of Charleston. "Poverty, sickness, filth, crime, and wretchedness meet him full in the face at every turn; and if he has a heart to feel for the misery of his fellow-creatures, it will be wrung with agony, by the shocking things he encounters."[25]

Southerners were especially pleased to point to any deficiency that could not be attributed to slavery. Urban filth, or filth in any form, was one of them. "In our rash youth," one of them said, "we used to believe that this criminal inattention to all the proprieties of house, chamber, bed, table, body, and apparel, was one of the thousand ills attributable to slavery or association with slaves.

---

23. See above, Chapter I.
24. Myers, *Sketches on a Tour*, 50.
25. [William M. Bobo], *Glimpses of New York City, by a South Carolinian (Who Had Nothing Else to Do)* (Charleston: J. J. McCarter, 1852), 32.

We have outlived that error. We have seen such dirt in Ohio and New York, and such slovenliness and disregard for comfort in Maine and Vermont, and the Canadas, and 'all alongshore' on the free northern frontier, that we are compelled to ascribe it to some wide and more universal cause."[26] Apparently, the writer derived strange comfort in bringing other areas into a common association with the filth whose existence he conceded in the slaveholding areas.

Begging, professional and amateur, was one display of wretchedness about which southerners frequently spoke. Bobo told of an old woman who had a regular spot—on the corner of Lispenard and Broadway—that she had occupied for more than twenty-five years. He learned that she had amassed a considerable fortune and owned the building across the street that rented annually for $2,500. He had been informed that there was a well-organized association of beggars, with a president, secretary, treasurer, and board of directors, that hired persons by the month to beg, and Bobo believed it.[27] Representative John A. McQueen of South Carolina had a similar experience in 1847. In New York he saw a blind man holding a plate in his hand and being led by a dog. The plate contained nothing, and none of the many passers by, except McQueen, who "stopped to add a trifle," took any notice of him. On the steps of the "notorious Astor House," he saw a woman with a "writhing infant on her knee." When McQueen stopped to give her a pittance, a citizen told him that she was "doubtless an imposter, who had borrowed the child and bandaged it . . . to impose upon strangers."[28]

There was real poverty—not merely pretended poverty—in

26. *Magnolia*, IV (June, 1842), 264. Most of the severest critics of wage slavery in the North were not among the frequent visitors. See Wilford Carsell, "The Slaveholders' Indictment of Northern Wage Slavery," *Journal of Southern History*, VI (November, 1940), 504–20.

27. [Bobo], *Glimpses of New York*, 34–35.

28. *Congressional Globe*, 31st Cong., 1st Sess., Appendix, Volume 22, part 1, p. 735. McQueen told of his experiences during a speech in the House, June 8, 1850, on the need for the North to attend to its own problems instead of attempting to destroy southern institutions.

the North, southerners argued; and the North should be ashamed of it. McQueen told his colleagues in the House of Representatives that some eighteen hundred human beings lived underground in cellars, "packed together in rags and horrible wretchedness in the great city of New York."[29] William Caruthers said that if the lame, blind, poor, dumb, aged, and diseased could be "poured out along one side of the gay promenades, while fashionables were parading along the other, a much truer picture of life in a city would be seen."[30] When Paul Hamilton Hayne visited New York in 1854 he was pleased to inform his wife that the reports about the cholera epidemic had been greatly exaggerated. Then, in an interesting association of filth and poverty with the disease, he said:

> In fact, it has not prevailed *at all*, except among the lowest labourers, and in those horrible localities, where it is not infrequent to observe a man seizing on the carcass of a fowl thrown out for the scavenger, and bearing it into his hut, for the purpose of eating the atrocious thing at dinner. You don't know, my dear little wife, how particular I have been about my baggage, my money, and myself. I really begin to wonder at my own prudence.[31]

If Hayne was being prudent because of any suspicion of the prevalence of crime, he was not the only southerner who felt that way. Many of them were convinced that northerners would cheat them in every possible way, and even steal from them.[32] They were also convinced that crime was rampant in the North. A Mississippi planter congratulated himself for having reached New York safe and sound, "for there is scarcely a day that passes without some railroad or steamboat disaster and wholesale murder in this free country."[33] As Victor Chevillere pointed out, it seemed that every detestable form of vice and dissipation

29. *Ibid.*, 735.
30. Caruthers, *A Kentuckian in New York*, I, 50–51.
31. Paul H. Hayne to Mary Michel Hayne, August 25, 1854, in Paul Hamilton Hayne Papers, Duke University, Durham.
32. See above, p. 39.
33. James T. Harrison to Mrs. James T. Harrison, August 15, 1853, in James T. Harrison Papers, University of North Carolina, Chapel Hill.

flourished in the large cities of the North—"young females with bloated countenance—boys with *black* eyes and bruised faces . . . and filthy and ragged garments."[34] Even more to the point were the observations of William Bobo, who became something of an authority on depravity and crime in New York City. As he moved about the less attractive parts of the city, leaving Broadway and crossing Centre Street, the area sank into a sameness "like the degrees of crime, 'till you reach infamy, positive and hopeless." Small children early learned to steal, drink beer, and gamble. "It makes the heart of any good or kind-feeling man almost burst with pity."

Conditions such as these, Bobo contended, inevitably contributed to the statistics of crime in the great city: 9,087 arrests in the last quarter of 1851. Of these arrests, 1,291 had been for assault and battery; 1,337 for disorderly conduct; 818 for petit larceny, etc. There were more cases of crime in the city of New York alone than in the entire South. "In fact, there is more poverty, prostitution, wretchedness, drunkenness, and all the attending vices, in this city than the whole South." That was an eloquent comment on northern institutions at a time when northerners were expending so much energy in their attempt to reform the South. Only after the abolitionists had cleared their own house would they have the right to "hold up their hands in holy horror at the slaveholder, and the enormity of his sins."[35] Perhaps Bobo and the other critics were unaware of the prevalence of crime in the mid-nineteenth-century city in general, which was certainly not peculiar to the North. Unhappily, crime seemed to be an integral part of the disorganization and maladjustment that accompanied urban growth. It was as true in Baltimore and New Orleans as it was in New York and Philadelphia.[36]

34. Caruthers, *A Kentuckian in New York*, I, 154.
35. [Bobo], *Glimpses of New York*, 97.
36. See the lively description of nightly killings, stabbings, riots, and "murderous clashes of rival bands in New Orleans" in the 1850s in Harnett T. Kane, *Queen New Orleans, City by the River*, (New York: William Morrow and Company, 1949), 221–23.

The northern city was a wicked place, some southerners thought, and exerted a sinister influence on its visitors, including southern ladies! One young southern belle, "Eliza," visited her rich relatives in New York, where she became a frequent visitor at "balls, parties of various kinds, theatres, etc. Very soon she laid her Bible, prayer, and religious duties entirely aside." Upon returning home, she was no longer satisfied with the "quietness and many endearments" of the past. She wanted "whist parties, sitting parties, and dancing parties. The parents (erring mortals) would fain gratify her." Even as she recovered from the strange sickness which had sent her to her bed soon after her return from the city, she was "bolstered" up in bed to play cards with some of her associates.[37]

The gossip about the notorious Woodman case, purveyed by the fictitious Belle Brittan, was even more shocking than was the story of Eliza. Mrs. Caroline Woodman was the wife of a New Orleans druggist; and with her thirty trunks, containing a new dinner dress for each day during the season, she regularly visited Saratoga and Newport. She was usually pointed out as the one with the remarkably small waist "or, as it was said, for being laced within an inch of her life, no one at that time suspecting her guilty of 'loose habits.' Having made what the French call a marriage *de convenance*, of course 'a lover' was as necessary as a carriage." It seems that a young New York dandy, the son of a very wealthy family, occupied that "peculiar poodle-like" position for years.[38] The account may well have been as fictitious as Belle Brittan herself; but southerners could well believe that the wicked ways of the northern city did strange things even to their women.

When one southerner said that he was more interested in the character of the people of New England, their tone of thought

37. Junius, "Danger of Worldly Pleasures," *Southern Lady's Companion*, II (May, 1848).

38. [Hiram Fuller], *Belle Brittan on a Tour, At Newport and Here and There* (New York: Derby and Jackson, 1858), 229–30.

and feeling upon some important subjects, and their social institutions than in the physical lineaments of the area, he set for himself a quite difficult task. He succeeded remarkably well, because he was a thoughtful and careful observer who took considerable time both in his traveling and in recording his impressions, and he talked with a wide variety of people in many parts of the region.[39] Most southerners who visited the North did not take the time, nor did they have the advantages or opportunities that this particular southerner had. It is unlikely that they would heed his advice and do a bit of "foot-traveling." That was one of the few ways they could see a country thoroughly. By country, he did not mean "its rivers and mountains, cities, forests, and churches, but its *men and women*." They could not remain to themselves, as most southerners tended to do, or merely visit relatives if they were so fortunate, or restrict their contacts to those who served them or with whom they had business dealings. Most of them did, however; and that is why one can find a hundred descriptions of Niagara Falls or of the Crystal Palace Exposition to every single discussion of the people, their institutions, or the quality of life in the North. And, most unfortunately, a considerable number of those few discussions are superficial or uninformed. Happily, some of them are incisive, informed, and perceptive.

Since southerners took great pride in their own physical appearance and sought to improve it both by physical activities and by grooming, it is not surprising that some of them would comment on the appearance of northerners, especially women. New Yorkers in the economic and social groups to which southerners paid attention were always impressive, even when southerners did not find them especially attractive. It was their supreme self-confidence, their vivacity, and their sure knowledge that they were the pacesetters of the Western World that southerners

39. "Letters from New England—1," *Southern Literary Messenger*, I (November, 1834), 84.

found so tantalizing.[40] There was a certain lavishness of dress bordering on gaudiness that southerners did not always wish to emulate but were slow to condemn. "I saw more extravagance in one day than I ever expected to see in all my life," a North Carolina planter remarked to his wife regarding the dress of New York women in 1826.[41] Perhaps the apparel that he saw would have looked a bit out of place on a Caswell County plantation, but he was not prepared to say that it was not suitable for a Broadway promenade.[42]

If Paul Hamilton Hayne's complaints in 1854 were at all justified, the women of Boston were no match for those of New York or Charleston or, indeed, anywhere else. One suspects, however, that his observations were not at all serious or that he desired to entertain his wife with his descriptions and give her a greater sense of security regarding his prolonged absence. "Do you know I have not seen one pretty girl, since I came to Boston," he exclaimed. "An uglier set of devils never walked the streets of a Christian City." Perhaps Hayne protested too much, for two weeks later he said, "I think I told you before the dreadful urgliness of the Boston women. Really it is distressing. Sandy hair, and freckles are the most common type of this sin." He would not let go. In his next missive he complained of being lonely and added "all the Boston girls are humbugs, large feet and a horrid brogue."[43] Hayne's contacts were apparently quite limited, and his disposition was not improved by the tasks of editing and reading proof that his publisher assigned him.

There was an elegance of style and demeanor about the people of Philadelphia that won the admiration of most southerners. The city yielded to "none in the Union in the wealth, industry and

40. Myers, *Sketches on a Tour*, 57–58.
41. James M. Jeffreys to Mrs. James M. Jeffreys, April 9, 1846, in Mrs. James M. Jeffreys Papers, Duke University, Durham.
42. For a Charlestonian's refusal to purchase dresses designed for the New York "look," see above, p. 95.
43. Paul Hamilton Hayne to Mary Michel Hayne, August 29, September 16, 30, 1854, in Paul Hamilton Hayne Papers.

intelligence of its citizens," J. C. Myers observed.[44] The men
were good looking and well dressed and there were many handsome faces among the women. But the temptation to compare
them with southerners was irresistible. "Contrasting their com-
plexions with the Southern ladies, you will not find them so fine
and delicate, but more showy in the distance. Their feet are
large, which is almost a characteristic. The Southern lady may
justly boast of the neatness and delicacy of her hands and feet."
The women of Philadelphia were intelligent and accomplished,
according to this southern observer, reflecting the advantage of
select and well-conducted schools from which they were not
withdrawn at the age of fourteen in order to "come out" as was
often the case in the South. Even here, the advantage was not
altogether on the side of the women of Philadelphia:

> Their manners are pleasant and agreeable, and their conversation
> interesting and instructive. They want the liveliness, the vivacity, the
> simplicity, the ease and expression of the Southern lady when en-
> gaged in conversation. They have the *substance* but want the *soul*.
> Hence the conversation of the latter, although not so instructive, is
> more attractive and winning. All who have been so fortunate as to
> converse with both, must acknowledge the superiority of the South-
> ern in this particular.[45]

Compliments to northern women were not always so grudging
as that paid to women of Philadelphia. One southerner in New
England not only found "handsome" women, but it was also "his
good furtune to meet with some admirable female minds." One
in particular, he thought, was most accomplished intellectually.
She was no pedant, "harping on books, authors, and sciences."
She would never reveal that level of her knowledge except by

44. Myers, *Sketches on a Tour*, 439.
45. *Southern Literary Messenger*, IV (April, 1838), 250. Even regarding the physical
build of northerners, one southerner had to qualify his praise. In Connecticut he found
the men "of good size and remarkably healthy." It was a pity that "they are almost
invariably homely. Since my residence in Connecticut I do not recollect to have seen
more than three or four persons of comely features." William D. Martin, *Journal: A
Journey from South Carolina to Connecticut in the Year 1809* (Charlotte, N.C.: Heritage
House, 1959), 44.

cross-examination. "But let a subject be tabled, calling for ideas, or for exertions of intellect, to which a conversancy with books, authors, and sciences was indispensable—and you might see that she knew them well." The writer suppressed the rest of his encomium for fear that the reader should think that he was falling in love.[46]

Not all northern women were so accomplished, but many of them enjoyed an independence as well as opportunities that were generally denied southern women. As in Philadelphia, they went to better schools and remained in school longer. They could operate business establishments with no loss of status or respect. They had greater freedom of movement, and traveling alone was not regarded as unsafe or unusual. In the South, they perhaps enjoyed greater deference and respect, while traveling, because among New England men there was "less tender and obsequious manner . . . towards the fair sex than southrons shew." But it was an everyday occurrence in New England for "handsome young ladies, of refined appearance, to drive for miles with no male attendant whatever and be perfectly safe." This was due, in part, to the "sober, honest, and peaceful habits of the people, and to the certainty that any wrong or insult offered to a female would be promptly resented and punished."

There were other reasons why northern women enjoyed greater independence and freedom of movement, the observer suggested. First, there were more women than men, due to the emigration of men westward and "their resorting to the maritime cities and to the ocean, for trade and seafaring employment." New Englanders, moreover, had less time for pleasure, "and no Virginian will deny that 'to tend the fair' is a *pleasure*." Finally, New Englanders did not practice "those minute, delicate attentions—that semi-adoration—ingrained in the very constitutions of our well-bred men." The result was that northern women stood on their own much more than southern women; they were

46. "Letters from New England—1," *Southern Literary Messenger*, I (November, 1834), 87.

able to exercise an independence and demand a respect somewhat closer to that of equals than were southern women.[47]

Women were not the equals of men in the North, but what southerners saw suggested a far greater egalitarian spirit between the sexes there than what they were accustomed to at home. Nor was there real egalitarianism in other spheres, although what southerners saw was sometimes strange and even awkward. The lack of an adequate number of porters, waiters, maids, and other personal servants never failed to be noticed by southern visitors; and that must certainly explain in part the desire of some to bring their servants with them. The Virginia observer in New England was somewhat ambivalent on the matter and conceded that the attention of servants in the South was often "superfluous and cumbersome." Even so, he did not like having to brush his clothes and clean his shoes, even in some of the best hotels. And he noted that in some places where the servants had not yet retired to the factories or commercial houses they preferred not to be referred to as "servants."[48]

All too often, when southerners did encounter servants in the North they were white; and they found such a situation especially awkward. Traveling through Illinois in 1859 with his son and some other young southerners, Benjamin L. C. Wailes of Natchez was served by a "well clad interesting young white girl." He was revolted by the very thought of one of his own race acting in a menial capacity. This was only natural for persons "accustomed to Negro servants and who regard every [white] female with deference and respect."[49] The southerner in New England also found it strange to be served by whites. He was inclined to treat them as equals, but realized both from their reaction and from his own sensitivity that "it was incompatible with the relation." In the Old Dominion, he said, the blighting

47. *Ibid.*, (January, 1835), 218.
48. *Ibid.*, (December, 1835), 167.
49. Quoted in Charles S. Sydnor, *A Gentleman of the Old Natchez Region: Benjamin L. C. Wailes* (Durham: Duke University Press, 1935), 282.

curse of slavery was mitigated by the regard the master had for his slaves, as, indeed, he had for all of his inferiors. This was a thoroughly acceptable and understandable mode of conduct in a society where the status of the superior class was not and could not be challenged. Under the circumstances, therefore, a master could show a regard for his slaves that would be entirely out of place in an employer-employee relationship between two white persons.[50]

There was one area in which, even in the early antebellum years, southerners boasted an unchallenged superiority. That was in their regard for their fellow man and in the hospitable treatment of all persons, even complete strangers. They were so certain of this that they tended to call attention to every incident they witnessed in the North that confirmed their view. In 1806, a young Georgian passing through New York en route to the law school in Connecticut, fretted about the lack of regard New Yorkers had for others. "Here," he said, "great attention was paid to every man, but it was to himself." He regretted that, even in Litchfield, "the inhabitants possess neither the refinements of hypocritical politeness, nor the warm feelings of country hospitality."[51] Years later a visitor in New York complained that in that "peculiar court of Mammon" called Wall Street, almost no one paid any attention to a funeral procession as it passed and, in fact, the mourners themselves "did not seem inconsolable in their grief."[52] One can hardly be surprised that New York's arch critic, William Bobo, would have something to say on the general subject: "No person knows or cares anything of his neighbor, so long as he does not interfere with his affairs or interest." Everything turned on the dollar in Yankeeland, and so long as one did not outstrip his neighbor he was passed by, and just as soon he

50. "Letters from New England—3," *Southern Literary Messenger*, I (January, 1835), 218.
51. W. C. Cumming to Thomas Cumming, June 8, and September 15, 1806, in Alfred Cumming Papers.
52. "A City Incident," *Southern Literary Messenger*, XVII (October and November, 1851), 667–68.

passed out of memory. To sum up his case, Bobo added: "The Yankee character is an industrious, energetic, and persevering one, without much, if any, sublimity of purpose; if I may so express myself, no lofty aspirations, no nobleness of spirit, none of that warmheartedness, and generosity of sentiment and feeling which pervades the soul of the Southerner."[53]

If one had no friends or even contacts in the North and no opportunity to cultivate them or no interest in doing so, he could well spend many months there, as many southerners did, and never experience the warmth of friendly hospitality. The most certain way to experience hospitality was to have friends or relatives, as Charles Fraser of Charleston had in Boston. He knew many people there—some who had lived in Charleston and others whom he met through them. Consequently, he had nothing but praise for the friendly nature of the Bostonians. "It seems that hospitality is so natural to the character of the people," he wrote to his mother, "that the lowest class will incommode themselves to direct or oblige a stranger. I have not dined at home but once for upwards of a week and that was the day after I arrived." One suspects that Fraser's acquaintances and friends were so numerous that he had no feeling of being a stranger in Boston. In fact, he said, "I may be in Charleston whenever I please, as far as regards society."[54]

The test of northern hospitality lay not so much in the enjoyment of the generosity of friends as in the possibility of discovering generosity and thoughtfulness in new acquaintances or even strangers. On such a test, northerners scored surprisingly well; and when they did southerners gave them full credit for it. After traveling for several weeks in New England one Virginian warned southerners, "Curl not your lip sardonically" when referring to Yankee hospitality, for there was a great deal of it, "according

53. [Bobo], *Glimpses of New York*, 144–45.
54. Charles Fraser to Mary Fraser, August 29, 1800. Mary Fraser Papers.

to the condition and circumstances of society." For southerners, hospitality was a "cheap, easy, and delightful virtue," especially since most of the work devolved to the slaves and since the
wasteful cooking habits of southerners made it perfectly easy to
feed one or two more mouths. He wondered whether the Virginian would be quite so hospitable if, like the New Englander, he
had one hundred acres instead of a thousand, which he and his
sons cultivated, then fed and milked the cattle, cut the wood and
made fires, rubbed down and fed the horses, while his wife and
daughters did the laundry, cleaned the house, washed, ironed,
made the clothes, tended the garden, and cooked the meals. It
was an "audacious heresy" even to compare northerners with
southerners regarding the South's "most prominent virtue." Yet,
he admitted in all candor, the southerner did not excel the
northerner in "the kindliness of soul, which soothes and
sweetens human life."

This Virginian in New England had been the recipient of the
most generous outpouring of hospitality that he had ever seen.
Men who were busy with their own pursuits, some of them of
advanced years, had spent hours showing him all that could
amuse and interest a stranger, going with him on foot or driving
their own vehicles to show him some scene of interest, answer-
ing his many questions, and explaining with care whatever required explanation. Everywhere he found "guides, enlighten-
ers, and hosts" such as he could never hope to see surpassed.
During his walking tour, a farmer provided him comfortable
quarters the first night, refused all compensation, and invited
him to stay for breakfast. The next day a farmer, intelligent and
friendly, invited him to ride with him in his jersey wagon. Along
the road, he was always offered refreshing drinks—"cider,
switchell, and water." One "gudewife," on learning that his
object was seeing the country and learning the ways of the
people, made him sit down, then treated him "abundantly to

cider," gave him many items of information, and wished him great success.

Nor was he a special case, he insisted. A fellow Virginian whom he knew visited Boston with a letter of introduction. For three days, the addressee gave himself up entirely to the visitor and his family. He brought his carriage to the hotel and showed them the entire city and its environs. In short, "he seemed to think that he could not do enough to amuse and gratify" the visitors. Still another example was the case of the deserter from the British navy—"moneyless, shoeless, with only yarn socks on; feet blistered and actually suffering from a fever and ague." He told the Virginian that he had walked from Bath, Maine, to the neighborhood of Hartford, entirely on charity and that he had never asked for food or shelter in vain. One woman had even given him a clean linen shirt. Thus, the Virginian concluded that "the New Englanders have in their hearts as much of the *original material* of hospitality as we have. . . . And although their mode of using it is less *amiable* than ours, it is more *rational*, more *salutary*—better for the guest, better for the host, better for society."[55]

Not all young southerners found life as dull and the people as cold as the law student found the people of Litchfield. Indeed, one of them had an experience on Long Island Sound that was quite the opposite. He was not surprised that some southerners believed that the Yankees were a "cold-hearted, selfish people." But this was a view that was as inaccurate as it was malevolent. "If you will only give credence to *my* word," he argued, "you will immediately lay aside those ill-founded prejudices that have taken possession of your mind." One needed only the pleasure of visiting their homes, partaking of their food and drink, and sharing their recreational activities to see that an injustice had been done the New England people. "There is no land where the

---

55. "Letters from New England—2," *Southern Literary Messenger*, I (December, 1834), 166–67. See also "New England Character," *ibid.*, III (July, 1837), 412, in which the author referred to "the elegant hospitality of the burghers of Boston."

stranger is more welcomed, or where the hand of friendship is more freely extended," he concluded.[56]

Even in the 1850s, southerners continued to concede that New England was warm and hospitable. In 1852 James Henly Thornwell, president of South Carolina College, spent several weeks in Boston. One of the errands he was to perform for his wife was to find their friends from South Carolina who had placed their child in a Boston hospital for special treatment. Having no success in inquiring at the several hospitals, he then began to inquire of physicians. In Roxbury, he found a physician who knew the place and who insisted on taking him there in his own buggy. He then waited for Thornwell and drove him "for two hours among all the villages and fine scenery around Boston. . . . Now can South Carolina beat that? My heart was touched at the unostentatious kindness which was heaped upon a stranger." Despite the fact that Paul Hamilton Hayne complained bitterly to his wife about his loneliness in Boston, he admitted to others, on occasion, that things were not really all bad. In a letter to his New York friend, Richard Henry Stoddard, whom Hayne had missed seeing during his two-month sojourn in the North in 1853, he said that in Boston he "met with so much kindness and sympathy, that I can never forget the good old city."[57]

S. H. Dickson of Charleston was a real Yankeephile. He was educated in the North and visited there frequently. But he was also strongly attached to his beloved South and would say nothing to sully its "most prominent virtue." In 1854 this did not prevent his acknowledging and praising New Englanders for their many kindnesses to him. "This very season past," he told the New England Society of Charleston, "I have been enjoying the warm and kind hospitality of a Yankee poet, one of the

56. A Southron, "Vacation Scribblings," 438.

57. Benjamin M. Palmer, *The Life and Letters of James Henley Thornwell* (Richmond: Whittlet and Shepperson, 1875), 362–63; and Paul Hamilton Hayne to Richard Henry Stoddard, January 1, 1854, in Paul Hamilton Hayne Papers.

brightest stars in this country's constellation of undying names, and of a Yankee millionaire, with a heart large in proportion to his fine athletic person and his immense wealth." He came away from the lavish treatment and warm fellowship fully convinced that "not all the powers of darkness . . . are destined to prevail against the strength of this glorious Union."[58]

Dickson strongly believed that if southerners and northerners would continue their "free communion" with each other and if they would visit each other regularly, they would forge bonds of friendship and understanding that no political or economic crisis could destroy.[59] This was a view, not always expressed with such optimism, that many southerners held. William Caruthers urged every southerner to visit New York, for it "would allay provincial prejudices, and calm his excitement against his northern countrymen."[60] The Virginian who wrote a series of letters from New England even surpassed Dickson in his discussion of the benefits that southerners could derive from their visits to the North. In 1835 he called for delegations, "exploring parties," to go to observe and report on all areas of northern life "deserving our imitation." Surely, planters, housewives, statesmen and "lawgivers," businessmen, and teachers would greatly benefit from such an experience. But the most important benefit, he insisted, would come in the "unlearning of our long cherished prejudices, from seeing the Yankees *at home*—that place where human character may always be the most accurately judged." This was all the more important if the effort to preserve the union was to succeed. "There cannot be a simpler *recipe*," he concluded. *"The North and the South need only to know each other better, to love each other more."*[61]

58. S. H. Dickson, *Address Delivered before the New England Society of Charleston, S.C.* (Charleston: J. Russell, 1855), 18.

59. *Ibid.*, 186.

60. Caruthers, *A Kentuckian in New York*, I, 181.

61. "Letters from New England—5," *Southern Literary Messenger*, I (April, 1835), 425–26. A Philadelphian, Joseph Hopkinson, warmly praised the "Letters" for promoting good feeling and showing that "there is no important difference of character,

The enthusiastic visitor had fallen for the simplistic notion that if the North and South knew each other better there would spring up—almost automatically—a warm bond of friendship between the sections. But knowledge of each other was not the last step but the first one toward building intersectional understanding. Until more northerners visited the South, even this first step would remain incomplete. Beyond that lay a whole range of problems—economic, social, and political—that would require for their solution more than travel or even knowledge. What the visitor seemed to mean was that as northerners and southerners tackled their mutual problems of industry, agriculture, trade, education, and social reform, knowledge of each other would greatly mitigate the inevitable stresses and strains. Meanwhile, for their part, southerners were taking the first important step of getting to know the North.

Even James D. B. De Bow, at least in 1847, asserted that the example of the North provided much for the southerner to admire and even emulate. On that occasion he was full of enthusiasm for what he had seen on a recent visit. He especially admired the remarkable enterprise and industry in Massachusetts, which, he believed, would place her in the first rank of ancient or modern states. He spoke well of the colleges and schools and of the general elevation of the people to which various organizations such as the agricultural and horticulural societies had contributed so much. He was not unaware of the attitude of many people in Massachusetts toward the South and its institutions, but he refusd to permit that to blind him to her virtues:

> Whatever displeasure as a Southerner we may have expressed, and however often we may have expressed it, in relation to the unauthorized and illiberal course pursued by Massachusetts in reference to our institutions and our rights, we cannot but admire her in the

education or habits, between gentlemen of the same grade in the South and North." *Ibid.*, I (February, 1835), 322–23.

position in which she is truly admirable, and publish her honor to the world. As a great sister of our confederacy, we are bound to respect and love her, despite even her faults.[62]

Despite his own frequent visits to the North, De Bow did not urge southerners to follow his example. As a matter of fact he was inclined to counsel them against it.[63] But there would be others who would continue to urge their fellow southerners to visit the North. In 1849 J. C. Myers said that he wished that some of the intelligent and more enterprising farmers of Virginia would visit western New York and take lessons from the farmers there, "and return using their influence and exertions in sustaining and carrying forward the great agricultural improvements of this region."[64] Benjamin F. Perry, the South Carolina editor and politician who visited the North on several occasions, thought that southerners could learn much by studying the northerners and their ways. "Let the Southern people take lessons from the Yankees," he urged, "in industry, wisdom, and economy, and strive to become their equals as merchants and manufacturers, as mechanics and scientific men." This would be better than their boasting of their superiority over the Yankees when it was obviously not true.[65] Even in November, 1860, G. W. Bagby, editor of the *Southern Literary Messenger*, was urging southerners to visit the North, hopeful as he was for "happier days to come. . . . Make up a party next summer. . . . If you have plenty of time, leave home at the beginning of August. . . . Aim to spend the whole of September in the North, so as to reach New York while the Opera is in season, and to return home about the 10th of October. . . . Make the tour as we have advised, come back and thank us for the six happiest weeks of your life."[66]

62. *De Bow's Review*, IV (December, 1847), 459–60.
63. See above, pp. 40–41.
64. Myers, *Sketches on a Tour*, 158.
65. Charleston (S.C.) *Southern Patriot*, May 11, 1854, quoted in Lillian Kibler, *Benjamin F. Perry, South Carolina Unionist* (Durham: Duke University Press, 1946), 302–303.
66. *Southern Literary Messenger*, XXXI (November, 1860), 390–91.

It was actually the quality of life in the North that appealed to many southerners, though they would never use language that made this concession. To do so would have come close to implying the inferiority of life in their own section; and this they could never do. They were content to speak of the industrious and steady habits of the people, of their democratic practices, of their educational and religious institutions, and the like. But if one looks at certain aspects of northern life for which southerners expressed admiration, one is impressed not only with the areas to which they pointed, but also with the manner in which those areas enriched northern life in a way that was lacking in the South.

Although many southerners argued that their colleges and universities were not inferior to those in the North, it appears that most of those who could do so sent their sons to the North to be educated.[67] Many of them admitted that the North was ahead of the South in the establishment and maintenance of public schools, but conditions in the South—a scattered population and the consequent emphasis on private academies and tutoring— made public education difficult to support. Even so, many communities and several states were initiating programs of public education. But what was important in the North was the general attitude toward learning and how that affected what northerners achieved and, ultimately, the quality of life.

William D. Martin of South Carolina seemed to sense the effects of the North's attitude toward learning when he visited Connecticut in 1809. The importance and necessity of education were held in the highest esteem, he reported. That was why the state had such a high number of scientific men in proportion to her population. It was rare to find a person who did not write an intelligible hand, and he believed it was not possible to find one who could not read. Compare that with South Carolina, where one-third of the white people were illiterate. There were, he

67. See above, Chapter II.

said, "more graduates in Connecticut than grammarians in Carolina. Alas! at what an ebb is education. I feel for my country and blush at the comparison."[68] A generation later the editor of the *Southern Literary Messenger* was agreeably surprised to discover a lively interest in his magazine wherever he went in the North. That was because of the widespread interest in learning in general. The magazine was already in the hands of the most intelligent, and others were anxious to become acquainted with it. "The glory of the North," he concluded, "is her public and private Institutions for the promotion of knowledge. In some of her cities all classes have the opportunity of attending courses of lectures, such as few of our Colleges afford."[69]

The general effect of what was becoming universal education in the North appeared quite salutary to the Virginian traveling in New England in 1834. Nine-tenths of the whole population in Massachusetts took newspapers or at least read them, whereas not more than half of the population at home did so, he regretfully observed.[70] Lectures, social libraries, and similar institutions were "among the chief glories of New England." In all the cities and in many of the towns, he found lyceums, young men's societies, or associations for "mental exercise and improvement." Everything to improve the mind was done and apparently by everyone. Not only did public-spirited leaders offer lectures, but even farmers and mechanics—gratis and "in a style plain enough to be understood by all classes of society who flock to hear them." Even distinguished personages such as Joseph Story, Edward Everett, and Daniel Webster had presented free lectures for the general public. The Virginian wondered when the great men of his state would join in such a "noble race of usefulness," which had done so much to stimulate and advance the quest for knowledge in the North.[71]

68. Martin, *Journal*, 44–45.
69. *Southern Literary Messenger*, IX (November, 1843), 698–99.
70. "Letters from New England—1," *Southern Literary Messenger*, I (November, 1834), 85.
71. *Ibid.*, I (February, 1835), 273–74.

The relentless pursuit of learning had even raised the moral tone of the North, despite the depravity that could be found in its large cities. There was little interest in horse racing and similar "vices" as in the South, and there seemed to be not a fourth of the "tippling" that existed in Virginia.[72] Lectures were as likely to be on temperance as on poetry or new farming methods; and it appeared to some that the movement for temperance reform in the North was directly related to the accelerated interest in improving the mind and the body. In the late 1830s a southerner was present at a large temperance meeting in Boston. An ode was written for the occasion, and there was special music by the organist and a military band. The entire experience was one that the visitor would not soon forget—the several well-spoken orations, the orderliness of the meeting, the rapt attention of the listeners, and "the spectacle of such an immense assembly, breaking up and moving towards the doors, all in perfect order."[73] There was something in the total effect that surely raised the southerner's respect for the quality of life in New England.

Religion was an aspect of life in the North with which few southern visitors seem to have had much acquaintance. For one thing, church going while on vacation was not their idea of diversion; and few of them, if they had a desire to worship, felt disposed to enter a strange church where they knew no one, for their idea of worship was to be among friends and relatives. Thus, in many diaries and letters, Sundays pass with no mention of church attendance; but in some of them reference was made to visiting church edifices as a part of the sightseeing. Some of the buildings, Trinity Church in New York, Grace Church in Boston, and Christ's Church in Philadelphia, were interesting for their history and architectural style. Southerners visited them as they would the cemeteries and water-works.[74] Some fortunate visitors

72. *Ibid.*, I (November, 1834), 85.
73. "Eloquence in New England," *Southern Literary Messenger*, VIII (January, 1842), 68–69.
74. In 1830 Simri Ross found the new churches in New Haven—Baptist, Presbyterian, and Episcopal—interesting structures that had been erected since her previous

had northern friends who took them to church services as a part of the social activities of the day.[75] Some went out of curiosity to services for the deaf mutes in New York or the Quakers in Philadelphia.[76]

Perhaps so few southerners attended church in the North because they associated all or most northern ministers with abolitionism. They had heard of Henry Ward Beecher and Theodore Parker, of course; and they were hearing of others who seemed even more extreme.[77] Some southerners, moreover, attended the national meetings of their denominations, where they frequently heard slavery and slaveholding ministers roundly denounced.[78] Had they been more enterprising they could have found many northern ministers expressing sympathy for the South and calling for the enforcement of the fugitive-slave laws. As Samuel May said in 1869, "When the true history of the antislavery conflict shall be fully written . . . no one will fail to see that, practically, the worst enemies of truth, righteousness,

visit. See Journal of Simri Ross, in Hermione Ross Walker Collection, University of North Carolina, Chapel Hill. For another description of New Haven churches see Paul H. Hayne to Susan Hayne, September 14, 1843, in Paul Hamilton Hayne Papers. Myers mentioned most of the important churches in the North in his *Sketches on a Tour, passim*. See also Gideon M. Davison, *The Fashionable Tour: A Guide to Travellers Visiting the Middle and Northern States and the Provinces of Canada* (Saratoga Springs: G. M. Davison, 1830), *passim*.

75. In the summer of 1814 Mrs. Ann Wagner of Charleston, visiting in Boston, attended church with her friend Mrs. Curtis, before going on to spend the afternoon with Mrs. McClain. She made no mention of what the church services were like. Ann Wagner to Effingham Wagner, July 17, 1814, in Cheves-Wagner Papers, University of North Carolina, Chapel Hill.

76. Arney Robinson Childs (ed.), *The Private Journal of Henry William Ravenel, 1859–1887* (Columbia: University of South Carolina Press, 1947), 28. For an account of a South Carolina rice planter's visit with Quakers see J. Harold Easterby, *The South Carolina Rice Plantation As Revealed in the Papers of Robert F. W. Allston* (Chicago: University of Chicago Press, 1945), 135. Benjamin Wailes of Natchez visited Christ's Church in Philadelphia for sentimental reasons. His father had worshipped there in 1797. Sydnor, *A Gentleman of the Old Natchez Region*, 279.

77. See, for example, Hayne's account of the rantings of a Presbyterian minister in Boston. Paul H. Hayne to Mary Michel Hayne, October 27, 1854, in Paul Hamilton Hayne Papers.

78. John Donald Wade, *Augustus Baldwin Longstreet: A Study of the Development of Culture in the South* (New York: The Macmillan Company, 1924), 271, contains an account of the denunciation of southern slaveholders at the historic meeting of the Methodist Conference in New York in 1844.

and humanity were of those who professed to be the friends and followers of Christ."[79] If southerners had heard sermons by such northern divines as John Chase Lord of New York's Central Presbyterian Church or Samuel Thayer Spear of Brooklyn's South Presbyterian Church or such Unitarian ministers as Henry H. Fuller and Francis Parkman of Boston, they would have felt much more at ease in northern churches.

Some, of course, would not have been pleased with the theological doctrines of certain northern churches. For example, there were a few Unitarians in the South, but their influence was so minimal that they were not taken seriously. And, of course, there were wide differences among Presbyterians in various parts of the country. When young James Henley Thornwell went to Andover Theological Seminary in 1834, he could not bear the theology taught there. It was "awfully New School," he wrote his mentor in South Carolina. The reply he received should have been comforting: "I do not fear for your principles in religion; they withstood the insidious approaches of Dr. [Thomas] Cooper, and they cannot now give way to error in a less dangerous form." The words came too late, for Thornwell had already transferred to Harvard, where he would take German and Hebrew. He had to live in Divinity Hall with Unitarian students, "for there are no others here." He enjoyed the classes, but he disliked the Unitarian beliefs; "I look upon the tenets of modern Unitarianism as little better than downright infidelity," he wrote. "Their system, as they call it, is a crude compound of negative articles, admirably fitted to land the soul in eternal misery." The Unitarians even countenanced dancing. "Just think of it soberly," he said, "and at the least, it cannot but appear ridiculous." In a few weeks he left for his South Carolina home. When he returned to New England eighteen years later, as president of

79. Samuel Joseph May, *Some Recollections of Our Antislavery Conflict* (Boston: Fields, Osgood and Company, 1869), 332. See also Stanley W. Campbell, *The Slave Catchers: Enforcement of the Fugitive Slave Law, 1850–1860* (Chapel Hill: University of North Carolina Press, 1968), 69–70.

the South Carolina College, he was still deploring the Unitarians of Boston and Cambridge. "It makes me sad," he wrote his wife, "to see such men, so accomplished, so elegant, at once such finished gentlemen and such admirable scholars, sunk into so vile a faith."[80]

There were southerners, however, who looked beyond narrow denominationalism and doctrinal differences to appreciate the role of religion in elevating the quality of life in the North. Private life was not disturbed "by the bitterness or sectarian dogmatism," and the spirit of religious toleration in Massachusetts was accompanied by "more Christian charity than is generally found in many other sections of the Union." The Sunday schools, moreover, were excellent vehicles for inculcating in the children of the community a spirit of sober and thoughtful concern for their fellows. This was far better than permitting them to "run about the highways and streets, where they have ample opportunities of having not only the various shades of mischief, but also a draught of brandy ground into them."[81]

A Virginia visitor was pleased with the kind of religion that flourished in New England. It was unobtrusive, yet effective. It was a "quiet, Sabbath-keeping, morals-preserving, good-doing, and heaven-serving religion, free from several extravagancies, that have elsewhere crept into Christianity." There were no protracted meetings or revivals such as were common in the South, and religious obligations did not intrude themselves unduly into the secular life of the people. Dancing, which young Thornwell so greatly deplored, was not proscribed; and churches took the initiative in providing wholesome recreation for the young people. Nor was it unusual for church services to be enlivened by the playing of violins and flutes to accompany the

80. James H. Thornwell to General James Gillespie, August 13, 1834; W. H. Robbins to James H. Thornwell, August 23, 1834; James H. Thornwell to A. H. Pegues, August 14, September 18, 1834; James H. Thornwell to his wife, July 21, 1852; all in Palmer, *The Life and Letters of James Henley Thornwell*, 115–17, 124, 361.

81. Myers, *Sketches on a Tour*, 368, 390–91.

choir. Thus, he could conclude that "in the formalities of piety, the descendants of the Pilgrims are radically changed from the puritanical strictness of their fore-fathers." [82] It was this spirit of change and a willingness to change that gave religion a continuing and, indeed, an enlarged role in the life of New England.

Southerners were generally proud of their own system of law and order which, they believed, protected their social institutions and raised the moral tone of their community. But they were not unmindful of certain attitudes toward the law and certain customs and traditions in the North that deserved close observation if not emulation in every instance. The Virginia visitor was attracted to the Massachusetts system of the careful impaneling of lists of jurors, from which were drawn by lot those who were to serve during a particular sitting of a court. Since they were paid for their services and since they were not expected to serve more often than once in three years, it seemed eminently fair to all; and it was certainly superior to the practice in Virginia of gathering "the sweepings of the court-yard" or "strangers from other counties" or "tipplers from the tavern porch" whenever twelve men were needed to sit in judgment of their peers.[83] Perhaps this is why the people seemed to have confidence in the administration and enforcement of the law and why they did not strongly object to new laws designed to promote the general social welfare. S. H. Dickson was thus able to understand how, in a rail car on which he rode in the North, "not only smoking, but spitting was absolutely forbidden, and the prohibition efficiently carried out, and the *unclean abomination*, for the first time in my large experience of public travel, entirely got rid of."[84]

No amount of law enforcement and respect for the law in the North could persuade most southerners that the level of morality

82. "Letters from New England—3," *Southern Literary Messenger*, I (January, 1835), 219.
83. *Ibid.*, I (April, 1835).
84. Dickson, *Address Delivered before the New England Society of Charleston*, 187.

was higher there than in the South. Olmsted thought that northerners and southerners agreed that although the *facilities* for
licentiousness were much greater in the South, the *evil* of licentiousness was much greater in the North, where it was "far more
captivating, irresistible, and ruinous than at the South."[85] Wage
slavery was bad enough in the northern factories, but the immorality in the factories, about which many southerners were convinced, was even worse. Even so ardent a supporter of New
England as the Virginia visitor who saw less immorality in the
New England factories than he had expected admitted in 1834
that vice and immorality had to be fought constantly. "The
natural course of these establishments . . . seems to be *down the
stream of vice*. Great exertions may enable them to resist, nay to
surmount and ascend the current; but so soon as those efforts
cease, that instant the downward tendency prevails."[86] In the
next decade a southerner visiting the factory village of Willimantic, Connecticut, asserted that long hours of work with no wholesome diversions led to the kind of degradation he had seen at the
local tavern the previous evening.[87] Southerners were convinced that industrial pursuits that brought large numbers of
people together in an urban setting or under other circumstances
that discouraged probity and restraint inevitably led to the kind
of immorality that their rural existence could not promote and
which, in any event, they would not tolerate.[88]

Many southerners were so preoccupied with making comparisons that they were unable to judge the North on its own terms.
While their own section was understandably their point of reference, it quite frequently clouded their perception of the North as

85. Frederick Law Olmsted, *The Cotton Kingdom*, edited with an introduction by
Arthur M. Schlesinger (New York: Alfred A. Knopf, 1953), 239.
86. "Letters from New England—4," *Southern Literary Messenger*, I (February,
1835), 273.
87. A Virginian, "One Day of a Foot Tour in Connecticut," *Southern Literary
Messenger*, XIV (June, 1848), 384.
88. For a discussion of wretchedness frequently associated with licentiousness, see
above, pp. 149–51, 177–79.

a place whose differences could be positive. To say that the town of Princeton was "a pleasant healthy situation something like ... Charlotte in North Carolina" was merely to use a familiar place for orientation with one that was not familiar.[89] To say in 1852 that the Charleston Hotel was as good as any of the hotels in New York City could merely arouse suspicion of the observer's sound judgment or, indeed, of his seriousness.[90] When southerners made an effort to turn all comparisons in the South's favor, they were playing a game fraught with the inevitable danger of missing the mark by a wide margin, some of the time, and coming closer to reality at other times. It would be difficult to trust young James Thornwell's assessment of Harvard when he wrote in 1834, "I had just as soon send a son to Columbia as to Cambridge."[91] He was much more believable, but not necessarily accurate, in 1852 when he wrote his wife about the Harvard commencement and said, "The exercises of the young men were not equal to those we have in our own College."[92]

Most of the time, whether the comparisons were unfavorable or not, southern visitors concluded that the North was so different from their beloved Southland that being there was like being in a foreign country. Some confessed to being homesick, even as they were overwhelmed by what they saw in the North. The distance from home seemed all the greater because the differences were so remarkable. After marveling at all the wonders of New York City for several days, a Louisiana planter declared, "I

89. Joseph Brevard Diary, June, 1791, in Alexander and Joseph Brevard Papers, University of North Carolina, Chapel Hill.

90. [Bobo], *Glimpses of New York*, 80.

91. James H. Thornwell to Alexander H. Pegues, October 1, 1834, in Palmer, *The Life and Letters of James Henley Thornwell*, 126.

92. James H. Thornwell to his wife, July 21, 1852, *ibid.*, 360. Thornwell was president of South Carolina College at the time. In 1850, William Gilmore Simms thought that it was entirely possible to carry the matter of comparisons too far. In reviewing Charles Lanman's *Letters from the Alleghany Mountains*, Simms said that Lanman did not have words to describe the beauty of the South; and he was particularly outraged by Lanman's assertion that Deane's Sulphur Springs in the Smoky Mountains was "worthy of Saratoga." See "Summer Travel in the South," *Southern Quarterly Review*, XVIII (September, 1850), 32.

am getting homesick and am determined to leave soon."[93] Whenever he was away, Paul H. Hayne was constantly declaring his loneliness and his desire to return home. "It seems to me," he wrote his wife from Boston in 1854, "That if one desires to gain the power of appreciating fully the inestimable blessings of *home* . . . he should sojourn as I have done for weeks in a great city like this. . . . I long, most sincerely—I long to return to the South. Kind as many persons have been to me here, I am *not at home*. I feel as an alien, and sojourner in the land."[94]

Loneliness and homesickness were at times the occasion to declare one's attachment to the South, as though the sojourn could have raised the question of loyalty. "After all the places I have seen," wrote a young southerner who was visiting in Philadelphia, "I still prefer 'Old Virginia', and would not exchange Holly-wood [his ancestral home] for all the fine buildings, and stupendous edifices I have yet met with."[95] A southern editor felt a similar compulsion to declare his loyalty to his home after writing at length in praise of the progress of science in the North, "but though we delight to see the North or the West advancing in these things, we love our own Virginia more!" What he hoped, however, was that his state would imitate those things that the North had accomplished so that Virginia would elicit an even greater loyalty from her sons.[96] But Clement Clay of Alabama saw little to imitate or admire. His experience in the North merely served to alienate him from the North and strengthen his loyalty to the South. "Every step I take and every word I hear makes me more Southern in feeling and principle," he wrote from Philadelphia in 1850.[97]

93. A. F. Rightor to Andrew McCollam, August 9, 1851, in Andrew McCollam Papers, University of North Carolina, Chapel Hill.

94. Paul H. Hayne to Mary Michel Hayne, September 16, 1854, in Paul Hamilton Hayne Papers.

95. Arthur A. Morson to Alexander Morson, September 14, 1818, in Morson Papers, University of North Carolina, Chapel Hill.

96. *Southern Literary Messenger*, VII (July, August, 1841), 553.

97. Clement C. Clay to Hugh Lawson Clay, July 22, 1850, in Clement Comer Clay Papers, Duke University, Durham.

This sense of alienation, of feeling that the North was more like
a foreign land than a portion of their own country, increased in
the decade before the Civil War. Perhaps it was related as much
to the real or fancied increase in economic and social differences
as to the increase in political strife between the sections. Southerners who were not hostile to the North shared this feeling with
their fellows who hated everything northern. Benjamin Wailes,
who, according to his biographer, never gave a hint of any hostility to the North, was certain that the agricultural, slaveholding
civilization of which he and his Natchez neighbors were a part
simply was not the same as that in the North. The North was, in
fact, a "strange land," which Wailes never succeeded in understanding.[98] When one South Carolinian visited the new, bustling
towns in New England, he said quite frankly that he felt that he
was in a new country. Upon returning to the South through
settlements that had "no bustle, no eager panting after the dollar," and across a countryside where there was hardly a human
face to remind one that he was not alone in the world, it was easy
to believe, "by the time you reach Cheraw, that you have passed
into a totally foreign country."[99]

The ultimate in alienation was the call for all southerners to
refrain from visiting the North. The call was made by editors,
politicians, managers of southern resorts, educators, and commercial conventions. It was as strident as it was unequivocal, as it
questioned the wisdom, judgment, and common sense of any
southerner who went north for any reason whatsoever. Southerners denounced the practice of sending their youth to the
North for an education, where their minds were "likely to
be . . . poisoned by denunciations and anathemas against their
parents."[100] They should by all means cease visiting the northern
watering places, as useless and extravagant a venture as could

98. Sydnor, *A Gentleman of the Old Natchez Region*, 282–83.
99. *Southern Quarterly Review*, XXVI (October, 1854), 432.
100. *De Bow's Review*, IX (July, 1850), 123. For an extensive discussion of the
campaign against northern education for southern youth, see above, pp. 70–78.

possibly be imagined. "Let our people cease their annual migrations to the North," De Bow railed in 1851, "in which they squander millions, which, if retained at home, would give new life to every branch of domestic employment with us. We have watering places that need but *fashion* to make them equal, if not superior to Saratoga or Cape May, with none of their disadvantages."[101]

Southerners opposed to northern travel seemed to believe that if they could dissuade their fellow southerners from visiting the northern watering places, most of the battle would have been won. They could rail against Saratoga and Cape May and all the other places, as indeed they did; but that would only demagnetize them without providing southerners with an attractive alternative. What was needed was a positive program to improve the southern resorts and "sell" southerners the idea of patronizing them. The first phase of the program was to praise the physical beauty and other attributes of the prospective and embryonic places of rest and recreation. As early as 1840, for example, Habersham, Georgia, received the attention of the *Southern Literary Messenger* as a place where the excellent climate and "salubrious hills" created for it a real possibility of competing successfully with those in the northern states.[102]

In later years other articles appeared praising the beauties of southern scenery. One in 1843 drew attention to a work by a South Carolina physician that painted the "features of his own native land" in a manner that commended it to tourists north and south.[103] A year later W. H. C. of Carroll County, Virginia, expressed the view that western Virginia would become available to more visitors upon the completion of a good road that would pass within a mile of some of the most sublime scenery to be found anywhere.[104] But isolation was turned to good advantage

---

101. *De Bow's Review*, X (January, 1851), 107.
102. *Southern Literary Messenger*, V (November, 1840), 776.
103. *Ibid.*, IX (September, 1843).
104. *Ibid.*, X (December, 1844), 736.

in 1851 by one of the strongest advocates of southern tourism. Conceding that the South had no great waterfall like Niagara or "heights as elevated as the White Mountains," he argued that the White Sulphur Springs were, however, as fine as any of the northern watering places; and "the very difficulties of getting there have had the effect of rendering the society more exclusive." In his attempt to clinch his argument regarding the virtues of southern travel, he said:

> We come now to assure the reader who has not journeyed much in the highlands of the Southern States, that they contain some of the wildest and most beautiful scenery that ever inspired a poet; spots sequestered from the busy routine of commercial life, where the spirit may find repose and revel in a satisfied sense of the grandeur and loveliness of Nature; valleys of surpassing richness and slopes of the most refreshing verdure—all of which might have been rendered to us by description, had our people sooner discovered their attractions.[105]

It was one thing for the South to have the physical features that compared favorably with those of the North; but it was quite another for the South to develop facilities that would transform some of its more desirable locations into attractive and fashionable resorts that could compete successfully with Saratoga, Niagara, Newport, Ballston, Lebanon Springs, and Cape May. To be sure, White Sulphur Springs in western Virginia was already an established resort as early as 1788; and in 1854 the state chartered a new White Sulphur Springs Company, capitalized at $1,500,000. James De Bow hoped that this would encourage others to follow the example set by Virginia and the supporters of White Sulphur Springs.[106] There were numerous resolutions to encourage travel in the South, but this was not enough.[107] Who would take the initiative for securing public or private support for Limestone Springs in South Carolina, Catawba Springs in North Carolina, or Warm Springs in Georgia, or the scores of

105. "Domestic Tourism," 378.
106. *De Bow's Review*, XVI (June, 1854), 653.
107. *Ibid.*, X (January, 1851), 83; and XX (March, 1856), 351.

other possible sites throughout the South?[108] They needed roads for access (even if the resorts would thereby become somewhat less exclusive); they needed living, dining, and bathing facilities, as well as personnel with skill and experience to operate them. They even needed to improve their cuisine. "Bacon and greens half cooked, corn bread and venerable butter, coffee and tea which have a smack of each other, but a greater smack of smoke and hot water will not do," De Bow advised those who would reform the "distant travel" propensities of southerners.[109] In the absence of these necessary resources, southerners could only promote their own resorts as best they could and remonstrate against those who persisted in being disloyal to the South.

A few watering places in the South enjoyed a limited prosperity. Tyree Springs in Tennessee was "a fashionable resort" near Nashville that some Natchez citizens visited regularly.[110] Henry Clay frequented several places in the upper South, including Graham Springs, called by some the "Saratoga of the West," Blue Lick Springs, and, of course, White Sulphur Springs.[111] Only White Sulphur Springs approached the success that its several northern counterparts enjoyed. When Edmund Ruffin went there in 1858 he was delighed to find visitors from the Carolinas, Alabama, and Louisiana. In August of the following year he found about 1,200 visitors from every part of the South, including James De Bow and "Parson" William G. Brownlow. In August, 1860, with some 1,650 visitors there, Ruffin was somewhat dismayed that the forthcoming election seemed to "excite but little zeal" and regretfully admitted that, as

108. For discussions of the numerous springs and other recreational sites in the South, see Lawrence F. Brewster, *Summer Migrations and Resorts of South Carolina Low-Country Planters* (Durham: Duke University Press, 1947), 82–89; and Billy M. Jones, *Health-Seekers in the Southwest, 1817–1900* (Norman: University of Oklahoma Press, 1967), 18–20.

109. *De Bow's Review*, X (March, 1851), 352.

110. D. Clayton James, *Antebellum Natchez* (Baton Rouge: Louisiana State University Press, 1968), 141.

111. Clement Eaton, *Henry Clay and the Art of American Politics* (Boston: Little Brown and Company, 1957), 157.

far as he knew, he was the only "avowed disunionist" there.[112] Even if some southerners began to prefer White Sulphur Springs to Saratoga, it did not follow that they had become ardent secessionists. It was, perhaps, its improved facilities more than its southern exposure that attracted an increasing number of southern visitors.[113]

By 1856 De Bow believed that southerners were gradually learning not to visit the North. They had become incensed by the abuse which northerners "heaped upon them" and they had become insulted by the creeds and platforms of the antislavery parties. Despite their predilections for the northern watering places, the shock of abuse and insult had come faster and faster, awakening them "at last from their dreams of security and repose and from their fixed confidence in the conservative classes of that section of the Union." Consequently, southerners had found on their own coasts, in their own mountains, "health, pleasure, intellectual pastime, and fashion, when it was vainly imagined they existed only afar off."[114] In 1857 he reported that the southern watering places were "full to overflowing, and few go to the North to be insulted by the helps in their hotels." And in the southern resorts people were coming together in stronger bonds of amity, more determined than ever to support southern institutions.[115]

If southern resorts were filled—and one suspects that De Bow was merely referring to White Sulphur Springs—there were still large numbers of southerners who went North either from preference or because they were unable to secure accommodations in the southern watering places. If they went to Blue Lick or Old

112. William Kauffman Scarborough (ed.), *The Diary of Edmund Ruffin* (2 vols. projected; Baton Rouge: Louisiana State University Press, 1972), I, 228, 330, 337–38, 450.

113. Perceval Reniers, *The Springs of Virginia: Life, Love, and Death at the Waters, 1775–1900* (Chapel Hill: University of North Carolina Press, 1941).

114. "Southern Travel and Travellers," *De Bow's Review*, XXI (September, 1856), 323.

115. *De Bow's Review*, XXIII (October, 1857), 340. See also *Southern Literary Messenger*, XVII (August, 1851), 518.

Sweet Springs or even White Sulphur Springs, there was no New York or Philadelphia en route where they could do their shopping, attend the theater and concerts, and enjoy the diversion that only large cities could provide. Perhaps J. A. Turner was making those concessions in 1860 when he wrote, "Admit . . . that under ordinary circumstances, an occasional visit to the land of black-republicanism is admissible; still, what are we to think of those who after the late developments, will continue to go every summer to expend their means among those who treat them with apparent respect, merely for the sake of their money?"[116]

The stay-at-home campaign, based largely on political arguments, seemed not to have persuaded large numbers of southerners. If southern planters and businessmen went to cities and summer resorts to find amusement and attractive items to purchase as much as to escape the fever and the torrents of political controversy, many of them still preferred the North. The example of James De Bow spending his honeymoon in New York in 1860 spoke at least as eloquently in favor of northern travel as anything he said against it in the pages of his *Review*.[117] And with the editor of the *Southern Literary Messenger* advising his readers in 1860 to go north the following summer and spend the "six happiest weeks" of their lives, the picture was, at best, confusing.[118] Perhaps the North was, indeed, a far cry from Eden, but southerners continued to find it sufficiently attractive to spend much time there down to the final weeks before the beginning of the secession movement in 1860.

116. J. A. Turner, "What Are We To Do," *De Bow's Review*, XXIX (July, 1860), 72.
117. See above, p. 107.
118. *Southern Literary Messenger*, XXXI (November, 1860), 391.

VI

Crusaders
Among
Infidels

In 1782 Hector St. Jean de Crèvecoeur, the French admirer of American life, argued that a new man had emerged in the New World—the American. He was, said Crèvecoeur, "either an European, or the descendant of an European; hence that strange mixture of blood, which you will find in no other country." The American was one, he continued, "who had left behind him all his ancient prejudices and manners" and had received new ones "from the new mode of life he has embraced, the new government he obeys, and the new rank he holds."[1]

There is reason to question the accuracy of Crèvecoeur's assessment at the time he made it, for blacks were surely not included in the amalgam of races that he described, and southern whites had already begun to show those distinctive traits that were, in time, to contribute to their alienation. As the northern states abolished slavery and moved toward a new economic base, emphasizing commerce and industry, their contrast with the southern states, more deeply committed than ever to agriculture, became more pronounced. In another place Crèvecoeur unwittingly came closer to describing how the North-South estrangement would occur when he said: "Men are like plants; the goodness and flavor of the fruit proceeds from the particular soil and exposition in which they grow. We are nothing but what we derive from the air we breathe, the climate we inhabit, the

1. J. Hector St. Jean Crèvecoeur, *Letters from an American Farmer* (New York: Fox, Duffield and Company, 1904), 54.

government we obey, the system of religion we profess, and the mode of our employment."[2] Even as the two sections remained under the same government, they went their separate ways and developed quite different points of view, resulting in no small degree from the social "climate" they inhabited and the "mode of employment" they adopted.

In due course the people of the two sections would become harshly critical of each other, with northerners condemning southerns for slavery and their general backwardness and southerners criticizing northerners for their crass materialism and their intolerance. Not only did northerners preach antislavery doctrines from their own pulpits and in their presses, but they even attempted to spread these doctrines into the South. It would be an insensitive southerner who would not take umbrage at such northern postures; and southerners were anything but insensitive.

As early as 1820, during the debates over Missouri, southerners heard northerners in Congress condemn slavery and the treatment of blacks in the South. This was grossly unfair, southerners felt, for it was clear to anyone who cared to look that free Negroes in the North were treated harshly and did not enjoy many of the privileges of citizenship. By the time that abolitionism gathered full steam, the anti-Negro riots in Philadelphia, Pittsburgh, and New York suggested a northern hypocrisy on the race question that was especially reprehensible to southerners. Soon, northerners would blanket the South with antislavery tracts, condemning slaveholders and calling on slaves to throw off their yokes. Abolitionists, meanwhile, were debating the propriety and wisdom of admitting blacks into their own ranks on a basis of equality. In time abolitionists would seek political office in order to influence the federal government to attack the South and slavery; but they launched no campaign to enfranchise the Negroes in their midst. Southerners regarded

2. *Ibid.*, 56.

such actions and inactions as evidences of northern capriciousness and inconsistency.

It is difficult to appreciate fully the reactions that many southerners had to what they came to regard as northern insults, the acts of intelligent men "eager to throw stones, though living themselves in glass houses."[3] Already southerners had begun to formulate some positive views of their own social order, and, more and more, they were unwilling to apologize for it. Northerners could rail all they pleased against southern crudity, southern ignorance, and southern slavery. Their railing would not eradicate the filth, poverty, crime, and wage slavery that abounded in northern cities and which so many southerners had seen.[4] What northerners saw as southern backwardness and inadequate development, southerners saw as the quietude and gentility of a bucolic existence. The South had, indeed, promoted a culture and civilization that had no equal in the New World, perhaps not even in the Old World. At worst, the northern view was calculated and sinister; at best it was uninformed and irresponsible. In any case, southerners would not let the northern position go unchallenged; and they would do whatever they could to correct it.

There were numerous ways of doing this, and the sons of the South neglected none of them. In their own press, they answered northern strictures in loud, clear tones, to reassure any doubting southerners—hoping, meanwhile, that northerners would get the message. In the last two decades before the Civil War, journals such as the *Southern Quarterly Review*, *De Bow's Review*, and the *Southern Literary Messenger* assumed the role of official spokesmen for the South. They poured forth millions of words to show that northern impressions of the South were erroneous and that southern civilization was something to be admired and even emulated.

3. J. C. Myers, *Sketches on a Tour Through the Northern and Eastern States, the Canadas and Nova Scotia* (Harrisonburg, Va.: J. H. Wartmann and Brothers, 1849), 367.
4. See above, pp. 177–79.

Southern ministers and politicians defended southern civilization in the pulpit and on the hustings, in conventions and in the
legislatures. Southern political giants promoted the cause of the
South in their electoral canvasses and on the floor of the United
States Congress. The combined effect gave the impression not
only that the South was right on questions of slavery and the
general social order, but that there was a southern unanimity on
these matters that should well be the envy of any group or section
that had a cause to espouse. There was nothing, however, comparable in its effectiveness, to taking the fight to the enemy's own
territory, to "nailing the lies" in the places where they were
perpetrated. This became an important undertaking of southerners in the years immediately preceding the Civil War.

It had not been unusual for southerners to participate in political or religious activities in the North. Politicians like Hugh S.
Legaré and Henry W. Hilliard, both regular visitors in the North,
appeared before numerous political groups in the middle states
and New England.[5] Such laymen as R. F. W. Allston and Benjamin L. C. Wailes attended the general conferences of their religious denominations when they met in the North, while such
clergymen as William G. Brownlow and James Henley
Thornwell did likewise.[6] They were cordially received and entered into the deliberations with ease, at least until the churches
became centers of the slavery controversy and the political parties all but collapsed under the strain of the intersectional strife.

A portent of what northerners could expect from southerners
in response to abolitionist attacks was a meeting of southerners
in New York's Tammany Hall on July 20, 1835. A group of about
three hundred persons from various parts of the South, dismayed

5. For northern visits of Legaré and Hilliard see Linda Rhea, *Hugh Swinton
Legaré: A Charleston Intellectual* (Chapel Hill: University of North Carolina Press,
1934), 190–98; and Henry W. Hilliard, *Politics and Pen Pictures at Home and Abroad*
(New York: Putnam's, 1892), 200–203, 235–37.

6. For northern visits of Brownlow and Thornwell, see E. Merton Coulter, *William
G. Brownlow, Fighting Parson of the Southern Highlands* (Chapel Hill: University of
North Carolina Press, 1937), 26–27; and Benjamin M. Palmer, *The Life and Letters of
James Henley Thornwell* (Richmond: Whittlet and Shepperson, 1875), 361–63.

by the abolitionist agitation that they witnessed in the North, called a meeting to discuss the matter. They were not satisfied with the assurances that northerners in attendance attempted to give them, i.e., that the abolitionists were few in number and belonged generally to a low order of society. The group passed resolutions declaring that slavery, though an evil, was an inherited complex social problem. The abolitionist assault was merely tightening the bonds of the institution. They hoped, therefore, that the intelligence and sound public opinion of the North would put down the fanatics. Some wanted to set up a committee to correspond with prominent southerners with a view to calling a southern convention, but a resolution embodying that sentiment was put aside.[7] While the action itself had little significance, the meeting was an indication that southerners were prepared to speak out, even in the North, in defense of their institutions.

The controversy over fugitive slaves and over the disposition of territories acquired during the Mexican War was the occasion for southerners to attempt once more to go north and present their case. They regarded the Wilmot Proviso, which proposed to exclude slavery from all land acquired during the war, as a direct attack on them and their institutions. The manner in which abolitionists were protecting fugitive slaves, moreover, demonstrated their fundamental lack of regard for property, to say nothing of the South. Northern action based on such views must be checked. That is what Elwood Fisher undertook to do when he spoke before the Mercantile Library Society of Cincinnati in 1849. Taking as his subject "The North and South," the editor of the *Southern Press* argued that during the colonial and early national years the South was superior to the North in wealth, commerce, and population. Thanks to the policy pursued by the federal government after 1816, "The grass is growing in the

7. The proceedings of the meeting were printed in the New York *Daily Advertiser*, July 22, 1835. See also, Henry H. Simms, *Emotion at High Tide: Abolition as a Controversial Factor, 1830–1845* (Baltimore: Moore and Company, 1960), 66–67.

streets of those cities of the South, which once monopolized our colonial commerce." Some northerners, therefore, had concluded that the South was falling behind and should "abandon her peculiar institution in order to avoid the disastrous condition of ignorance and barbarism that awaits her."[8]

It would be a mistake, Fisher declared, for anyone to conclude that the South was declining merely because she had no great cities comparable to those of the North. The great display of wealth and luxury in the northern cities leads to the popular error "that they are the peculiar abodes of wealth." In the city the temptation to indulgence is incessant, because every object of desire is in the market, and this leads to wastefulness and prodigality. But real wealth does not necessarily reside in the cities. The wealth of the South, concentrated in its rural areas, is superior to that of the North; and the North is, indeed, dependent on the South for its own prosperity. "The superior productiveness of agricultural labor, the great intrinsic value of the articles of necessity, of its products, the extravagant style of living in towns and cities, and finally the ruinous waste of human life and labor they occasion, are reasons enough for the fact . . . of the triumph of the agricultural States of the South over the more commercial States of the North."[9]

It was in the middle 1850s that several prominent southerners, despairing that ordinary means of persuasion would have any effect on northern attitudes, decided to accelerate their crusade among the infidels. The Compromise of 1850 had been undermined by abolitionists who disregarded the intent of the Fugitive Slave Act by aiding slaves to escape, by rescuing apprehended slaves from law-enforcement officers, and by harboring them in their homes. Mrs. Stowe's celebrated and widely

8. Elwood Fisher, "North and South," *De Bow's Review*, VII (August, 1849), 135–37.

9. *De Bow's Review*, VII (September, 1849), 264–66. Edmund Ruffin was immensely pleased with Fisher's effort in Cincinnati, and in February, 1857, he told him so. William Kauffman Scarborough (ed.), *The Diary of Edmund Ruffin* (2 vols. projected; Baton Rouge: Louisiana State University Press, 1972), I, 35.

read novel, *Uncle Tom's Cabin*, had given a view of southern slavery that outraged even the lukewarm supporters of the institution. The debates over the Kansas-Nebraska bill suggested to many southerners that the abolitionists were as unwilling to stand by the spirit of that bill as they had been to obey the provisions of the Fugitive Slave Act. Consequently, some of the ablest and most articulate southerners set out to correct northern misconceptions of the South and to persuade northerners of the justice of the South's position.

Among those southerners willing and able to do battle with the enemy on his own grounds, none was better prepared than George Fitzhugh, a small slaveholder and accomplished writer from Port Royal, Virginia. He had thought a great deal about southern problems, had contributed articles to leading southern journals, and in 1854 had published his first book, *Sociology for the South*. Fitzhugh was not among those southerners who had spent a great deal of time in the North and knew it firsthand; but he had made an intensive study of northern institutions and practices and felt that he knew the North well enough to pronounce it a failure. Its frantic, but serious consideration of such radical movements as socialism, communism, and anarchism was a clear admission of its failure. The antirent riots of the forties in New York, the extreme radicalism of the Oneida Colony and similar utopian communities, the fad of spiritualism that was sweeping the North, and the "Bloomerism" of the women's liberation movement attested to the utter social bankruptcy of the North. And yet, it was the North that had launched a campaign to destroy the South by seeking to impose its impossible concepts and practices on the South.[10] "For thirty years," Fitz-

10. For discussions of George Fitzhugh's ideas see his *Sociology for the South* (Richmond: A. Morris, 1854); Harvey Wish, *George Fitzhugh, Propagandist of the Old South* (Baton Rouge: Louisiana State University Press, 1943); C. Vann Woodward, "George Fitzhugh, *Sui Generis*," in George Fitzhugh, *Cannibals All! Or, Slaves Without Masters*, ed. C. Vann Woodward (Cambridge: Harvard University Press, 1960); and Eugene Genovese, *The World the Slaveholders Made* (New York: Pantheon, 1971), Part Two.

hugh argued, "the South has been a field on which abolitionists, foreign and domestic, have carried on an offensive warfare. Let us now, in turn, act on the offensive, transfer the seat of war, and invade the enemy's territory."[11]

Fitzhugh's opportunity came in the form of an invitation to speak in New Haven in March, 1855. "The People's Course of Lectures," a popular series, was managed by a Yale graduate, Joseph Sheldon, and attracted large crowds. Ralph Waldo Emerson and Henry Ward Beecher had already appeared, and the series undoubtedly provided an excellent platform on which to set forth one's views. In casting about for a speaker to give the South's views on slavery, Sheldon sought the advice of Moncure D. Conway, a former Virginian who had not returned to his home after becoming an ardent antislavery man during his years at the Harvard Divinity School. Conway said that his mind "fixed on George Fitzhugh of Kings County, Virginia."[12] Fitzhugh accepted the invitation with pleasure. Although he was in debt, he declined Sheldon's offer of a fee for the lecture. En route he stopped off in New York and visited the abolitionist Stephen Pearl Andrews, with whom he had been corresponding. Together they discussed for several hours their common views regarding the "cult of objectivity as the solvent of social controversies."[13] But they continued to hold strong and antithetical opinions on slavery. In New Haven the Fitzhugh lecture was to be followed the next day with a reply from Wendell Phillips. Since Phillips had been detained in Boston by a lawsuit, Fitzhugh agreed to postpone his discourse until Phillips arrived. Meanwhile, he visited his distant kinsman, Gerrit Smith, the wealthy abolitionist and philanthropist who resided in baronial splendor in Peterboro, New York. Despite the different worlds in

11. Fitzhugh, *Sociology for the South*, 222.
12. Moncure D. Conway, *Addresses and Reprints, 1850–1907* (Boston: Houghton, Mifflin Co., 1907), 112. Port Royal, where Fitzhugh lived, was actually in Caroline County.
13. Wish, *George Fitzhugh*, 82.

which they lived and the diametrically opposite views they held on many social and economic questions, the visit was both pleasant and memorable.

There was great interest in Fitzhugh's appearance in New Haven, and there was assurance that he would be received respectfully and even cordially. Many students and professors at Yale were interested in what he would say. The New Haven carriage-makers, with a lively southern trade, would surely not offend him. The town moreover, was not a hotbed of abolitionism; and antislavery candidates for public office had not fared well there. "He may rest assured," said the editor of the New Haven *Palladium*, "that he will be treated to no mobbing or any invitation to leave the city, however radical may be the difference between his ideas and those of his auditors. We could hope that such a proffer of 'free discussion' may not be without its influence in opening a way for like encounters of reason and morality among our Southern brethren."[14]

Although Phillips had not yet arrived from Boston, Fitzhugh spoke to a large and attentive audience in Brewster's Hall on March 21, 1855. Using as his subject "The Failure of Free Society," Fitzhugh spoke largely about the natural origin of slavery, the misguided views of Jeffersonian liberalism, and the superiority of southern civilization. He had not prepared a special paper, and most of what he said was taken directly from his recently published book, *Sociology for the South*. "Although my lecture was double the usual length," he wrote the following month, "and a metaphysical and statistical argument instead of an evening's entertainment (as they are used to) it was often applauded, and listened to politely throughout."[15] Not having previously visited the North, Fitzhugh based his conclusions regarding its failure on a most extensive study of the problems of free societies

14. Quoted *ibid.*, 132.
15. George Fitzhugh to "G. C.," April 12, 1855, quoted in Moncure D. Conway, *Autobiography* (2 vols.; Boston: Houghton, Mifflin Co., 1904), I, 224.

throughout the history of mankind. "But I was 'carrying coals to Newcastle' in proving the 'Failure of Free Society,'" he later recalled. "They admit all that, but say they have plans for social organization that will cure all defects."[16]

The *Palladium* was correct in predicting that Fitzhugh would be treated civilly. Indeed, he received marked attention from Professor Benjamin Silliman and other members of the Yale faculty. Sheldon congratulated him, remarking that no other lecture had aroused so much talk and speculation. But the *Palladium*'s appraisal of the lecture was not very complimentary. It did not report the speech in its entirety because it contained "much assertion, much fog, and much nonsense, with many disgusting appeals to the perceptions of his hearers, intended to elicit responses 'from the heart.'" The newspaper went on to assure Fitzhugh's southern friends that he was listened to with fairness throughout his remarks, which were "prolonged through two hours." But "no one was convinced by his attempted arguments; many were amused by their novelty; a few were saddened that a man whom nature evidently intended for a genial gentleman, possessing common sense, and ordinary mental ability, should have the end of his production thwarted by the mere fact of tropical location under the influences of slavery."[17] Moncure Conway, who had suggested Fitzhugh to the New Haven group, was hardly more charitable. "Fitzhugh's method of proving Free Society was by theories and speculations which had got into crevices and under the eaves of his brain, like the bats in the rickety old mansion, situated on the fag-end of a once noble estate in which he resided."[18]

Fitzhugh had two other experiences while in New Haven that he would not soon forget. On the morning after his lecture he was

16. *Ibid.*, 225.
17. Quoted in Wish, *George Fitzhugh*, 135.
18. Conway, *Addresses and Reprints*, 112. Conway was inaccurate in recalling that Fitzhugh spoke "on the evening of his arrival" and that Wendell Phillips was "present and heard it."

visited by Samuel Foote. Foote, formerly of Cincinnati and now living in New Haven, was an uncle of Harriet Beecher Stowe. He had heard Fitzhugh's lecture, and when he called upon him the following morning, Foote offered to take Fitzhugh on a tour of New Haven and environs, apparently to show him how free society had failed. On the drive Foote made it a point to show him houses and cottages, owned by mechanics and even some day laborers, that would have been considered "marvels of elegance in Virginia." Fitzhugh saw the suburb of Fair Haven, whose residents were quite prosperous in the oyster trade; their prosperity was made possible by transporting oysters from Virginia and planting them near the mouth of the Quinnipiac River.[19] That Fitzhugh was impressed is clear. That he was not too greatly influenced by what he saw is also clear from his remarks in *Cannibals All,* where he spoke of the doubtful effects of small, individual successes in the North while the masses of people remained in poverty.[20]

Foote also took the Virginia visitor on a tour of Yale University. Among other things he saw a monument commemorating the deeds "of a regicide, who had sought refuge in New England, from that merited punishment with which he was threatened in England." Fitzhugh could feel no sympathy for the parliamentarians who had ordered the execution of Charles I, and he was interested to learn from Foote that southern students occasionally threw stones at the statue. "Thus," he thought, "is the quarrel kept up. The South sustains religion, order, subordination, law, and government." Foote ended the tour by taking Fitzhugh to his home to meet his niece, Mary Beecher Perkins, the sister of the author of *Uncle Tom's Cabin.* She was considered the "sensible" member of the Beecher family, and Fitzhugh declared privately that he was "much pleased with her."[21]

19. *Ibid.,* 112–13.
20. Fitzhugh, *Cannibals All!* 50–51.
21. Wish, *George Fitzhugh*, 136–38.

The other experience in New Haven was hearing the address by Wendell Phillips, who arrived the morning after Fitzhugh spoke. That evening, the famous abolitionist, champion of women's rights, Irish independence, and the end of capital punishment, spoke to a large audience that was "delighted and instructed for an hour and a quarter." He did not offer a direct reply to the southerner, who was in the audience; rather, he spoke on "The Lost Arts." He disposed of Fitzhugh rather briefly by remarking:

> I rejoice especially to stand here and succeed the lecture you had last evening, for the highest attribute to a free society is that it allows men to speak fearlessly, and that society cannot be accounted a failure, although it should fail to give food to the hungry or shelter the desolate.
>
> Last night you listened to a Virginian, defending Virginia and her institutions. When I and many more like me, are welcomed to Richmond to defend New England and her institutions, without danger of the penitentiary, then may Massachusetts and Connecticut be weighed in the balance with Virginia.

Apparently Phillips was aware that Fitzhugh had been on a tour of New Haven, for he offered the view that if one spent an hour looking down from the hills on New Haven, with its churches, its industry, its educational institutions, and its other worthy features, and reached the conclusion that New Haven had failed, then he "must look elsewhere than upon this earth for success." If Fitzhugh needed any evidence of northern disdain for the South, Phillips gave it to him by neglecting the Fitzhugh arguments and devoting the greater portion of his address to the failure of the northern churches to take a stand against slavery and other evils.[22]

Fitzhugh's foray into the land of the infidels had as profound an effect on him as his remarks had upon his listeners. On his return to Virginia, he brooded over what he had heard and seen;

22. New Haven *Weekly Palladium*, March 31, 1855, quoted in Wish, *George Fitzhugh*, 139.

and this brooding is clearly reflected in his subsequent book, *Cannibals All! Or Slaves Without Masters*. He wrote a lengthy letter to the editors of the Richmond *Enquirer* summarizing the views he had set forth in New Haven. Apparently he wanted Virginians to know that he had not failed them, even if he had not convinced New Englanders. He also dispatched letters to William Lloyd Garrison and Horace Greeley, pointing out that nothing had changed his opinion that slavery was both natural and indispensable.[23]

Fitzhugh was persuaded that the northern reformers, especially those in the Liberty party, were as intent on "subverting and reconstructing society at home as on abolishing slavery" in the South. Some of them were "infidels who find the Bible no impediment to their social reforms, because they assert that it is false." Others, Fitzhugh said, "are the best allies of the South because they admit, and continually expose, the utter failure of Free Society."[24] Among them was Wendell Phillips himself, who had said in his New Haven lecture that "governments are not formed by man, but are the gradual accretions of time, circumstances, and human exigencies." Fitzhugh accepted this theory and argued that he would do all he could to "deter men from applying the axe to the root of our Southern institutions" for the "worst institutions that ever *grew up* in any country are better than the best that philosophers or philanthropists have ever devised." As for Phillips, Fitzhugh conceded that in private life, aside from his abolition and sectional prejudices he was "a worthy, accomplished gentleman. . . . He seems to distill manna and ambrosia from his lips, but is all the while firing whole broadsides of hot shot."[25] But the crusading George Fitzhugh would never be the same again.

Most southerners would have agreed that if any place in the

23. The letters are reprinted in Fitzhugh, *Cannibals All!* 104–106.
24. *Ibid.*, 98–99.
25. *Ibid.*, 257–58.

North needed a corrective of its views of southern civilization it was Boston. In this cradle of liberty Garrison published the *Liberator*, Wendell Phillips inveighed against slavery, and Charles Sumner carried on a running fight against most southerners and all southern institutions. It was in Boston, moreover, that the Fugitive Slave Act of 1850 had been effectively nullified by large numbers who defied the southern slave catchers as well as the federal marshals. And in 1855 the legislature had desegregated the public schools of the state. The passing of time had dimmed the memory of those Bostonians who, together with their ancestors, had built their fortunes on the African slave trade. And if great profits were still to be made from the institution of slavery, the textile mill owners, who were the principal beneficiaries, stood apart from the crowd. Thus, if the Garrisons and Sumners and Phillipses were regarded as overly zealous, they did not offend great numbers who had a direct interest in slavery; and the general climate of Boston was becoming increasingly antislavery.

Yet, the spirit of the community that was committed to examining the burning issues of the day was inclined to tolerate discussions of both sides of controversial questions. There were, moreover, some Bostonians who felt that the southern point of view deserved a respectful hearing. Among them was the wealthy banker and textile manufacturer, Nathan Appleton, who regarded Garrison as a "fanatical monomaniac" and whose support of Zachary Taylor in 1848 moved Sumner to remark that there was an "unhallowed union" between the "lords of the lash and the lords of the loom."[26] Appleton believed that slavery was a local problem and that the interests of the nation as a whole should not be hampered merely because slavery existed in the South. He hoped, therefore, that his own New England would adopt a more tolerant attitude toward the South. In the hope that

26. Arthur Burr Darling, "Nathan Appleton," *Dictionary of American Biography*, I, 330–31.

he could be instrumental in accomplishing this objective, he invited Senator Robert Toombs of Georgia to come to Boston to participate in a series of lectures designed to present "various shades of opinion on the explosive issue."[27]

At the time he received the invitation from Boston, Toombs was one of the best-known defenders of southern rights. After a rather modest career as a Whig member of the Georgia legislature and the United States House of Representatives, he rose to prominence by his bitter attack on the North during the debates over the Compromise of 1850. "The first act of legislative hostility to slavery is the proper point for Southern resistance," he exclaimed in the debate on whether slavery should be excluded from the territories acquired during the Mexican War. "Those in advance may fall . . . but the cause will not fall with them; no human power can avert the result; it will triumph. Though hostile interference is the point of resistance, non-interference is not the measure of our rights."[28] These were the words of an emerging southern "fire-eater." Four years later he was in the United States Senate, a prominent and respected spokesman for the southern cause. Unlike Fitzhugh, Toombs was no stranger in the North. After a tumultuous three years at the University of Georgia, from which he was expelled for misconduct, he had graduated in 1828 from Union College in Schenectady, New York. In 1848 he had campaigned for Zachary Taylor in New York, where his speech was interrupted by shouts of "slaveholder." In 1855 he had visited Boston before sailing for an extensive tour of Europe.[29]

A large audience was present when, in the company of Nathan Appleton, Senator Robert Augustus Toombs of Georgia mounted the platform to speak at Boston's Tremont Temple on January 24,

27. William Y. Thompson, *Robert Toombs of Georgia* (Baton Rouge: Louisiana State University Press, 1966), 104.
28. *Congressional Globe*, 31st Cong., 1st Sess., Appendix, Volume XXII, part 1, p. 201.
29. Thompson, *Robert Toombs*, 47, 103.

1856.[30] Toombs, known for bombast and even profanity in his public harangues, fully appreciated the significance of the occasion, and he had carefully prepared his remarks. The following month he was to write a friend that his letter had reached him just before he "left for Boston to lecture the Yankees, and found me much engaged in preparation for that work."[31] His preparation to "lecture the Yankees" resulted in a carefully written lecture of one hour and a half, a lecture that he would rework before publication. And it was as carefully reasoned as it was written.

Toombs first spoke of the constitutional powers and duties of the federal government relative to domestic slavery. He argued that slavery was an established fact at the time of independence and that the Constitution clearly recognized this fact. The Constitution did not give Congress the right to "abolish, limit, restrain, or in any other manner to impair the system of slavery in the United States." Every clause in the Constitution touching on the subject of slavery "was intended either to increase it, to strengthen it, or to protect it."[32] Consequently, Congress did not have the power to exclude slavery from the territories, a point he had made most impressively in his celebrated speech in the House of Representatives in 1850.

Toombs then spoke on the influence of slavery upon the slave and upon American society. Speaking for most southerners and, indeed, many other Americans, he held that the whites were clearly superior to the blacks. If the two races were to coexist, the subordination of the blacks was the "normal, necessary, and proper condition, and . . . such subordination is the condition

30. Pleasant A. Stovall, *Robert Toombs: Statesman, Speaker, Soldier, Sage* (New York: Cassell Publishing Company, 1892), 130.
31. Robert Toombs to Thomas W. Thomas, February 9, 1856, in Ulrich B. Phillips (ed.), "The Correspondence of Robert Toombs, Alexander H. Stephens, and Howell Cobb," *Annual Report of the American Historical Association for the Year 1911* (Washington, D.C.: Government Printing Office, 1913), II, 359.
32. Robert Toombs, *Lecture Delivered in the Tremont Temple, January 24, 1856* (Washington, D.C.: John T. and Lem Towers, 1858). The full lecture is reprinted in Alexander H. Stephens, *A Constitutional View of the Late War Between the States* (Philadelphia: National Publishing Co., 1868), 625–47.

best calculated to promote the highest interest and the greatest happiness of both races, and consequently of the whole society." He was not concerned with whether Africans should have been removed from Africa and enslaved. That was an accomplished fact, thanks to the English and other Europeans, by the time of independence. Since Africans were "unfit to be trusted with political power, incapable as freemen of securing their own happiness, or promoting the public prosperity," their slave status was recognized and perpetuated. More than that, they were given all the benefits of social security—the protection of life; provision for food, clothing, and shelter; and benevolent treatment when old or infirm.

Toombs insisted that slavery was neither a wasteful nor an unprofitable system of labor. In arguing that the social system of the South was stable, he said:

> For nearly twenty years, foreign and domestic enemies of [Southern] institutions have labored by pen and speech to excite discontent among the white race, and insurrections among the black. These efforts have shaken the national government to its foundations, and bursted the bonds of Christian unity . . . yet the objects of their attacks . . . have scarcely felt the shock. . . . The desire for organic change nowhere manifests itself. Within less than seventy years, out of five feeble colonies with less than one and a half millions of inhabitants, have emerged fourteen republican States, containing nearly ten millions of inhabitants, rich, powerful, educated, moral, refined, prosperous, and happy; each with republican governments adequate to the protection of public liberty and private rights, which are cheerfully obeyed, supported, and upheld by all classes of society.[33]

The New York *Express* declared that the speech by Toombs was "earnest and deliberate, presenting his argument with great power." A biographer later observed that "there was some conduct in the audience at the close which the Boston *Journal* was forced to denounce as 'ungentlemanly.' " After his remarks, the speaker was given three cheers, not unmixed with dissent; and

33. *Ibid.*

one person in the audience shouted, "When will Charles Sumner be allowed to speak in the South." One paper declared that "if Toombs and other hotheads would lecture in Syracuse, Oswego, Ashtabula, and other points of 'Africa' they would do a great deal of good in educating the innocents and becoming themselves educated and freed from fire, froth, fury, and folly."[34] It was a memorable experience for Bostonians to have among them a Georgia fire-eater who would speak with such restraint and candor. Crusading among infidels was still a one-way street, however.

As the intersectional strife became more heated during 1856 and as the adversaries on both sides became more senstive, virtually any remark by one side was the occasion for vehement refutation by the other. In such cases where their section was offended, southerners stood ready to go into the North to argue their case; and frequently they did precisely that. The Reverend Fred A. Ross of Huntsville, Alabama, delighted in taunting his colleagues at the 1857 meeting of the New York Presbyterian Assembly in Buffalo. When a member introduced a resolution condemning slavery, Ross sought to amend it to include the antislavery leaders as well. He argued that if they purchased cotton, rice, and sugar "sprinkled with blood, literally you say, from the lash of the driver," they were just as guilty as those who held slaves. When a speaker challenged anyone to defend slavery on scriptural grounds, Ross accepted the challenge. He was not a slaveholder, he said. Indeed, he had emancipated his slaves, perhaps $40,000 worth. But he proceeded to offer the classic defense of slavery, based on the Bible, to the astonishment of his northern listeners.[35]

In the early autumn of 1856, as the presidential contest between John Fremont and James Buchanan moved to a climax,

34. Stovall, *Robert Toombs*, 131–32.
35. Fred A. Ross, *Slavery Ordained of God* (Philadelphia: Lippincott, 1857), 17, 34–35.

southern political leaders went north to join in the fight against Fremont. As the first presidential candidate for the new Republican party and as an outspoken opponent of slavery, Fremont represented everything that southerners opposed; and since there was little need for their talents in the South they went to the land of abolition to do their part. John Slidell, the prominent Louisiana politician, worked desperately to secure the election of Buchanan. He moved quietly among party leaders in New York to attempt to heal the dissensions there; and he gave strong anti-Fremont speeches in several places. He remained apprehensive; and a few days before the election he told Buchanan that he would be only half satisfied "if your triumph is not overwhelming."[36]

If John B. Floyd, former governor of Virginia, was not as effusive as Slidell in his support of Buchanan, he was no less determined to persuade northerners to defeat that archenemy of southern institutions, John C. Fremont. Since Nathaniel P. Banks, Speaker of the House of Representatives, had appeared in New York in support of Fremont, some twelve hundred Democratic merchants engaged Floyd to speak for Buchanan. When he appeared at the Exchange in October, 1856, Floyd eschewed fire-eater oratory and devoted most of his speech to "an analysis of the economic issues at stake in the election."[37] There had been much talk by Banks and others of the lack of efficiency and productivity in the South. Floyd rejected such claims and insisted that much of the northern economy was dependent on the products of the South. "Take away from New York the exchange which Southern States give to her, and every interest and every pursuit here, would be thrown into chaos."[38] Floyd was pleased with this sectional interdepen-

---

36. Louis M. Sears, *John Slidell* (Durham: Duke University Press, 1925), 136–37.

37. New York *Times*, October 3, 1856. See also Philip S. Foner, *Business and Slavery: The New York Merchants and the Irrepressible Conflict* (Chapel Hill: University of North Carolina Press, 1941).

38. Foner, *Business and Slavery*, 133.

dence; but he wanted to leave no doubt among the New York merchants that the South's role was not only important but indispensable.

That was essentially the theme of the speech that Virginia's R. M. T. Hunter made to the citizens of Albany, New York, during the campaign of 1856. He was less cautious than Floyd in pointing to the consequences of the reckless abolitionist policy of attacking slave property. If institutions and property, recognized and guaranteed by the Constitution, can be overthrown, Hunter asked, "how can any government, or any constitution, be secured and protected, otherwise than by force?" He then pointed out that virtually everyone, in one way or another, was committed to some form of servitude:

> Fellow citizens, what is property in man, and what is involuntary servitude? Property may be absolute or limited; it may be in fee or for a term of years. In practice one man may hold property in the services of another for life, as in the law of slavery; for a term of years, as in apprenticeship; or for months, weeks, days, and hours, in case of domestics, or mechanics, or lawyers or doctors. . . . All of it is servitude. The evils which are ascribed to one form . . . are common to them all.

Hunter warned that if the war against slavery was successful, it could easily lead to a war against the institution of property itself. Perhaps even worse, if the North won a war against the South, the two races would still be a problem. Would the South be converted into one great Jamaica, "one vast Nigritia," he asked. This was a question that every responsible northerner should ponder. For "what then would become of the vast commerce and rich customers who now contribute to your power and wealth." He then warned his listeners not be tempted to try to scatter ruin over the land and destroy it. The best course for the North and South was to seek unity and understanding.[39]

39. R. M. T. Hunter, "An Appeal to the North," *De Bow's Review*, XXI (November, 1856), 530–38.

The controversy over the comparable contributions of the two sections to the War for Independence was about as acrimonious as any debate in the period and extended over most of a decade, culminating in 1856. In 1847 Lorenzo Sabine, the Massachusetts historian, published his *The American Loyalists*. In one place in his book Sabine observed, quite incidentally, that the Loyalist sentiment in the South was so strong that the section's contribution to the winning of independence was extremely limited and, on the whole, without effect. In singling out South Carolina, the author conceded that there was some patriotic zeal in that colony but cautioned that "one swallow does not make a summer nor *one* feather make a bed, and so, a Laurens, father and son, a Middleton, a Rutledge, Marion, Sumpter, and Pickens do not prove that the Whig leaven was diffused throughout the mass of her people." He added that one of the reasons for the southerner's inability to commit himself more fully to the revolutionary cause was the presence of large numbers of slaves who might become troublesome during a time of upheaval.[40]

If Sabine had deliberately planned it, he could not have wounded the pride of southerners more deeply or evoked a more spirited retaliation from them. The provocation came at a time, moreover, when southerners were already insisting that their position more nearly reflected a spirit of national unity and well-being than the disruptive activities of northern abolitionists. Southerners had also been pressing their argument that slavery, the cornerstone of their civilization, greatly contributed to the stability and prosperity of the entire country. The Sabine attack appeared to southerners to be part of a grand northern design to dispute their loyalty and challenge their institutions. They could not ignore it any more than they could ignore the

40. Lorenzo Sabine, *The American Loyalists* (Boston: C. C. Little and J. Brown, 1847), 30, 32.

frontal assaults of the abolitionists. They would refute Sabine in the press, on the platform, on the floor of Congress, and even in the North.

Literally scores of southerners insisted that their ancestors were the leaders in the War for Independence. Virginians were responsible for securing Illinois from Britain, Elwood Fisher told his Cincinnati audience; and then they magnanimously ceded it to the Confederation.[41] Another argued that the number of southern enlistments and the length of service by southerners clearly proved that they "suffered more of the privations of war than their Northern co-patriots."[42] Another proud southerner said that the Revolution in South Carolina had been "conceived and organized by the native population" and that from the first the people "never wavered nor faltered throughout its progress."[43] Southern troops, another argued, were more loyal than New England troops, who would not march into Virginia with Cornwallis "until they had received in hard money, one month's pay in advance."[44]

As for the slaves, southerners insisted that they were an asset during the Revolution. Even when whole districts of the country were left entirely to women, children, and slaves, the bondsmen, "far from proving treacherous, or deserting their masters, continued their labors upon the plantation, and no faithful watchdog was ever more true in giving the alarm, on the approach of an enemy."[45] They denied that their slaves deserted them and went over to the British. They claimed that the British only got slaves from the southern colonists by seizure.[46]

41. Elwood Fisher, *Lecture on the North and the South, Delivered before the Young Men's Mercantile Library Association of Cincinnati, Ohio, January 16, 1849* (Charleston: A. J. Burke, 1849).
42. Edward B. Bryan, *The Rightful Remedy, Addressed to the Slaveholders of the South* (Charleston: Walker and James, 1850), 87.
43. Lawrence Massillon Keitt, "Patriotic Services of the North and South," *De Bow's Review*, XXI (November, 1856), 491.
44. Joseph Johnson, *Traditions and Reminiscences, Chiefly of the American Revolution in the South* (Charleston: Walker and James, 1851), 556.
45. Bryan, *The Rightful Remedy*, 47.
46. *Ibid.*, 46.

Judge Augustus Baldwin Longstreet said that he had never heard of such a thing as slaves taking sides against their masters. "But I heard of thousands of instances, wherein they served them in battle, took care of the wives and children, [and] bore them away from peril."[47]

The argument over the South's valor and the role of her slaves in the War for Independence finally found its way to the floor of the United States Senate. Among the ardent defenders of the South's contribution to the War for Independence was South Carolina's Senator Andrew P. Butler. As early as 1850 he had declared that the "quarrel of Boston was espoused without calculation by the people of Charleston"; and he expressed the view that it would now be strange "if those who had a common history should be the parties to destroy the bonds of a union formed in a spirit of cordial confidence."[48] During the debates on Kansas, when Butler spoke against the move to make Kansas a free state, it was Charles Sumner who answered him.

> But it is against the people of Kansas, that the sensibilities of the Senator are particular aroused. Coming, as he announces "from a State"—ay, sir, from South Carolina—he turns with lordly disgust from this newly formed community, which he will not recognize even as "a body politic." Pray, sir, by what title does he indulge in this egotism? Has he read the history of "the State" which he represents? He cannot surely have forgotten its shameful imbecility from Slavery, confessed throughout the Revolution, followed by its more shameful assumptions for slavery since.[49]

Sumner had already overreached himself. He went on, how-

47. Augustus Baldwin Longstreet, *A Voice from the South: Comprising Letters from Georgia to Massachusetts, and to the South* (Baltimore: Western Continent Press, 1847), 25. For quite different versions of the role of slaves during the Revolution, especially their going over to the British, see Benjamin Quarles, *The Negro in the American Revolution* (Chapel Hill: University of North Carolina Press, 1961), and John Hope Franklin, *From Slavery to Freedom: A History of Negro Americans* (New York: Alfred A. Knopf, 1974), 90–93.

48. Andrew P. Butler, *A Speech of A. P. Butler, of South Carolina, on the Bill Providing for the Surrender of Fugitive Slaves. Delivered in the Senate of the United States, January 24, 1850* (Washington, D.C.: Globe Office, 1850), 11. For a vivid account of the Sumner-Butler-Brooks controversy see David Donald, *Charles Sumner and the Coming of the Civil War* (New York: Alfred A. Knopf, 1960), 259–311.

49. *Congressional Globe*, 34th Cong., 1st Sess., May 20, 1856, Appendix, 543.

ever, to make remarks against Senator Butler that offended most southerners. This led to the canning of Sumner on the Senate floor by Butler's cousin, Representative Preston Brooks. Butler, however, made his own reply by suggesting that "ingratitude is the monster of vices, and when it is associated with injustice, it ought to be condemned by the consuming indignation of even those who may tomorrow be our adversaries. . . . The man who now reproaches South Carolina is a degenerate son reproaching the dearest and nearest comrade of his mother. You cannot get over the errors he has committed in history; you cannot obviate the malignity with which the arrow has been shot. . . . I challenge him to the truth of history. There was not a battle fought south of the Potomac which was not fought by southern troops and southern slave holders."[50] There was no rebuttal, for Sumner lay critically ill from the thrashing that Brooks had given him.

William Gilmore Simms, South Carolina's leading novelist and man of letters, had watched this tragic dispute for years, and his temper rose with every exchange between the North and South. He had been among the first writers of the South to praise the South's role in the War for Independence, and as early as 1843 he had delivered a lengthy oration on the subject. On that occasion he said that the history of South Carolina in the Revolution did not need to be written. "It is deeply engraven upon the everlasting monuments of the nation. It is around us, a living trophy upon all our hills. It is within us, an undying memory in all our hearts. It is a record which no fortune can obliterate—inseparable from all that is great and glorious in the work of the Revolution."[51] The unionist of the 1830s had become by 1844 an ardent champion of the South.[52] When

50. *Ibid.*, 627–28. See also *De Bow's Review*, XXI (August, 1856), 197–98.

51. William Gilmore Simms, *The Sources of American Independence: An Oration, on the Sixty-Ninth Anniversary of American Independence* (Aiken, S.C.: The Council, 1844), 22.

52. John W. Higham, "The Changing Loyalties of William Gilmore Simms," *Journal of Southern History*, IX (May, 1943), 210–23.

Sabine's book appeared Simms was no longer certain that South
Carolina's role in the Revolution did not need to be written. He
had published a history of his state in 1840, and he had given
much attention to the Revolutionary era.[53] Apparently that was
not enough. He would set the record straight, once and for all.

First, Simms made a blistering attack on Sabine in his review
of *The American Loyalists*, which appeared in two issues of the
Southern Quarterly Review in 1848. He asserted that the present generation of public men of South Carolina had no doubt
that the colony's "patriotic devotion in the revolution was inferior to none and was superior to most of the states of the
Confederacy." Sabine had found this not to be so, but he did not
prove his claim, for he could not do so. "The claims of Carolina
to the distinction which her public men assert," said Simms,
"may be slurred over by ingenuous misrepresentation, but she
cannot be defrauded of them. They are to be estimated relatively with the difficulties with which she had to contend, the
deficiencies of her numbers, the purity of her purpose, the ran-
cor of her enemies, the spirit and wisdom of the favorite sons
who swayed her councils and fought her battles, and the se-
verity and frequency of the fields of fight." Simms then proceeded
to argue that the southern army was composed largely of men
from the five colonies of Virginia, Maryland, South Carolina,
North Carolina, and Georgia. Not a dozen patriots from New
England fought in the South; and the generals from the North
who led southern armies, Benjamin Lincoln and Nathanael
Greene, were scarcely better than mediocre.[54]

Next, Simms contributed an article, "The Morals of Slavery,"
to the *Pro-Slavery Argument*, which appeared in 1852. It was a
revision of an article that had first appeared in the *Southern*

53. William Gilmore Simms, *The History of South Carolina, From Its First European Discovery to Its Erection into a Republic* (Charleston: S. Babcock and Company,
1840). More than one-half of the book treats the period 1775–1783. See, especially, pp.
133–319.

54. *Southern Quarterly Review*, XIV (July, 1848), 45–51, and (October, 1848),
261–337.

Literary Messenger in 1837. In the revised version Simms gave special attention to the role of slaves during the Revolution. Despite the efforts of the British to lure the slaves away, they were unsuccessful, Simms contended. "The entire mass of the slave population adhered, with unshaken fidelity, to their masters—numbers followed or accompanied them to the field, and fought at their sides, while the greater body faithfully pursued their labors on the plantation, never deserting them in trial, danger, or privation, and exhibiting, amidst every reverse of fortune, that respect, that propriety of moral, which did not presume in adversity, and took no license from the disorder of the times."[55]

Then, in 1853, Simms brought out, in revised and extended form, his article on Sabine's book, which was itself a book. The intervening years had not cooled Simms's ardor or quieted his temper. He therefore launched a bitter personal attack on Sabine. He was not prepared, he said, to quarrel with the "taste, or passion for novelty, which of late, seems disposed to busy itself in rescuing the memories of the American Loyalists from obscurity." Perhaps it was natural, or perhaps even necessary, for the person engaging in such a work. He admitted, moreover, that such researches were essential to the "unity and completeness of our records, if not to their authority and value. . . . But to employ history, as Mr. Lorenzo Sabine seems to have done, as a sort of universal dragnet; and to arrest, and to preserve together in the reservoir, without discrimination, the fish, flesh, and fowl of this mixed multitude, is to make a 'hell-broth' of it, indeed, such as the witches of Shakespeare and Middleton might be led to admire and envy for the various loathesomeness of the ingredients." Simms, tempted to dismiss the whole Sabine undertaking, said that it was a waste of type and paper and declared, "That Mr. Sabine's book will be found readable in the

55. *The Pro-Slavery Argument: As Maintained by . . . Chancellor Harper, Governor Hammond, Dr. Simms, and Professor Dew* (Charleston: Walker and Richards, 1852), 243.

proportion of one page to fifty is quite beyond the range of literary probability."[56] Small wonder that some years later a biographer of Simms concluded that his petulance and want of courtesy led him to "gross indiscretions and injured his own cause."[57]

Finally, Simms decided to take his crusade into the North. As a young man he had lived in New York City for several years and in 1833 had published one of his early novels, *Martin Faber*, while residing in New Haven. In later years he went to New York almost every year to visit friends, among them his oldest New York friend, William Cullen Bryant, and to discuss literary matters with such associates as James Lawson and Evert A. Duyckinck of Scribners.[58] Bryant and Duyckinck, along with George Bancroft, the historian, were among the nine New Yorkers who extended an invitation to Simms to give three lectures in November, 1856.[59] Simms had arrived in New York early in November, and in accepting the invitation he was frank to say that he hoped to "disabuse the public of the North of many mistaken impressions which do us wrong."[60] He felt that he was among friends and they would give open-minded attention to what he had to say. Before giving the course of lectures in the city, however, Simms had engagements to speak in Buffalo, Rochester, and Syracuse.

On November 11, Simms addressed a Buffalo audience of more than twelve hundred people on "South Carolina in the Revolution." The material for the lecture, which he would repeat in Rochester and New York City, was drawn from his sev-

56. [William G. Simms], *South-Carolina in the Revolutionary War: Being a Reply to Certain Misrepresentations and Mistakes of Recent Writers, in Relation to the Course and Conduct of This State*, by a Southron (Charleston: Walker and James, 1853), 2–9.

57. William P. Trent, *William Gilmore Simms* (Boston: Houghton, Mifflin and Company, 1892), 205.

58. See above, pp. 103–104.

59. Simms had delivered a few lectures on purely literary subjects in Philadelphia in 1854. William R. Taylor, *Cavalier and Yankee: The Old South and American National Character* (New York: George Braziller. 1961), 293–94.

60. Mary C. Simms Oliphant and T. C. Duncan Eaves (eds.), *The Letters of William Gilmore Simms* (5 vols.; Columbia: University of South Carolina Press, 1954), III, 454.

eral works on the subject. One newspaper said that the lecture was interesting and instructive, and the only portion giving dissatisfaction "was his severe animadversions on a portion of the North." Another called it "an ill-digested, bitter, and to at least nine-tenths of the audience, offensive defense of South Carolina politicians of the Brooks school." A third newspaper was even less restrained:

> Mr. Simms was invited by a Library Association to address them as a literary man, the only one of note in the South. It was supposed he would choose a subject proper for the occasion. With an impudence unsurpassed, he comes into our midst and makes an harangue abusive of a Northern State and running over with fulsome and false praise of the least deserving State in the Union. Certainly he was listened to quietly, because if Mr. Simms is no gentleman, the audience were too good-natured and civil to notice it, and they seemed to be rather amused than otherwise at his discourse.

Simms fared no better in Rochester, where an editor said that as a literary production the lecture was "destitute of merit" and as a lecture before a literary association it was "an imposition."[61]

It was in New York City that Simms hoped to make his greatest impression. He was well known in literary circles, he had a distinguished list of patrons, and the lectures were to be given at Dr. E. H. Chapin's Universalist Church of the Divine Unity. Furthermore, Simms would have ample opportunity, in three lectures, to get his message across. The first lecture, on November 18, would be on "The South in the Revolution," to be followed on November 21 and 25 by "The Appalachians, A Southern Idyll, Descriptive of Southern Scenery, Life, Manners, etc."[62] A small audience of not more than one hundred was "scattered through Mr. Chapin's Church" at the appointed

---

61. Reports on the Buffalo and Rochester appearances are in Oliphant and Eaves (eds.), *Letters of William Gilmore Simms*, III, 456–58. The lecture, as delivered in Buffalo, Rochester, and New York City, is printed in this volume, 521–49. The Syracuse version of the lecture is not included.

62. The notice of the Simms lectures appeared in the New York *Tribune*, November 17, 1856. They were sponsored by the Young Men's Lecture Association.

hour on November 18. Simms spoke for an hour and a half, at the end of which "he received a round of applause."[63]

It is reasonable to assume that Simms alienated a considerable portion of his audience at the beginning when he launched an attack on Charles Sumner, still recovering from the assault by South Carolina's Preston Brooks. For some eighty years, Simms began, the people of South Carolina had reposed securely in the faith that the fame of their ancestors was beyond reproach. "The Past, they were confident, was secure—safe equally against the dull hoof of the ass, and the slimy trail of the reptile!" It was not to be so, for there had been allegations made "by a Senator in the Senate House" and he had regaled his listeners of the unmanly deeds of South Carolinians who were "false to their duties and their country;—recreant to their trusts . . . traitors in the cabinet and cowards in the field!" And this cruel history was "poured forth with a malignant satisfaction, seemingly with no other purpose than to goad and mortify the natural pride and sensibility of a hated party!"[64]

The remainder of the address sought to correct the notion that South Carolina had not contributed its full share to the winning of independence. Simms gave his audience statistics to show how extensive South Carolina's commitment was to the War for Independence; and he recounted events to show the valor of the men of the South in their effort to defeat the enemy. In passing, he asserted that his state had done nothing to cause anyone from Massachusetts to claim that South Carolina had not done its share. He closed by saying, "Forgive me, my friends, if I have spoken warmly; but you would not, surely, have me speak coldly in the assertion of a Mother's honour!"[65]

It was Horace Greeley's New York *Tribune* that delivered the

63. New York *Tribune*, November 19, 1856. The New York *Herald*, November 19, 1856, blamed the small attendance on "the unusual number and peculiar excellence of other places of attraction . . . and, to some extent perhaps, to the high price of the tickets." The tickets were 50¢ per lecture or $1.25 for the three.

64. William Gilmore Simms, "The South in the Revolution," in Oliphant and Eaves (eds.), *Letters of William Gilmore Simms*, III, 521–22.

65. *Ibid.*, 549.

most blistering attack on the Simms lecture. It praised Simms for seeking to give an accurate picture of the numbers of men that South Carolina furnished in the War for Independence, although it had some reservations about their accuracy. But it called him to task for making no mention of South Carolina's Negroes "who, after all, were her greatest drawback, and, since they served as plunder, the chief instigation to the ferocious civil war, by which she was ravaged and disgraced." This was all the more notice-able, the *Tribune* continued, "since it was this particular draw-back of slavery, alluded to in the speech of Mr. Sumner, which drew down upon him the ferocious attack of Bully Brooks, well worthy of a cowardly South Carolina Tory, and to which Mr. Simms also saw fit to allude in the beginning of his lecture, in terms reproachful to Mr. Sumner, and, we must be allowed to say, very little creditable to the head, heart, or taste of Simms." The article closed by advising Simms to delete his attack on Sumner the next time he gave the lecture and to give some attention to "the weakening effect produced by the institution of slavery; and to prove, if he can, that it was not the direct and principal cause of the disastrous subjection into which South Carolina fell. It will be quite enough to vituperate Mr. Sumner after having first refuted him."[66]

The New York *Post*, edited by William Cullen Bryant, long-time friend of Simms, regretted to notice "several instances of lack of courtesy in our contemporaries in their remarks upon Mr. W. Gilmore Simms, of South Carolina, in connection with a lecture recently delivered in Buffalo and in this city. It is an entire mistake to confound Mr. Simms with the vulgar political agitators of every portion of the country. He is neither a politician by habit or profession. . . . Having chosen for the subject of his lecture, the history of his native state, he has complimented his audience by taking a topic on which he is thoroughly prepared. Surely northern ears are not so delicate as to take offense at an

66. New York *Tribune*, November 24, 1856.

occasional outbreak of local and very natural feeling in an exceedingly elaborate, painstaking, and, upon the whole judicious
performance."[67] It was too late for Bryant to repair the damage
that his old southern friend had done to his reputation among
New York audiences.

On the evening of the next lecture there were only "thirteen
gentlemen and four ladies" present at half past eight. Simms,
deeply disappointed, refused to give the lecture. The New York
Herald saw nothing unusual in the way that Simms's "quixotical
undertaking was received." After all, it would perhaps not be
possible for any person from the North to go to South Carolina
and "lecture upon the intellectual preeminence of Massachusetts and the wrongs of Charles Sumner."[68]

Following the disappointment that Simms suffered in the failure of his second New York lecture, he canceled all other engagements. To his New York sponsors, he wrote, "I am greatly
mortified at being compelled to forego the pleasure of lecturing
before you, as you were so good to request continuing the course
which I began on Tuesday night." He was persuaded, however,
that he would do himself and the committee on arrangements
"an equal injustice" were he to persevere. He understood that
his first lecture had produced such a "rancorous feeling" that the
committee "could not only sell no tickets, but could not succeed
in giving them away."[69] He sent similar communications to the
Troy Young Men's Association and the New Haven Young Men's
Institute, for whom he was to lecture following his New York
engagement. He told the group at Troy that he was compelled to
forego his engagements "in consequence of the singular odium

67. New York *Post*, November 21, 1856. The New York *Times*, November 19, 1856,
called the lecture "eloquent and interesting" and said that Simms would always be
listened to "courteously and respectfully. . . . These courtesies are the more creditable,
because they are never reciprocated."
68. New York *Herald*, November 24, 1856. The *Times*, November 22, 1856, reported
that "as neither the lecturer nor any member of the Committee of Management presented himself within twenty minutes after eight o'clock . . . the ladies and gentlemen
present dispersed.
69. Oliphant and Eaves (eds.), *Letters of William Gilmore Simms*, III, 460–61.

which attends my progress as a South Carolinian, and the gross abuse which has already assailed myself personally, and my performances."[70]

It was a shattering experience for Simms. He had not expected to be censured so sharply by some newspapers or ignored by the general public. To a friend he had planned to visit while in the North, he sent a brief note of apology, saying, "I had been so defeated, so disappointed of my expectation, that I was in no mood for society, even that of friends; and I hastened home to my forest cover, with the feeling of a wounded hare flying to the thicket."[71] Even James Henry Hammond was distressed and wrote to Simms, "You have gone North at a somewhat critical time for *you* and martyred yourself for South Carolina who will not even buy your books and for Brooks whose course could at best be only excused and who in his supreme vanity will think your sacrifice only a slight oblation. What demon possessed you, mon ami, to do this?"

Hammond's letter awaited Simms when he returned to South Carolina in early December. In his reply Simms poured out his heart to Hammond. He saw nothing in his lecture that could give offense. He had made no allusion to Brooks, he pointed out, directly or indirectly. "I did to Sumner, as the wanton assailant of South Carolina . . . when she was not a subject of discussion. I had to do this, in order to show why, and on what points I had undertaken to correct the vulgar mistakes or misrepresentations of her history." On reflection, it became clear to Simms that nothing he could have said would have changed anything. "But such is the rancorous temper of Black republicanism; so completely does New England rule New York; and so malignantly do they all regard South Carolina that the very object rearoused all the hostility. Besides, the Black republicans were grateful for any new occasion for keeping up the excitements by which they live."

70. New York *Post*, November 21, 1856.
71. Quoted in Trent, *William Gilmore Simms*, 224.

Simms told Hammond that after the first lecture in New York, it was determined that he should "abandon the field" and the church was not even opened at the appointed time for the second lecture. He then released the committee from its obligation. Meanwhile, he decided against attempting any lectures elsewhere. "Could I hope that if I could not secure a hearing in New York I should be more successful farther East." He could have chosen other subjects that would have given no offense, but "would not that have made me appear as shrinking from the mission which I came upon?"

Then, in a rather bitter response to Hammond's assertion that he was not appreciated at home:

> I expect nothing from South Carolina, but I have been too long accustomed to toils and sacrifice from her, to feel her injustice now. My losses are all pecuniary. She will never make them up to me. She will probably never acknowledge my performance. But I have the precious consciousness of both the toil and the sacrifice, and the proud feeling that if I have never received her favours, I am free from obligations; and though she may allow of none to me, I, at least, have a conviction on that score which is singularly compensative.[72]

A hurt and broken crusader had returned home, having utterly failed to conquer the infidels. In the failure of his mission and in his abject and bitter disappointment, Simms, like other southern crusaders before him, had just begun to take the measure of the adversary. It would take more than self-satisfaction or self-esteem or even naked courage to carry the day. Somewhere along the line, if the southern crusaders would hope to succeed, they would need to assay the strength of their adversary, understand its resources, and gain some insight into the complexity of its people and way of life.

72. Oliphant and Eaves (eds.), *Letters of William Gilmore Simms*, III, 465–69. In obvious reference to Simms's New York appearance, Paul Hamilton Hayne wrote his New York friend, Richard H. Stoddard, "There is much truth undoubtedly in what you say of Simms. He had no tact, discretion, or judgment. But if you knew the circumstances of his career—what, from boyhood he has had to contend against here, your surprise at his conduct would be vastly modified." Paul H. Hayne to Richard H. Stoddard, December 15, 1856, in Paul Hamilton Hayne Papers, Duke University, Durham.

Southern crusaders also needed to be tougher, more cynical than the sensitive, idealistic Simms. They could not become enraged or even discouraged by heckling or other forms of disagreement; and if they were to be effective and successful, they had to parry or disregard the taunts of their listeners. William G. Brownlow, "the fighting parson of the Southern highlands," possessed many of the qualities required of a southern crusader in the North. A vigorous Whig leader and editor in East Tennessee, Brownlow was at once a strong advocate of slavery and an ardent supporter of unionism. He could be as fervent in his advocacy of certain political and social causes as in his espousal of his brand of religion at a Methodist camp meeting. In the 1850s Brownlow developed an especially strong antipathy for the abolitionists whom he regarded as hypocritical and destructive. He decided to challenge them to come out and fight. He preferred to cross swords with Theodore Parker or Henry Ward Beecher; but he would settle for any worthy gladiator. When Frederick Douglass, the former slave turned abolitionist, was suggested, Brownlow rejected him "as an untouchable."[73]

In the late spring of 1858 Abram Pryne, a radical Garrisonian from McGrawville, New York, answered Brownlow's challenge and indicated a willingness to debate him. Since a Negro college was located in McGrawville, Brownlow demanded assurances on Pryne's religion and his race. After some heated exchange regarding possible arrangements, Pryne finally told Brownlow that he was a Congregational minister and that "my father is a Hollander by descent, and my mother's father was a Scotchman, and though not a very white man, there is not a drop of Negro blood in my veins."[74] Brownlow was thus satisfied and indicated that he would debate Pryne in Philadelphia as soon as he

73. Coulter, *William G. Brownlow*, 97.
74. Abram Pryne to W. G. Brownlow, April 28, 1858, in *Ought American Slavery to be Perpetuated? A Debate between Rev. W. G. Brownlow and Rev. A. Pryne, Held at Philadelphia, September, 1858* (Philadelphia: J. B. Lippincott, 1858), 9. This volume contains a complete account of the arrangements leading up to the debate as well as the speeches of Pryne and Brownlow. Coulter's biography of Brownlow has an excellent account of the debate.

fulfilled some other engagements. "This will give you more time for preparation," he wrote Pryne, "and you will please not accuse me of egotism when I advise you to be fully ready, as I purpose to give you battle after a style you have not been accustomed to—not intending to be outdone by you, however, in courtesy and fairness."[75]

The debate began on September 7, 1858, at the National Guard Hall in Philadelphia and continued for five successive evenings. On the first evening there were about four hundred persons present, "a mixture of black and white, Southern students, Quakers, Black Republicans, abolitionists and negro barbers and bootblacks."[76] Each man was to speak for an hour at each meeting, with no interruptions. Brownlow told Pryne that he could surround himself with abolitionists, if he so desired, but only *he* could speak.

As he invaded "enemy territory" the crusading parson from Tennessee was confident that he would win the day. On succeeding evenings he argued his case with vigor, at times offering "evidence," at times seeking to intimidate his opponent, and at other times "lecturing" the obviously partisan audience. Slavery, he said, was an established and inevitable condition in human society, was sanctioned by divine authority, and would exist to the end of time. Drawing on the Old and New Testaments, he gave numerous examples to show that slavery had been divinely ordained. It was clear to anyone who cared to look that slavery had greatly improved the moral, mental, and physical condition of blacks. It was for this reason that many who had gained their freedom wanted to be reenslaved, he claimed. Slavery was indeed "a blessing to the master, a blessing to the non-slaveholders of the South, a blessing to the civilized white race in general, and a blessing to the negro slaves in particular."[77]

Brownlow pointed out that people like Pryne "stirred things

75. *Ibid.*, 9.
76. Coulter, *William G. Brownlow*, 100.
77. *Ought American Slavery to be Perpetuated*, 102. The summaries of the arguments come from the five lectures that Brownlow delivered.

up" by seeking to paint a picture of the horrors of slavery and misrepresenting the happy relationship between master and slave. Instead, he and other abolitionists should be concerned with the deplorable conditions in the North. Brownlow devoted most of his third lecture to a discussion of the low aspects of northern life: crime, prostitution, insanity, free love, and the many "issues" that clearly underscored the absence of stability. It was most unfortunate that northerners spent their time and talents trying to undermine southern life, for the worst consequences accrued to the North. Southerners would not continue to do business with people who sought to destroy them. For example, "Boston, the hot-bed of sedition, and Abolition slang-whanging, has done a little more than *half* her usual business with the South, the last two seasons."[78]

Brownlow seemed to derive special delight in taunting Pryne and the audience. At the beginning of his second talk, he said, "I hope the gentleman has recovered his composure after the discussion of yesterday evening. And if the *joints* of his armor crack under the power of truth tonight, it shall not be my fault; but the fault of the *cause he advocates.*"[79] In response to Pryne's praise of black abolitionists, Frederick Douglass and Samuel Ringgold Ward, saying that they were his (Pryne's) superiors, Brownlow retorted that he did not doubt it, "after the exhibition he has made of himself on the stand! I do not think it follows, as a matter of course that they are giants in intellect. They may be intellectually his superiors, and still be moderate men!"[80] In observing that Pryne strayed from the subject, Brownlow commented condescendingly, "I am willing to overlook the *aberrations* observable in the truly desultory remarks of my worthy friend."[81]

Nor did the audience escape the wrath of the southern parson.

78. *Ibid.*, 259.
79. *Ibid.*, 77.
80. *Ibid.*, 129, 170.
81. *Ibid.*, 77.

At the beginning of his third talk Brownlow recalled that on the previous evening he had been interrupted repeatedly by cries of "time expired," an announcement that came from "ruffians and insolent free negroes." He insisted that he had not gone beyond the outside limit of one and one-half hours on which he and Pryne agreed. "I ask no favors—no quarters—no sympathy from Abolitionists—and I expect none; but I demand *justice*." He realized that the South was well represented at the debates, "but the friends of the South have not interrupted Mr. Pryne and will not do so. . . . Southern men, unlike Abolitionists, are men of good breeding! If *persons*—I will not say gentlemen, friendly to the cause of Abolition—are sick of this discussion, and of the facts and figures I am laying before them, and wish to break it up, let them say so, through their reverend spokesman, and we will discontinue it quietly, and disperse as becomes gentlemen."[82]

While Pryne was a courageous combatant, he was hardly a match for the rough and tumble tactician from the South. When Pryne said he spoke for religion, justice, law, and "an outraged God," Brownlow threw the Constitution and the Bible at him. When he said that he spoke for the "voiceless maidens sold in the shambles, for millions of strong men rendered mute by chains," Brownlow said that such utterances merely revealed Pryne's ignorance of slavery. Brownlow's reply was weak, however, when Pryne declined his invitation to debate him in the South. "The *brave* South meets Northern ministers with mobs," Pryne said. "Let a man attempt to address the Southern mind sentiments with which the people of that section differ, and the *brave* South gathers hundreds of her roughest citizens to argue him down with brickbats, and bowie knives, and pistols, and bludgeons."[83]

Pryne refused to be intimidated by Brownlow; and he was fully prepared to exchange blow for blow. He called the southern

82. *Ibid.*, 140–41.
83. *Ibid.*, 282.

slaveholders the greatest criminals of the age and asserted that
the South was $12 billion poorer because of slavery.

> What a sum to sink into the fathomless maw of such a monster crime!
> All for the purpose of letting 250,000 slaveholders to lord it over their
> negroes, keep race horses, and vary the amusements of gambling,
> fighting, and drinking, by an occasional dash into politics, to play the
> game of Southern statesmanship, and, when weary of that, to astonish
> waiters and attachees of Northern hotels by blustering about North-
> ern watering places.[84]

At the conclusion of the debate, the two adversaries prepared
their manuscripts for publication. In a joint preface they said that
they had spoken "honestly and with a sincere desire to do good."
They admitted that they both had some prejudices arising from
their education, habits and associations. They hoped, nevertheless, that the reader would appreciate their principles and opinions, "as he may deem them entitled to favor."[85] Brownlow had
the last word, however. After John Brown's raid on Harpers
Ferry, Brownlow declared that Brown was a vile creature but
that Pryne was even worse. In an open letter to Pryne, published
in his *Tri-Weekly Whig*, Brownlow let loose his final malediction:
"Had you, as a 'Preacher of Righteousness,' exhorted the old
scoundrel, and his villainous boys, to repentence and faith, they
might have become religious, instead of dying in their disgrace-
ful act of rebellion and going to Hell, as they doubtless have
done. Shame on you, you vile hyprocrite."[86]

The one final opportunity that southerners had to present their
case to the northern people came during the presidential cam-

---

84. *Ibid.*, 107–108.
85. *Ibid.*, iv. When this volume on the Brownlow-Pryne debate appeared Edmund
Ruffin read it with interest and declared that it was "entertaining and also instructive. . . .
But it is obvious that the two disputants had previously prepared their arguments, and
that neither troubled himself much to answer his opponent." Scarborough (ed.), *The
Diary of Edmund Ruffin*, I, 339.
86. Quoted in Coulter, *William G. Brownlow*, 126. The classic southern denunciation of John Brown was made by Captain H. Clay Pate of Virginia in a lecture at New
York's Cooper Institute, December 7, 1859. When Brown was his prisoner, Pate quoted
Brown as saying that he "would as soon take a man's life as a common dog's, if that man
stood in the way of his principles." New York *Herald*, December 9, 1859.

paign of 1860. With the Democratic party divided and the Republican party all but captured by the abolitionists, southern leaders went north not so much to mount a crusade in behalf of southern institutions as to issue a solemn warning of the impending doom. "It cannot be disguised that both the safety of the South and the integrity of the Union are seriously threatened," wrote Howell Cobb, the Georgia leader who was President Buchanan's secretary of the treasury. "It is my honest conviction that the issue depends on the action of the Southern people at this important juncture."[87] After all, the Republican nominee, Abraham Lincoln, was making forays into the Northeast hammering away at the moral wrong of slavery. At Cooper Union in February, he had said that "if slavery is right, all words, acts, laws, constitutions against it, are themselves wrong, and should be silenced and swept away.... If it is wrong, they [the slaveholders] cannot justly insist upon its extension—its enlargement."[88] Southerners would have to go north and make their position clear and unequivocal. That is what Howell Cobb and Herschel V. Johnson of Georgia, Leslie Combs of Kentucky, Henry W. Hilliard, William L. Yancey, and others sought to do between September and November, 1860.[89]

Henry W. Hilliard, long-time member of the House of Representatives, was from Alabama, but had numerous close connections in the North. He passed the summer of 1860 in Saratoga Springs with his family; later he took apartments at the Fifth Avenue Hotel in New York City. In September the conservative men in the city decided to hold a meeting in Cooper Institute to be addressed by men supporting the claims of the presidential candidates opposed to Lincoln. Hilliard accepted the invitation

87. Quoted in Emerson D. Fite, *The Presidential Campaign of 1860* (New York: The Macmillan Company, 1911), 108.

88. Roy P. Basler (ed.), *The Collected Works of Abraham Lincoln* (8 vols.; New Brunswick: Rutgers University Press, 1953), III, 549.

89. Foner, *Business and Slavery*, 194. For an account of Herschel v. Johnson's appearance in New York, Philadelphia, and other northern cities, see Percy Scott Flippin, *Herschel v. Johnson of Georgia: State Rights Unionist* (Richmond: Dietz Printing Company, 1931), 140–47.

and spoke on September 17. He warned of the dangers of the times and gave particular attention to the danger posed by a sectional party. He reminded his listeners of the economic and social consequences of the disruption of the Union.

Hilliard was especially bitter as he denounced the unreasonable abolitionists and William H. Seward's "higher law" morals; he argued that slaveholders had as much right to expect protection of their property under the Constitution as owners of other types of property. He warned that if the "fierce sectional league" succeeded in coming into power and using the government to destroy the institutions of one section, that would be "the beginning of the end. The day that witnesses the election of Mr. Lincoln, if that calamity is to be visited upon us, will witness a convulsion which shakes the institutions of this country to its deepest foundations. (Tremendous enthusiasm.)" He pleaded with the people of New York to save the Union by crushing its enemies.[90]

A few days after the successful meeting at Cooper Institute, Hilliard received an invitation from a group of conservatives in Boston to speak there. He accepted and was the house guest of Edward Everett, the vice-presidential candidate on the ticket with John Bell. He spoke at Faneuil Hall to a packed house; and, as he later recalled, "I presented the claims of the eminent men whose cause I represented in strong terms, and appealed to all who heard me for another illustration of the attachment of Massachusetts to the Constitution, by giving them their support."[91] Hilliard spoke in other cities in New York: Utica, where his host was the former governor, Horatio Seymour; and Buffalo, where he called on former President Millard Fillmore. Everywhere he was cordially received. Instead of returning to Alabama, he was in New York City on election day.

The most spectacular crusade by a southerner during the cam-

90. Hilliard, *Politics and Pen Pictures*, 292–302. The full text of Hilliard's speech appeared in the New York *Herald*, September 18, 1860.
91. *Ibid.*, 303.

paign of 1860 was made by the leader of the southern movement, William Lowndes Yancey of Alabama. Sometimes called "The Great Precipitator," Yancey accepted an invitation to speak in the North in order to dispel the rumor that slaveholders really desired the election of Lincoln in order to have an excuse for seceding.[92] Beginning in Kingston, Georgia, he worked his way north, and on October 10, he spoke to an overflow crowd at Cooper Institute. He was in his best form—eloquent, witty, logical—and did not embarrass himself and his audience as he had done at the southern convention in 1858 when "he was under the influence of strong drink, and his speech suitable to his condition."[93] "I trust an Alabamian may yet speak to the citizens of New York in a spirit of fellowship," he began. "I trust that hour has not arrived when an Alabamian, speaking to his brethren of the city and state of New York as brothers, will be received with jeers and hisses."[94]

Yancey told his audience that he believed that truth, "at all times, will win its way to hearts that are swayed by the love of truth, generosity, and justice." He would speak the truth about his home, state, and section that he loved better than any other. It was a mistake, he said, to claim that the institutions of the South were inimical to the highest attainments of civilization. He praised the South's way of life and its institutions that were protected by the Constitution and the laws of the land. Why should the North begrudge the South's way of life, he asked, when it has developed its own way as the result of climate and economy. Mutual toleration and mutual respect were all that the South desired.[95]

There were other high points in the Yancey tour. At Faneuil Hall in Boston, where he spoke on October 12 to a large and cordial audience, he recalled the lessons he had learned while a

92. Fite, *The Presidential Campaign of 1860*, 214–18.
93. Scarborough (ed.) *Dairy of Edmund Ruffin*, I, 188.
94. John W. DuBose, *The Life and Times of William Lowndes Yancey* (2 vols.; Birmingham: Roberts and Son, 1892), II, 499.
95. *Ibid*., 500–502.

student at Williams College and had not forgotten. He feared that Massachusetts would vote for a candidate dangerous to the South, but he hoped he was wrong. He pleaded with his listeners who had become prosperous from industry, not to fear honest competition with the slaveholder who had remained on the soil. When a voice interrupted to say that he could not go south, Yancey replied, "There isn't a man among you who is not welcome if he doesn't come to steal our niggers. We have plenty of Northern men in our city; they do not try to steal our property, or to incite rebellion, and they stay."[96] If he did not convince his audience, it must have been impressed with his candor.

Yancey then proceeded to Albany, where he spoke on October 15, then to Syracuse and Rochester, ending his northern tour in Cincinnati on October 22. Since he had left Alabama he had delivered more than twenty "elaborate addresses." His biographer called his feat "the most remarkable oratorical tour in American history."[97] It must have been a source of some satisfaction to Yancey to have carried the fight to the enemy and to have been listened to with interest and attention even if he did not significantly affect the outcome of the election. Perhaps his greatest satisfaction came from the compliment paid him by a fellow southern firebrand, Edmund Ruffin, who described the tour as a "brilliant campaign of political warfare and defense of the claims of the South . . . [with] displays of the power of eloquence and zeal, and ardent patriotism."[98]

In the end none of the southern crusaders really succeeded in winning over the northerners to their point of view. When they drew large crowds, their listeners were more likely to be curiosity-seekers than persons susceptible to change. There seemed always to be a feeling among northern audiences that they should attend if for no other reason than to remind

96. *Ibid.*, 507–10.
97. *Ibid.*, 513–17, 494.
98. Edmund Ruffin to William L. Yancey, October 29, 1860, in Scarborough (ed.), *The Diary of Edmund Ruffin*, I, 633–34.

themselves—and, often, the speaker—that the South would not tolerate the presence of abolitionists and other northern crusaders. They could hardly have been optimistic about what they could accomplish. For most of them their crusade among infidels was another part of the ritual of warning the North and giving it a final opportunity to save the Union from destruction by its fanatics.

VII

A
Renewal of
Faith

As the crisis deepened in the last two years before the disruption of the Union, southerners did not cease their northern travels. To be sure, some of them went to White Sulphur Springs instead of Saratoga; and some merchants, finding their northern credit canceled when they threatened not to pay their debts if the South seceded, began casting about for other sources. Most of those who were in the habit of going north, however, continued the practice right down to the beginning of secession. These included not only the politicians who campaigned so vigorously in the North in the autumn of 1860 but many who went on less critical missions. As Henry Hilliard pointed out in his speech at Cooper Institute on September 17, 1860:

> At this moment an extraordinary number of citizens of the Southern States are in New York; they fill the hotels, they throng the streets, they are seen in your great trading establishments; they come with the confidence of a kindred people. [Applause] And yet torches borne by men who denounce their institutions, and seek to turn all the power of a common government against them, glare upon them at midnight, and the tread of disciplined battalions shakes the very paving stones as they march in their training to prepare for a resistless assault upon the rights and honor of our section. [Loud applause][1]

Apparently, the other southerners in New York and elsewhere in the North were able to view such northern actions with as

1. Henry W. Hilliard, *Politics and Pen Pictures at Home and Abroad* (New York: Putnam's, 1892), 294.

much equanimity as Hilliard, who, after all, spent most of the summer and early fall of 1860 in the North. There were the James De Bows spending their honeymoon in New York and Philadelphia in the autumn of 1860.[2] Clement Clay was in Minnesota looking for a cure for his maladies even after the election of Lincoln.[3] Edmund Ruffin was touching the hated free soil of Ohio as he went from Virginia to Kentucky in September.[4] In the same month Henry W. Ravenel, the Charleston botanist, met with his peach factor in New York and went on a three-day excursion to Saratoga, where he met dozens of other southerners.[5] Benjamin L. C. Wailes, the Natchez planter, spent five and one-half months in the summer and fall retracing his steps of earlier visits to New York and Philadelphia.[6] William Gilmore Simms, far from boycotting the North after his ill-fated lecture tour of 1856, spent a month in New York in August and September and regretted that personal affairs in South Carolina made it impossible for him to remain longer.[7] And there were others, many others.

Even after John Brown's raid in 1859, which was the occasion for more than a hundred southerners to withdraw from northern medical colleges, most southern students in northern schools remained there until secession began. In September, 1860, De Bow estimated that "fully a thousand young men from the South" continued to attend medical colleges in the North.[8] In 1860 there

2. Ottis C. Skipper, *J. D. B. De Bow, Magazinist of the Old South* (Athens: University of Georgia Press, 1958), 111.

3. Ada Sterling (ed.), *A Belle of the Fifties: Memoirs of Mrs. Clay of Alabama* (New York: Doubleday, Page and Company, 1905), 153–54.

4. William Kauffman Scarborough (ed.), *The Diary of Edmund Ruffin* (2 vols. projected; Baton Rouge: Louisiana State University Press, 1972), I, 468.

5. Arney Robinson Childs (ed.), *The Private Journal of Henry William Ravenel, 1859–1887* (Columbia: University of South Carolina Press, 1947), 26–28.

6. Charles S. Sydnor, *A Gentleman of the Old Natchez Region: Benjamin L. C. Wailes* (Durham: Duke University Press, 1935), 278–80.

7. Mary C. Simms Oliphant and T. C. Duncan Eaves (eds.), *The Letters of William Gilmore Simms* (5 vols.; Columbia: University of South Carolina Press, 1954), IV, 238–40.

8. *De Bow's Review*, XXIX (September, 1860), 396.

were ninety-five students at Princeton from the slave states, a net increase of four over 1857.[9] Early in 1861 they began to leave "very quietly," and after Fort Sumter, the southern students from all four classes departed in a body, "the funds for their journey being supplied by President Maclean." Before leaving they requested that they might be permitted officially "for the last time to salute the flag. And one—John Dawson of Canton, Mississippi—asked that with his violin he might accompany the singing of the 'Star Spangled Banner'. . . . The flag was raised. The salute was given. The southern students then marched off the campus."[10]

The belated departure of southern students from Princeton symbolized, in a sense, the reluctance with which southerners gave up their northern connections. Even in the face of abolitionist taunts and the campaign of a sectional party, based in the North, it was not easy to forego a practice that had become regularized over the years. More than most southerners were willing to admit, they were dependent on the North for their economic, cultural, educational, and even physical well-being. If, as Thomas P. Kettell said, the South poured riches into the lap of the North, southerners themselves were drawn to the North in the process.[11] They followed their raw materials there, where credit had been established, where they could exchange the goods they produced for the things they needed or wanted, and where the North's sophisticated businessmen and economic institutions exerted seductive influences that southerners seemed unable to resist. If southern wealth did, indeed, produce northern profits, southerners who went north derived some profit of their own from the experience.

    9. Varnum Lansing Collins, *Princeton* (New York: Oxford University Press, 1914), 408.
    10. Edwin Mark Norris, *The Story of Princeton* (Boston: Little, Brown and Company, 1917), 186.
    11. Thomas Prentice Kettell, *Southern Wealth and Northern Profits, As Exhibited in Statistical Facts and Official Figures* (New York: George W. and John A. Wood, 1860), 126.

Southerners were not unique in their desire to enrich their own lives. And there was more art, music, theater, recreation, and other diversion in one major city of the North than in the entire South. If the North had the things southerners wanted, what was wrong with their going there to obtain them? If they wanted to, they could rationalize that the rural or small-town existence that most of them led made it impossible to develop the activities and institutions that they so much enjoyed in the North. Perhaps they could even say that they spent the better part of their lives in more productive and constructive tasks. As they developed the notion that their own civilization was both different from and better than that of the North, they could go—out of curiosity, if nothing else—to see and savor the alien culture. Thus, it was well for the North to divert them and entertain them on occasion; and when they had had enough of it, they could return to their more serious pursuits.

They desired the best possible education for their sons, of course. It would take more than an appeal to sectional pride and loyalty to convince them that the best educational institutions were not in the North. Thus, when they sent their sons to northern colleges and professional schools, they did not feel that they were committing acts of disloyalty. Indeed, many of them were quite active in programs to raise the level of education in the South. Until their own institutions reached the point where those in the North were, southerners seemed determined to send their offspring to Yankeeland for an education. When editors and other southern spokesmen warned them that northern colleges were teaching heretical social and religious doctrines, the parents discounted the warnings. To southern parents northern professors, so solicitous of their sons and of them when they made visits, did not appear to be anti-Christ, antisouthern, or even antislavery. And when young southerners graduated and returned home, they showed no signs of serious contamination. Some editors and other southern spokesmen were products of such institutions and, in some instances, sent their own sons to the same northern colleges where they had received their own educations.

Visiting the North became a habit for many southerners, and, like most habits, it became increasingly difficult to break. Knowledge of the evils of the habit—extravagance, prodigality, over-indulgence—did not persuade them to give it up. The most that it did was to induce a certain amount of self-reproach for their inability to break the habit. Logic, as well as many promoters of the South, argued that they should remain at home, husband their resources, and develop their own resorts and centers of culture and amusement; but they went. James De Bow, the southern commercial conventions, and a host of persons in private stations urged them not to go, for the sake of the future of the South and of their own self-respect; but they went. And when they began to make their way home in the autumn of 1860, it was as much because the first frost was approaching as because the nation was falling apart. As they reached their respective homes and began to realize what was happening, they viewed in utter disbelief the spectacle of a nation, shattered by dissension and secession. For in a very special way, their own world had fallen apart.

Although they did not do so consciously, the travelers themselves had contributed to the polarization of the sections. They had made regular excursions to the North and had remained for months at a time. They insisted that they *knew* the North and could speak with authority about it. Whether or not they admired the North, they were generally agreed that it was a quite different civilization, an alien culture. The people were different from those of the South, they believed; and their economy, institutions, and general way of life were different. If the North was not a "totally foreign country," as more than one southerner insisted, most southerners felt that the things they had in common with northerners were minimal. The Virginia traveler who said in

1834, "The North and South need only know each other better, to love each other more" was excessively sanguine. With every passing year, as travel increased from south to north, southerners became better acquainted with northerners and their institutions; but every passing year witnessed a deterioration in relations between the two sections. Even if the travelers had wanted to, they could not have stemmed the tide. By the 1850s they could merely subscribe to the growing alienation that engulfed all of them.

But one of the things that caused the southern travelers to feel more alienated from the North was the attitude of the North toward them and their section. Few of them really felt comfortable among northerners. Perhaps it was because they tended to remain to themselves whenever they were in the North or because they sensed a certain condescension on the part of northerners whenever they were in their presence. Perhaps, also, it was because northerners not only did not reciprocate by visiting the South but also because they seemed to have no interest in looking at the South firsthand. A few of them did visit the South. William C. Bryant made three trips there in 1832, 1843, and 1849; and James Lawson visited his old friend William Gilmore Simms in 1859. Frederick Law Olmsted made his celebrated tours through the South in 1852, 1853, and 1854. And there were others. Some businessmen visited southern centers of commerce, and some of them remained for extended periods. But there was no general interest in observing the southern scene even on the part of northerners who wrote about the South; and there was no travel in the South comparable to the northern trek made annually by throngs of southerners. Northerners would argue, of course, that they were not welcome in the South. Southerners would respond that as long as northerners did not attempt to overthrow southern institutions, they were indeed most welcome.

Southerners could scarcely escape the feeling that when they were in the North the host section was the dominant power in the relationship. The more they traveled the more keenly aware they became of the colonial status of the South. They did not need Hinton R. Helper or Thomas P. Kettell to tell them that the North was the chief beneficiary of southern toil. They saw it at the New York wharves piled high with southern agricultural products to be processed in the North or exported to Europe by northern shippers. They saw it in the exorbitant prices they paid for goods there and in the South's generally unfavorable balance of trade with the North. It seemed to them that northerners were doing little more than providing a vantage point from which those who did the work and produced the raw materials could see their efforts transformed into northern wealth. As one hapless southern observer put it, "Northern wealth appeared daily to increase, and Southern wealth to diminish."[12]

Their sense of disadvantage gradually turned to outrage as they saw that northerners were too self-centered and too self-righteous to have any regard for the well-being of the very people, the southerners, who had contributed so much to their wealth. The North did not create its own wealth, southerners said; that wealth resulted from the happy circumstances of its developing trade. And that was not necessarily permanent, George Fitzhugh insisted:

> Whilst travelling through New England, viewing her poverty-stricken fields, her fine towns and cities, her mighty factories, her great commerce, her palatial private residences, and her stores and warehouses with rich merchandise from every region, the reflection forced itself upon us that a change in the course of trade might make all of this, except the worthless lands and untenanted houses, take wings and fly to countries where capital could be more profitly [sic] employed in commerce and manufactures.

The more Fitzhugh thought of this the more he was tempted to exclaim to the people of the North, "Your wealth is cosmopolitan,

12. *Southern Quarterly Review*, XXVI (October, 1854), 437.

your poverty indigenous! . . . The wealth of the South is permanent and real and that of the North fugitive and fictitious."[13]

In the final years before secession southerners who had lived or traveled in the North were among the leaders in denouncing the North. The more James De Bow visited the North the more bitter his strictures against the North became. In 1860, shortly before he went north on his honeymoon, De Bow denounced southerners who sent their sons to the "unhospitable climes" of the North to secure an education. Conceding that in the arts and manufactures the South was not yet ready for independence, he then said, "but let things go on as they have and we soon will be." He praised those who had established the Virginia Rights Association and called for the founding of similar organizations in other states.[14] William L. Yancey, Williams College graduate with good northern connections, founded the League of United Southerners and, in the 1850s, became the most active agitator against the North. Robert Toombs, Union College graduate and friend of Boston merchants, became one of the most eloquent advocates of a hard-line policy toward the North. On the floor of the Senate he warned the South in January, 1860, that the enemy was at its door. "Wait not to meet him at the hearthstone—meet him at the doorsill—and drive him from the temple of liberty, or pull down its pillars and involve him in a common ruin."[15]

Southerners who *knew* the North seemed at least as hostile as those who had never crossed the Mason-Dixon Line. Clement Claiborne Clay, frequent visitor to the North and collector of southern debts for northern merchants, said as early as 1850 that every step he took and every word he heard in the North made him "more Southern in feeling and principle."[16] An exponent of

13. George Fitzhugh, "Wealth of the North and South," *De Bow's Review*, XXIII (December, 1857), 587, 592.
14. *De Bow's Review*, XXVIII (February, 1860), 244.
15. *Congressional Globe*, 36th Cong., 1st Sess., Appendix, 93.
16. Clement C. Clay to Hugh Lawson Clay, July 22, 1850, in Clement Comer Clay Papers, Duke University, Durham.

the principles of Calhoun in the United States Senate, Clay alternated between visiting the North and denouncing it. Presbyterian leader, James Henley Thornwell of South Carolina, was one who never wavered in his antipathy toward the North. This was evident in his refusal to remain at Andover or Harvard during his brief northern sojourn in 1834. Even then he knew that northerners were godless. He only needed to discover that their political views were equally heretical. Subsequent visits brought him to that realization, so that by 1850 he could provide this assessment: "The parties in this conflict are not merely abolitionists and slaveholders—they are atheists, socialists, communists, red republicans, jacobins on the one side, and the friends of order and regulated freedom on the other. In one word, the world is the battleground—Christianity and atheists the combatants; and the progress of humanity at stake."[17] By the time of the outbreak of the Civil War Thornwell could firmly believe that God was on the side of the southern people.

During the war the people of the South, black and white, had many things to claim their energies and attention; and it is virtually impossible, even with all the testimonies, to describe what a drastic difference the war made in the lives of all of them. But none experienced a change in habits of movement, habits of consumption, and life-styles in general more than those southerners who had been in the habit of going north at regular intervals. Not only were they compelled by circumstances to remain at home, but they were no longer able to acquire the manufactured goods or to enjoy the amenities to which they had become accustomed during their northern sojourns. Worse still, regardless of social or economic standing, they—like all other southerners—were called upon to make sacrifices that, in many instances, reduced ordinary austerity to abject privation. With critical shortages of food, clothing, and virtually every item of

17. Quoted in Wilbur J. Cash, *The Mind of the South* (New York: Alfred A. Knopf, 1941), 80.

necessity, those who had enjoyed the luxury of extensive travel and the satisfaction of every conceivable desire found wartime living an extraordinarily painful experience. Those who had seen better days, including the travelers, could comfort themselves by remembering those days and looking ahead to the end of "this dreadful war."

If some southerners, at the end of the war, merely looked back to the antebellum days with a helpless longing, there were others who believed that the best way to return to the better life was to look to the future with resolution. There was so much to do: burying the dead, nursing the wounded, caring for the widows and orphans, rebuilding the sites of wartime devastation, working out a *modus vivendi* with the freedmen, developing a satisfactory legal arrangement with the Union government. But picking up the pieces and building a better life also involved the resumption of some of the prewar relationships with the people of the North. And the bitter feelings engendered by the war seemed not to preclude the resumption of such relationships—at least, some of them. As southerners ordered their priorities in the spring of 1865, visiting the North was not at the bottom of the list.

Within five weeks after the surrender of the Confederate forces, the possibility of southerners visiting the North was very real indeed. In mid-May a Richmond newspaper announced that the "fast and elegant steamers," the *M. Martin* and the *Georgiana*, were making daily trips from Richmond to Baltimore, "and there connecting with other fast lines to Philadelphia and New York, thus insuring a quick and pleasant trip to and from the Northern cities to all travellers."[18] Later in the month the paper announced that a direct, regular line to New York was expected shortly; and on the following day, it said that the *Carolina* would begin the run to New York the next Monday, with fare and meals at $15.[19] By the end of the month the *Blackstone* had begun

18. Richmond *Republic*, May 15, 1865.
19. *Ibid.*, May 25, 26, 1865. On June 1, the *Varuna* left Richmond for New York. *Ibid.*, June 1, 1865. In August the owners of the *George Leary, City Point, James T.*

regular service from Savannah to New York.[20] In August a Savannah paper said that the city could "now boast of her facilities of accommodation for freight and passengers to the cities of the North which is not surpassed by any other Southern port." There were three lines of "first class steamships to New York": the Star Line, with five vessels; the Pioneer Line, with two; and the Atlantic Coast Steamship Company Line, also with two.[21] By early fall the Star Line had ships making the run from New Orleans to New York.[22] Over the next three years, steamship service between southern and northern ports increased both in the number of vessels and frequency of trips.[23]

Because of their deterioration and destruction during the war the railroads had difficulty competing with the steamship lines in transporting southern passengers and cargo to the North. Since the managers and investors fully appreciated the importance of their speedy reconstruction it was obvious that they would not be at a disadvantage indefinitely. As early as July, 1865, the Orange and Alexandria Railroad Company was busily engaged in rebuilding the bridge across the Rappahannock River, which made possible the resumption of rail service between Richmond and Washington and the eastern cities in early August.[24] By mid-October three trains left Richmond daily for Washington, a feat which moved one observer to remark that "one of the busiest and most significant scenes in the daily life of Richmond is the arrival and departure of the trains to and from Washington, at the depot of the Richmond, Fredericksburg, and Potomac Railroad."[25] In

Brady, and Dictator leased a Richmond wharf from which their steamers would leave for Philadelphia. Ibid., August 12, 1865.

20. Savannah Daily Republican, May 30, 1865.

21. Ibid., August 29, 1865.

22. See the announcements in the New Orleans Times, November 18, 1865.

23. For news of increased steamship service see the Richmond Republic, May 15, 1866; Richmond Daily Dispatch, July 11, 24, 1866; Savannah Daily Republican, July 2, 4, 9, 13, 16, 1866, June 10, 12, 14, July 1, 19, 1867; and the New Orleans Daily Crescent, December 11, 1866.

24. Little Rock Arkansas Gazette, July 29, 1865.

25. Harper's Weekly, October 14, 1865.

July of the following year that company advertised that its line was the "great short route to the North, East and West," offering "elegant sleeping cars on all night trains." It boasted that it was the only railroad route issuing "through tickets and through baggage checks" from Richmond to "Alexandria, Washington, Baltimore, Philadelphia, New York, Boston and all the principal cities in the West."[26]

Rail transportation from the lower South to New York and other northern cities was available by midsummer, 1866. The trip from New Orleans to New York required ninety-eight hours; and if one desired to make the northern journey he could travel the Great Southern Mail Route, the Mobile and Ohio, or the Mobile and Great Northern.[27] In 1868 southern railroads were making a vigorous bid for the patronage of persons traveling north. The Western and Atlantic and the Virginia and Tennessee Railways offered daily passenger service between Atlanta and New York (requiring fifty-seven hours) and other eastern cities. "These lines," the advertisement announced, "pass through the finest portion of the country. Scenery not surpassed by any in the United States; and passengers will have all the advantages of comfortable cars, pure air, good water, and cheap rates of travel." The fare from Atlanta to New York and return was $37.[28]

If southerners needed encouragement to visit the North they found it in several actions that both the government and persons in private stations took in the years immediately following the war. The government's restrictions on movement were soon lifted, so that in early June, 1865, it was no longer necessary for citizens in Savannah "to make application to the Department of Headquarters . . . to go North."[29] Several southern newspapers

26. Richmond *Daily Dispatch*, July 11, 1866. See also the *Travelers' Guide and Illustrated Description of Central New York, Niagara Falls, Saratoga Springs, etc. Together with Railroad Time Tables* (Buffalo: Felton and Brother, 1866), which contains information on southern rail connections to the North.

27. New Orleans *Daily Crescent*, August 11, 1866.

28. Atlanta *Daily Constitution*, June 25, 28, 1868.

29. Augusta *Daily Chronicle and Sentinel*, June 3, 1865.

regularly printed dispatches from their own correspondents in northern cities, who kept prospective travelers informed regarding matters of interest there.[30]

To make southerners feel especially comfortable in New York, Henry Bruce, "late of Kentucky," announced that he had become proprietor of a new establishment called "The Southern Hotel," which he was "painting, frescoing, decorating, refurnishing, etc., in the most splendid and luxurious style." He hoped that it would appeal to southerners, since it was "of white marble, five stories high, fronting two hundred feet on the gayest part of Broadway, most commodiously and comfortably arranged for families and single persons, and is in the very midst of the most elegant stores and shops and the most fashionable places of amusements."[31] The Southern Hotel would have to compete with many other establishments, where southerners were warmly welcomed, including the Astor House, Brevoort House, the St. Nicholas, the St. James, the Metropolitan, and the New York Hotel, which was described in 1869 as "the staying place of Southerners and those who sympathize with them."[32]

With transportation and hotel facilities ready to receive them, southerners resumed the practice of going North at the first opportunity after the war. When the *Varuna* sailed from Richmond for New York on June 1, 1865, there were fifty-one passengers aboard. There were a few military personnel, such as Captain C. M. Coit, but the remainder of the list was not different from that of an antebellum vessel: "Mrs. Howell and two chil-

30. See, for example, the "New York Letter" and "Letter from Saratoga" from Moultrie in the Charleston *Daily News*, July 19, 21, 30, 1866; "Our New York Correspondence" in the Savannah *Daily Republican*, July 3, September 4, 1866; and "New York Correspondence" in *The Land We Love*, III (May, 1867), 82.

31. Savannah *Daily Republican*, July 2, 1866, and *The Land We Love*, I (May–October 1866), 450. See also the advertisement of Cincinnati's Burnet House in *De Bow's Review*, New Series, II (August, 1866), back cover.

32. Junius Henry Browne, *The Great Metropolis: A Mirror of New York* (Hartford: American Publishing Company, 1869), 394. The New York Hotel could count among its southern guests General Joseph E. Johnston, who was establishing several business relationships in the North. New York *World*, November 17, 1865.

dren . . . George W. Douglas and lady, R. P. Gabriel and wife, five children, and servant . . . N. Barridge, wife, and two children . . . A. W. Allen and son."[33] Meanwhile, the *Blackstone* had left Savannah for New York with fifty-four passengers. One major and one captain were aboard; the others were civilians traveling alone or with families and servants.[34] Before the end of the season there were visitors in New York from the Carolinas, Tennessee, Alabama, Mississippi, Arkansas, and Kentucky.[35]

While the visitors in 1865 were something more than a trickle, those in the following year may well have been regarded in some quarters as approaching a flood. In early July, 1866, the New York correspondent of the Savannah *Daily Republican* seemed to feel that way. "New York City is undoubtedly at present very healthy, very lively, and exceedingly hot," he reported. "Southerners are pouring in and the natives pouring out."[36] But the month of July saw an even greater number of southerners going north, especially to New York. On the first day of the month some 99 passengers left Savannah for the North.[37] By the end of the week 347 persons had taken steamship passage from Savannah to New York, a pace that continued for the next several weeks.[38] There were similar departures from Charleston and Richmond.[39]

As in the prewar years, New York held the greatest attraction for southern travelers. They were stopping at the fashionable hotels, shopping at the elegant mercantile houses, seeing the usual sights, and going to the various places of amusement. "A number of Southerners are here spending their money as freely

33. Richmond *Republic*, June 1, 1865. The list of passengers is in the New York *Times*, June 3, 1865.
34. Savannah *Daily Republican*, May 30, 1865, and the New York *Times*, June 1, 1865.
35. See the hotel registrations and shipping news in the New York *World*, June 15, July 28, September 29, 30, 1865; New York *Daily Tribune*, September 5, 1865; New York *Times*, September 7, 1865.
36. Savannah *Daily Republican*, July 3, 1866.
37. *Ibid.*, July 2, 1866.
38. *Ibid.*, July 9, 13, 16, August 2, 1866.
39. Charleston *Daily News*, June 2, 1866; Richmond *Daily Dispatch*, July 24, 1866.

and enjoying themselves as freely as before the war," a New York correspondent for a southern newspaper remarked in 1866. Southerners were as impressed with the hustle and bustle and noise of the great city as they had been during the days before the war.[40] In 1868, when a Georgian visited the city, he marveled at its size, its many attractions, and the noise that pervaded their rooms at the St. James Hotel: "That we had little rest, I deem it unnecessary to say. To anyone judging only by the sound of the little bells of the street-cars, the noise of other vehicles, and the tread of pedestrians, I might be permitted to believe that sleep has no place in New York."[41]

While most ships sailed from southern ports for New York, others were destined for other northern ports. In August, 1865, ships were beginning to make regular runs between Savannah and Philadelphia and Richmond and Philadelphia. Since the establishment of the latter line, "an immense quantity of freight and a large number of passengers have been conveyed to and from this city," a Richmond editor observed.[42] Steamship lines connecting southern ports with Boston began somewhat more slowly, but southerners were optimistic. As one of them commented, "The far-seeing merchants and ship-owners of Boston will no doubt enter the lists with her sister cities, and establish a line between that city and this port, in order to reap some of the advantages to be gained by such a course."[43] By the following summer the *William Tibbets* was making a regular run between Savannah and Boston.[44] Before the end of Reconstruction Boston seemed to be as popular as ever with southerners.

40. Savannah *Daily Republican*, August 30, 1866.
41. Edward Jenkins Harden, *Notes of a Short Northern Tour* (Savannah: Morning News Steam-Power Press, 1869), 11–12.
42. Savannah *Daily Republican*, August 29, 1865, July 2, 6, 16, 1866; Richmond *Republic*, August 12, 1865. The sum of $400,000 was subscribed in Philadelphia toward establishing a shipping line between that port and southern cities. Baltimore *Sun*, January 1, 1866.
43. Savannah *Daily Republican*, August 29, 1865.
44. *Ibid.*, July 6, 1866

It did not take long for Saratoga to resume its place as the favorite recreation spot for southerners. "The lifting of the cloud of war is already perceptible at Saratoga," wrote a correspondent in the summer of 1865.

> Southern faces are reappearing at the spring in the morning, at the balls in the night; and the Southern interest in all that belongs to racing, to horses, and to sport asserted itself today so handsomely both on the track and in the stands as to justify the remark of a Northern gentleman who observed General Hooker with his fiancée—a charming lady from Cincinnati, standing near a group of not less charming Marylanders, all equally excited by and absorbed in the animated preparations for the race, "this is the first palpable evidence I have had of peace and reconstruction."[45]

In the postwar years the Saratoga raceway seemed more attractive to southerners than the mineral springs. The 1865 racing season was described as brilliant, but there were early indications that the 1866 season would "eclipse even that." One important reason was that the "old sports" from the South and West "who have been kept away during the past four years 'by circumstances over which they had no control' promise to be on hand this year, with as much gold and brass as ever."[46] And the "old sports" did come. "The old Southern faces grow more and more frequent," a writer observed in July, 1866; "the South is proverbially billious, and Saratoga famously corrective."[47] Southerners not only attended the races but also entered their horses and served as officials.[48] Among the officials in 1869 were Governor Bowie of Maryland (judge), former Governor Hebert of Louisiana (official guest of judges), and Duncan Kenner (timer) and W. Conner (starter), both of New Orleans.[49]

There had been some complaints that Saratoga was not attract-

45. New York *World*, August 8, 1865.
46. New York *Times*, June 26, 1866.
47. *Ibid.*, July 16, 1866.
48. See, for example, the New York *Times*, July 14, August 1, 5, 1869, and *Harper's Weekly*, September 11, 1869.
49. New York *Times*, August 5, 1869.

ing as many southerners as expected.[50] If this was true, it may well have been the powerfully competing attractions elsewhere. They continued to frequent Niagara and Newport in considerable numbers.[51] The biggest new attractions were the New Jersey resorts and race tracks. Long Branch was scarcely known to antebellum southerners, but in the year of the war's end they went there to attend the races and to enjoy the social life characterized by "hops" and festive dinners. In August, 1865, there were Tennesseans, Georgians, Marylanders, Missourians, and Louisianians in attendance.[52] Seven years later they were still attending the Long Branch races in large numbers. It was remarked by one observer that one train carriage of men "probably had between them as much racing knowledge as America contains." They were from Maryland, Virginia, Kentucky, Louisiana, and Alabama.[53] Southerners also attended races at Paterson and, of course, continued to enjoy the social life of Cape May.[54]

A principal reason for traveling to the North remained, as in the past, to get away from the uninspired existence that was the lot of most southerners, to see the wonders of the North, and to enjoy the many diversions that could be found there. The very haste with which they resumed the practice suggested an absence of intense animosity on the part of those who traveled North or a feeling that the magnanimity of the victor would suffer them to express a hostile sentiment without fear of reprisal. The correspondent of the New York *Times* heard "some rabid rebel talk" at Long Branch in 1865. One southerner, it turned out, had been singing "We'll hang Andy Johnson on a sour-apple tree." The correspondent discounted the performance, however, saying

50. Charleston *Daily News*, July 30, 1866, and Savannah *Daily Republican*, August 2, 1866.
51. New York *World*, September 1, 1865, and New York *Times*, July 20, 1866.
52. New York *Times*, August 23, 1865. For a description of a Long Beach "hop" see *ibid.*, August 3, 1868.
53. *Ibid.*, June 30, 1872.
54. New York *World*, October 12, 1865; New York *Times*, June 2, 1867, June 16, 1873.

that he believed that the southerner did not mean it. "He had been hanging himself on the edge of several intoxicating beverages just previously."[55]

The feelings that northerners and southerners expressed to each other were amazingly warm. When the ball honoring General Ulysses S. Grant was held at the Congress Hotel in Saratoga in July, 1865, several southerners were in attendance, including one Mrs. Atoche of New Orleans whose attire was worth noting in the public press.[56] That same summer one southerner went north to see "what was the state of feeling there in regard to the South and her future." Upon returning, after a sojourn of two months, he wrote an open letter to the people of the North, saying in part: "Of your section I take great pleasure in saying that I was agreeably surprised and since my return I have been more than gratified to speak of it. Everywhere, and I may almost say among all classes of people, I found a universal feeling of conciliation."[57]

There were numerous touching incidents connected with some of these northern visits. Albert G. Mackey of Charleston, the "Grand High Priest of the General Grand Chapter of the Masons in the United States," arrived in New York in May, 1866. The New York Masons gave him a public reception to thank him for his kind treatment of Masonic soldiers in South Carolina prisons. During the war, when Mackey's funds were low he was compelled to sell a gold box that had earlier been presented to him in New Orleans. It later came into the hands of a Mason in Philadelphia, who, on the occasion of the reception, returned it to Mackey with one hundred dollars inside it. At about the same time, a southerner who had graduated from Harvard before the war, visited Boston "in a penniless condition, having lost everything by the rebellion." His Harvard classmates began a sub-

55. New York World, August 1, 1865.
56. New York Daily Tribune, September 1, 1865. See also Paul H. Buck, The Road to Reunion, 1865–1900 (Boston: Little, Brown and Company, 1937), 160–69.
57. Richmond Republic, May 25, 1866.

scription in his behalf, "and in a short time presented him with the handsome sum of $2,700 with which to commence the world anew."[58] A former Confederate soldier, on a visit to New York, mistook the editor of the Troy *Times* for General Robert E. Lee. The southerner was so overwhelmed that he said, "You cannot conceive, Sir, the warmth of my feeling toward you. . . . Were we not in the city of New York, and if I dared to do it, I would tear the hat from my head, and give three rousing cheers for old General Lee." Thereupon he wound his arms about the editor, kissed him twice on the right cheek, and "swept up Broadway with tears in his eyes." The stunned editor remarked to a friend, "Well, I declare this beats all. I have frequently been mistaken for Edwin M. Stanton, but never before for General Robert E. Lee."[59]

It may be assumed that most visits were relatively free of such memorable experiences. They were likely to be similar to that of Edward Jenkins Harden of Savannah, who spent three weeks in the North in 1868, accompanied by his oldest daughter and little son. After three days at sea, aboard the *San Salvador*, the Hardens were met at the New York pier by an old friend who had been a captain in the Confederate Army and who helped them get settled at the St. James Hotel. Harden had several letters of introduction to New Yorkers who were generous in their hospitality. They visited Central Park, Greenwood Cemetery, and the shops on Broadway. They went up the Hudson to Albany, then to Saratoga, Buffalo, and Niagara. Harden was as impressed with the Erie Canal, "burdened with riches," as he was with Niagara Falls—"No description of it will suffice." Commencement at Union College was another high point on the tour. It was the kindnesses of many friends that made the visit most enjoyable and memorable. Reconciliation was well underway, if the generosity of northerners was any measure.[60]

58. Augusta *Daily Chronicle and Sentinel*, June 5, 1866.
59. *Harper's Weekly*, June 5, 1869. Lee did not visit the North. He was said to have been "much bored by applications from proprietors of Northern watering places to spend the summer at their establishments free of charge." *Scott's Monthly Magazine*, II (October, 1866), 791.
60. Harden, *Notes of a Short Northern Tour*, 9–22.

Other northerners, some southerners believed, were more interested in "display and tinsel" than in anything else. That is why New Yorkers transformed the old brickfronts of their houses into handsome brownstone and then, if they could afford it, into marble palaces. A. T. Stewart, the merchant, purchased a fine brownstone that, in the view of one southern observer, was "fit even for the pampered scions of the effete aristocracy of the old world." But it was not fine enough for him. Consequently, he erected a palace of white marble, but his was neither as handsome nor as convenient in arrangement as the residence of William B. Johnson of Macon. This observer was entertained at luncheon in the palatial home of "one of the many of the lords of Wall Street." The "gorgeous table was decked in all the usual paraphernalia for a good dinner. But this was *lunch*, and we sat down at a little after one and rose at half-past five. . . . We *only* had *four* sorts of wine for lunch—for dinner there would have been more."[61] Such was the conspicuous consumption of New York's wealthy class; and such was the enjoyment of the guests from the South.

Southerners during the postwar years were quite willing to resume many important contacts with the North. They were even willing to increase some of them. But they were less inclined to place the education of young southerners in the hands of northern professors than they had been before the war. Despite the fact that some ardent sectionalists had railed against the northern education of southerners during the antebellum years, they admitted, apparently with some pride, that the northern influence had been minimal. "It is a powerful testimony to the strength of character and force of domestic affection at the South that they were utterly without influence in all their obnoxious and poisonous teachings," declared a Richmond editor. It was, nevertheless, a dangerous atmosphere to which young southerners should not be exposed, especially since northern professors had succeeded in contaminating the minds of young northerners

61. Augusta *Daily Chronicle and Sentinel*, August 24, 1866.

and raising a "crop of tares" that "became so deeply rooted there that ages will not eradicate them."[62]

The antebellum campaign to keep southerners out of northern colleges and universities was resumed and even intensified after the war. This time the principal feature of the campaign was the emphasis placed on the strength of southern colleges. James De Bow inaugurated a "Department of Education" in his *Review* in order to inform his readers of "what is being done by the large institutions of learning in the South." In succeeding issues the department gave pertinent information on the section's leading colleges and universities, including faculty rosters, expenses, and courses of study. In October, 1866, the University of Virginia was "in full tide of success again." Robert E. Lee had become president of Washington College, and the University of South Carolina had eight distinct schools. In the following month the *Review* called attention to the medical colleges in South Carolina, Georgia, Nashville, and the University of Tennessee. In the spring of 1867 there was great praise in a long notice on the University of Mississippi.[63]

An important factor in persuading southerners to patronize southern educational institutions was the introduction of new teaching materials. "The South should have its own books— books freed from bigotry, fanaticism, and sectionalism," declared the Richmond *Dispatch*.[64] That need was filled by Richardson and Company, incidentally a New York publishing house, which announced in 1866 the "Southern University Series of Textbooks for Schools and Colleges." The series enjoyed the imprimatur of the University of Virginia, several of whose professors were engaged in preparing the volumes. Among them were George Frederick Holmes (history and literature), Basil Gildersleeve (ancient languages), Schele De Vere (modern languages),

62. Richmond *Dispatch*, July 17, 1866.
63. *De Bow's Review*, New Series, II (October, 1866), 429–30, and (November, 1866), 535–37, and New Series, III (March, 1867), 318.
64. Richmond *Dispatch*, July 17, 1866.

and Charles S. Venable (mathematics). This was easily the most popular and most successful set of books for southern use that had ever been produced. By 1868 the series had been cordially endorsed "by the faculty of almost every Southern university and college," and had been generously praised by the southern press.[65]

The campaign worked better than its protagonists could have anticipated. Even the ardor for attending West Point had cooled a bit. No southerners entered the military academy in 1865. In the three succeeding years, only two, four, and seven entered respectively.[66] Of the class that entered in 1868, there were eight from the former slave states; and only two of these were still there when the class graduated four years later. There were even fewer in the class of 1871.[67] There remained the pride of accomplishment in military education, however. In the class that graduated in 1867 (some fifty-one southerners had been admitted in 1863!), each of the first six scholars was from the South. Indeed, nine of the first twelve places on the scale of general merit were taken by southerners, a source of great satisfaction to most southerners.[68] Not until 1874, when thirty-three cadets from the South were admitted out of a total of eighty-nine, did southern participation in military education approach the prewar proportions.[69]

Southerners seemed no more anxious to return to northern civilian colleges than they were to reenter "The Point." In 1914, one historian of Princeton asserted that "Princeton has never regained her Southern clientèle," while another stated in 1964

65. *Ibid.*, July 17, 1866; *De Bow's Review*, New Series, III (January, 1867), 93; *The Land We Love*, IV (March, 1868), 448.
66. *List of Cadets Admitted into the United States Military Academy, West Point New York, From Its Origins Till September 1, 1901* (Washington, D.C.: Government Printing Office, 1902), 112–15.
67. George Washington Cullum, *Biographical Register of the Officers and Graduates of the United States Military Academy* (Boston: Houghton-Mifflin, 1891).
68. Savannah *Daily Republican*, June 11, 1869. The item had been taken from the New York *Times*, June 5, 1867.
69. *List of Cadets Admitted into the United States Military Academy*, 112–15.

that "the students from the South never came back."[70] Bleak as the picture was, it was not quite as dark as these historians painted it. To be sure southerners were rather slow returning to Princeton; and in the fifteen years following the war, those from the former Confederate states never approached the sixty-eight who were there in 1860. The number climbed from nineteen in 1866 to a peak of thirty-nine in 1875 before falling back to twenty in 1878.[71] The picture was similar at Yale and Harvard, where there were twenty-nine and twenty students respectively in the colleges in 1860 and twenty-six and eleven in the 1866–1867 academic year.[72]

Southerners going north to school in the postwar years had to confront the unpleasant possibility of sitting "cheek by jowl" with some northern blacks or, worse still, some freedmen. Some Negroes had attended northern colleges before the war, and at least twenty-eight had graduated. But their opportunities for higher education had substantially increased during the postwar years. While most of them would attend the colleges that had been founded in the South by the Freedmen's Bureau and various religious and philanthropic groups, some blacks seized the opportunity to attend northern colleges. At Princeton, the "conservative and mildly pro-Southern character of college and town" operated to exclude blacks while encouraging southern whites to return. If they had any qualms about studying with blacks, they would not have been very happy at Harvard. In the late sixties several blacks were attending Harvard College as well as the schools of medicine, dentistry, and law. They were

70. Collins, *Princeton*, 162; George P. Schmidt, *Princeton and Rutgers: The Two Colonial Colleges of New Jersey*. (Princeton: D. Van Nostrand Company, 1964), 66.

71. Collins, *Princeton*, 408. In 1875 there were thirty-six students from Maryland, which had always been well represented in the southern group. There were twenty-four there in 1860, but they never really left during the war years.

72. John S. Ezell, "Southern Education for Southrons," *Journal of Southern History*, XVIII (August, 1951), 303–27; *Catalogue of the Officers and Students in Yale College . . . 1866–1867* (New Haven: E. Hayes, 1866); and *Catalogue of the Officers and Students of Harvard University for the Academical Year 1866–1867* (Cambridge: Sever and Francis, 1867).

also at Oberlin, Bucknell, Dartmouth, Wesleyan, the Newton Theological Institution, Yale, and other colleges and universities in the North.[73] Surely this could have been a factor in discouraging some white southerners from going north for an education.

Apparently, southerners were pleased with the results of their efforts to promote attendance at southern institutions. Enrollments at their principal colleges and universities were increasing steadily; and the notion that the South should develop a distinctive type of education was even clearer than before the war. The strengthening of southern colleges and universities was high on the agenda of postwar programs for southerners. South Carolina College became the University of South Carolina in 1865, with eight schools and seven new chairs. The Methodist church gave new support to Emory, and by 1868 the professors were receiving the highest salaries ever paid them. Trinity College was entering a new era, while the University of Georgia had a new school of engineering in 1866 and a reactivated law school in 1867. Both faculty and students in the 1865–1866 session of the University of Virginia have been described as "remarkable; and in 1867 the University had two new schools: The School of Applied Mathematics and the School of Chemical Technology and Agricultural Science."[74] These "happy" developments moved one observer to remark:

As yet comparatively few Southern students have so far forgotten the events of the last few years as to seek an education among those who are alien to them in blood, in habit, and in feeling. Such patronage as

73. See Rayford W. Logan, *The Negro in American Life and Thought: The Nadir, 1877–1901* (New York: The Dial Press, 1954), 329–31; William J. Simmons, *Men of Mark: Eminent, Progressive, and Rising* (Cleveland: Geo. M. Rewell and Co., 1887); and W. E. B. DuBois, *The College-Bred Negro* (Atlanta: Atlanta University Press, 1900).

74. Daniel Walker Hollis, *University of South Carolina* (2 vols.; Columbia: University of South Carolina Press, 1956), II, 16, 25, 32; Henry Morton Bullock, *A History of Emory University* (Nashville: Parthenon Press, 1936), 151, 153; Nora Campbell Chaffin, *Trinity College, 1839–1892: The Beginnings of Duke University* (Durham: Duke University Press, 1950), 250, 270; Robert Preston Brooks, *The University of Georgia* (Athens: University of Georgia Press, 1956), 47–48; Philip Alexander Bruce, *History of the University of Virginia* (New York: The Macmillan Company, 1921), III, 350, 353, 359.

the North received from the South comes mainly from Northern settlers who are Southerners in their post offices alone;[75] and even these, if they understood their true interests, would do well to look around them and see whether States, so rich in all material resources, are after all so poor in the appliances of higher education.[76]

Even as southerners turned increasingly to their own colleges and universities, their antipathy toward northern institutions persisted, as if to reinforce their faith in their own. Indeed, there was a tendency in some quarters to reject the idea that a northern education was of any value, even to those major southern figures of the prewar years who had studied in such places as Harvard, Yale, and Princeton. As one southerner put it:

> It is, to say the least, unwise in Northern colleges to brag so loudly of their achievements, in view of the fact that so many Southerners are alumni of Yale, of Harvard, and of Princeton, and know so well the constitution of those very schools which claim such vast superiority. How many of these Southern alumni would gladly buy back those years of misdirected effort, of sporadic study; how few of them send their own pupils to *Alma Mater*. For "Alma Mater" is no name to conjure withal. She can no longer win to her bosom the sons whom she cursed a few years ago with all the fervor of Mucklerath and all the venom of Sycorax. The hot breath of those curses burned up such slender ties as bound the Southerner to the Northern school and the Southern alumnus has as much love toward his Northern Alma Mater as toward a landlady who had feasted him with pumpkin-pies, charged him with pineapples, given him a photograph with her bill and then drenched him with soapsuds.[77]

If the resumption of educational contacts was slow and desultory, the same could not be said of the resumption of business contacts. From the war experience a great many southerners had learned one lesson well. It was that a broadly based economy was more likely to lead to stability and even sectional indepen-

75. This is hardly an accurate statement. The Lindsleys at Yale in 1867 were sons of a Nashville family that emigrated from New Jersey in 1824. Henry Wyre Scudder of Georgia and Richmond Pearson of North Carolina who were in the Princeton classes of 1871 and 1872 respectively were from old southern families.

76. "Our Southern Colleges," *The New Eclectic Magazine*, V (July–December, 1879), 217.

77. *Ibid.*, 217.

dence than one based on a few staple crops. They had also learned that their disadvantages during the antebellum years were nothing compared with the four war-years of want, privation, and economic isolation. They would, therefore, resume their business contacts and improve their general economic relations with the North at the earliest possible moment. There remained, of course, the danger of continued subordination and dependence on the North, especially in view of the enormous growth of the North's economic power during the war. That was a risk that the South would have to take, however, if it was to recover its own strength and build the kind of economic base that existing conditions demanded.

Northern businessmen were no less anxious to resume trade with the South than their erstwhile customers in the former Confederacy. And they were as aggressive in their own area as Sherman's troops had been on the battlefield. Indeed, even before the cessation of hostilities northern merchants were seeking to reestablish their contacts as rapidly as southern cities fell into Union hands. By 1865 trade between New York and New Orleans was "brisk and flourishing," and there was some activity between the great northern cities and other southern coastal cities such as Norfolk, Newbern, Savannah, and Richmond. There was even evidence of some new life in "ruined, half obliviated Charleston."[78] Once the war was over, business relations between the two sections developed rapidly. One had only to read the New York newspapers to find notices "of the sailing of all manner of vessels—mail and other steamers, barks, brigs, and schooners—laden with passengers and every kind of valuable freight, and bound from New York for some Southern port and a market. Never in the balmiest days of our traffic with the Southern States, were there so many steamships plying on the various lines of trade and travel as there are now."

Movement was by no means merely in one direction; but the

78. New York *World*, June 13, 1865.

northern businessmen were so anxious to promote the flow of goods and people northward that they could hardly wait. "Trade with the Southern States is beginning to open up," observed a New York correspondent in July, 1865, "though it has not reached any great magnitude; and the immense amount of cotton we have been led to expect has thus far not appeared."[79] By September, things looked better as shipments began to move northward. On the last day of August the *Zodiac* sailed from Savannah with seventy-four passengers, "1,584 bales of upland cotton, 75 bales of sea island and 49 bales of domestics."[80] A few days later a New York reporter commented that the city was "full of buyers principally from the South and West, buying up every piece of goods in the market. . . . The houses who formerly had large business relations with the Southern buyers before the war, and who have withstood the shock of disruption, report that all their old customers are coming back to them, willing to pay up old scores to the extent of their means, as the case may be, forty, fifty, or sixty cents on the dollar in order to renew old time business relations, and procure goods to replenish and restock their depleted warehouses."[81]

From the beginning of the new and special economic relationship between the North and South, there was a marked absence of the animosity that often characterized the political relationships. Each side seemed willing to adopt whatever attitudes and approaches were necessary to facilitate the flow of people, goods, and capital. If new business groups were called for, they were organized. If capital was necessary, southerners had only to make known their needs, and they were cheerfully met. Large numbers of southerners went north not to visit but to live and to

79. Little Rock *Arkansas Gazette*, July 15, 1865.
80. Savannah *Daily Republican*, September 1, 1865. A week later the *Varuna* left Savannah for New York with a cargo that included 992 bales of upland cotton, 41 bales of sea-island cotton, 23 bales of wool, 147 bags of dried fruit, 33 bales of domestics, 273 bags of ground nuts, and 4 packages of merchandise. Savannah *Daily Republican*, September 8, 1865.
81. New York *World*, September 5, 1865.

join business houses that hoped that the presence of a southerner in the firm would attract southern business. De Bow said in 1867 that not less than twenty thousand southerners had moved to New York since the war.[82] The Southern Land, Emigration, and Produce Company was organized late in 1865 "for the purpose of introducing capital, mechanical skill, emigration, and labor-saving machinery into the Southern States." The secretary was W. H. Quincy, "late of South Carolina," and it boasted among its references several former Confederate Army officers and a South Carolina railroad president.[83] "Confederate officers and soldiers are here in great numbers," one correspondent reported from New York. "In all the branches of trade and commerce, and in nearly all the pursuits of life here you will find a large number of greybacks. . . . They are active, cheerful, persevering and determined to recuperate their fortunes here in the land of the conquerer."[84]

There was no guarantee that a former southerner doing business in New York would attract southern business to himself or to the firm with which he was connected. In August, 1866, it was reported that there were more southern merchants in New York than at any time since the war and the number was increasing daily. "They all seem to have a full supply of money, and few are willing to make large purchases except for cash." Surely, well-placed southern businessmen could reasonably expect to enjoy their patronage. "Strange to say," remarked a reporter, "that instead of the Southern merchants giving their entire patronage to their fellow Southrons and sufferers, many of them give their trade entirely to the merchants whose money and influence was given freely to enslave them." The southern businessmen complained, but apparently to no avail. The reporter expressed the wish that "in the future the Southern man who comes here for

82. *De Bow's Review*, New Series, II (February, 1867), 215. See also the Atlanta *Daily Constitution*, June 18, 1868.
83. *De Bow's Review*, New Series, I (February, 1866), n.p.
84. Augusta *Daily Chronicle and Sentinel*, August 25, 1866.

goods will, all other things being equal, give his patronage to those who are of his blood, and who shared the trials and misfortunes of the lost cause."[85]

There were other places than the cities of the Northeast where southern businessmen could visit and establish important connections. Cincinnati was one of them. In the summer of 1866 James De Bow was a member of a delegation of Tennessee businessmen who visited Cincinnati in the interest of constructing a railroad between Nashville and Cincinnati. In addition to calling on bankers, other prospective investors, and the president of the Board of Trade, they visited the vast workshops of Lane and Bodley which made much machinery for the southern market. De Bow was quite pleased "to perceive a very liberal spirit existing in Cincinnati in favor of the South and a very general and anxious desire to enlarge its Southern trade." The group also visited, by invitation, the extensive wine cellars "of the late Mr. Longworth, where we were entertained with genuine hospitality by his grandson . . . who brought out every variety of his exquisite wines."[86]

A few years later the editor of the Atlanta *Constitution*, on a tour through the North, visited Cincinnati and nowhere was he so "agreeably disappointed as in Cincinnati." He was immensely pleased with the people and their city. The businessmen were the most "elegant" he saw anywhere. He never perceived "the slightest manifestation of sectional prejudice on the part of any of them." He was also surprised by the size and appearance of the city and the many evidences of "solid wealth" there. Some of his happiest moments were spent at the Merchants' Hotel. "This hotel is just what Southern gentlemen want, and just where it should be for those who visit on business."[87]

Despite the friendly hand that northerners extended to the

85. *Ibid.*
86. *De Bow's Review*, New Series, II (July, 1866), 106. When in Cincinnati later that year, De Bow again visited the Longworth wine cellars. *Ibid.*, II (February, 1867), 213.
87. Atlanta *Constitution*, April 19, 1870.

southern visitors, the guests could sometimes be critical of what they saw or experienced in the North. De Bow thought that Philadelphia never gave the appearance of making significant progress, although it continued to grow in population. "Were it of more cosmopolitan character, and was there less of radicalism existing, Philadelphia would be a most inviting and captivating place," he concluded.[88] In New York, one southern visitor found much that he could not approve "and much which every honest man, anxious to preserve the purity of life and the sacredness of the domestic relations, must unequivocally condemn and denounce." He had been informed that such activities and practices were the "necessary and unavoidable consequences of a high state of civilization." If this was true, then civilization was a "humbug, and is alike destructive of the physical and moral attributes of humanity and religion."[89]

Nor was the prosperous and progressive North without its destitute elements, its swindlers, and pickpockets. It seemed to one observer that wherever he went in the North, the rich seemed richer than ever while the poor seemed poorer than ever. "I have seen more careworn, hungry-looking, and shabbily dressed people in New York during my present visit than ever before."[90] There were, moreover, the "swindling benefit associations and lottery concerns" that were doing an immense business. Their patronage did not come from the wide-awake New Yorkers, but from "the innocent country people." The reporter regretted that many of the victims were from his own "Southern clime," who were constantly giving their money to "these thieving rascals" in the belief that they would receive dividends or prizes that were never forthcoming.[91] Even the pickpockets were thriving. One merchant, visiting New York from Chester, South Carolina, "went through the relieving process" and

88. *De Bow's Review*, II (February, 1867), 216.
89. Augusta *Daily Chronicle and Sentinel*, August 24, 1866.
90. *Ibid.*, September 4, 1866.
91. Savannah *Daily Republican*, July 3, 1866.

emerged from it "minus one hundred and fifty dollars in gold."[92] More fortunate was a young southern physician whose watch chain was lifted by a pickpocket. He discovered it immediately and, after a scuffle, recovered it on the spot.[93]

It is remarkable that southerners resumed their northern travels as quickly as they did after the Civil War. If the numbers were smaller and the categories of travelers somewhat fewer than before the war, these southern visitors indicated a willingness to emulate the spirit of Appomattox and take up where they left off in 1861. This time they were determined not to lose more than they gained. The most innocuous form of travel was sightseeing; and southerners entered upon this as soon as hostilities ceased. In doing this they gave up very little in return for their release from the inhibitions and restrictions of the war years.

Their attitude toward educating their youth in northern institutions was something else. The arguments of those who had railed against a northern education for southern youth during the antebellum years were as strident—and as fallacious—during the postwar years as they had been earlier. The abolitionists in northern academia had now been replaced by the Radicals; and the influence of the latter on the minds of young southerners was as mythical as had been the influence of the abolitionists. But the firm conviction of southerners to the contrary was enough to keep southern enrollments in northern institutions considerably below the antebellum figures.

Neither government activity in the South nor Radical preachments in the North could prevent southern businessmen from reestablishing contacts with their northern colleagues, however. In addition to the thousands of southerners who went to live in the North, there were many more who went there to conduct a variety of business transactions. Although many felt that they had been the victims of a northern colonial policy before the war,

92. Charleston *Daily News*, June 21, 1866.
93. *Ibid.*, July 19, 1866.

they refused to let bitter memories interfere with their general economic progress or with their determination to make a recovery from the war. If merchants looking for the best bargains, delegations of businessmen seeking to attract capital, and travelers accepting the blandishments of northern moguls were required, there were those who were quite ready to seize the opportunity.

No visits to the North, however frequent, involved the surrender of any of the South's self-esteem or its confidence in its own future. James D. B. De Bow, the South's promoter *par excellence* and inveterate northern traveler, died on February 27, 1867.[94] The new crusaders—the Henry W. Gradys and the Booker T. Washingtons—would not appear on the scene for another decade or so. Meanwhile, there were many who were willing to combine a cautious optimism regarding their northern contacts with a fierce loyalty to the principles for which they stood. They would get whatever they could from their northern contacts, but they had no illusions about the advantages *and* disadvantages of going north. The warning that one of Henry W. Grady's predecessors on the Atlanta *Constitution* gave to southerners who were going north to live was also worth considering by those who went north to visit. Some were making their mark in the northern business world. Others were becoming ornaments of their professions there, as they had been in the South. Then, there were the beautiful and accomplished ladies who had been "the magicians of society in Charleston, Augusta, and Mobile." All had carried their gallantry and politeness with them. "Thank God! we beat them in politeness if they beat us in Gold." Moving north symbolized, in a sense, the complete triumph of the North. And that is what all southerners, including travelers, should guard against. The lesson was clear, and the editor of the *Constitution* emphasized it to his readers:

94. A few weeks before he died, De Bow wrote that he had visited New York City some twenty times. *De Bow's Review*, New Series, II (February, 1867), 213.

But what have the Southerners gained by going North? . . . They ran away from negro supremacy and what have they got in exchange? The supremacy of a cold, heartless dissipated, vulgar social system, and the terrors of a poverty such as the South never knew, which takes more women and children by the brain and heart, without warning or pit, and presses and crushes them until they are glad to die. . . . No [instead of our men going North] let them stand by their imperiled homesteads; or if they are burnt, let them stand by the ruins, until the angel of God's mercy shall have come to us again.[95]

95. Atlanta *Daily Constitution*, June 18, 1868.

A Note
on
the Sources

—————————————— ❧ ——————————————

In view of the fact that I have provided extensive documentation in the footnotes, it seems unnecessary to offer here more than a general discussion of the nature of the sources, with examples, and some of the problems related to their use. It was not possible, of course, to read all of the materials related to southern travelers in the North. Some of them undoubtedly remain in private hands, and their existence can only be presumed. Much that is available in libraries and other depositories is repetitive; and beyond a certain point, its utility becomes minimal. There is a limit to the ways that one can say that New York is busy and noisy or that the people of Philadelphia are cultivated and cold or that the Boston abolitionists are conniving and hypocritical. I have attempted, nevertheless, to canvass every possible aspect of southern experience in the North; and this undertaking has involved the examination of a wide variety of sources.

Among the most thoughtful and valuable accounts of the southern experience in the North were those that were published. Some appeared in such newspapers as the Richmond *Enquirer*, the Charleston *Mercury*, the Raleigh *Register*, and the New Orleans *Picayune*. Some northern newspapers—including the New York *Times*, the New York *Post*, the New Haven *Palladium*, the Boston *Advertiser*, and the Boston *Courier*— contained accounts of southern visitors, especially well-known persons. Much more important than the newspapers were the magazines. Travelers frequently sent lengthy accounts of their experiences to the *Southern Literary Messenger* (1834–1860), and these many articles comprise one of the most important sources for this study. There were some travel accounts in *De Bow's Review* (1846–1867), including those of its peripatetic editor; but some of the sharpest criticisms of southern travel, frequently by the editor, also appeared in the magazine. The *Southern Quarterly Review* (1842–1857) opened its columns to southern travelers and seemed to favor discussions of northern travels that reflected unfavorably on the North. Other southern magazines that were of value, but only for portions of the period, were *Russell's Magazine* (1857–1860) and the *Southern Review* (1845–1860). Of northern magazines that took notice of southern travelers, *Hunt's Merchants' Magazine* (1845–1860) was the most important.

A few southerners published book-length accounts of their experiences in the North, which could well serve as guide books for the inexperienced traveler. Perhaps the outstanding work was J. C. Myers, *Sketches on a Tour Through the Northern and Eastern States, the Canadas and Nova Scotia* (Harrisonburg, Va.: J. H. Wartmann and Brothers, 1849). Somewhat more specialized was a smaller work that was widely reviewed and reprinted several times: Daniel Drake, *The Northern Lakes: A Summer Residence for Invalids of the South* (Louisville, Ky.: J. Maxwell, Jr., 1842). A quite perceptive early travel account is by the wealthy Baltimorean, Robert Gilmor, *Memorandums Made in a Tour to the Eastern States in the Year 1797* (Boston: Trustees of the Boston Public Library, 1892). A travel account filled with acerbic comments about the North is [William M. Bobo], *Glimpses of New York City, by a South Carolinian (Who Had Nothing Else to Do)* (Charleston: J. J. McCarter, 1852). Easily the most unique of the published accounts is [Joseph W. Wilson], *Sketches of the Higher Classes of Colored Society in Philadelphia, By a Southerner* (Philadelphia: Merrihew and

Thompson, 1841). An excellent early postwar account is Edward Jenkins Harden, *Notes of a Short Northern Tour* (Savannah: Morning News Steam-Power Press, 1869).

There were numerous guide books during the period; and some were written expressly for southern travelers. The best one was Gideon M. Davison, *The Fashionable Tour: A Guide to Travelers Visiting the Middle and Northern States and the Provinces of Canada* (Saratoga Springs: G. M. Davison, 1830), which was revised and reissued periodically. Others were Theodore Dwight, Jr., *The Northern Traveller, Containing the Routes to the Springs, Niagara, Quebec, and the Coal Mines* (New York: J. P. Haven [1841]) and an anonymous work, *The Eastern Tourist: Being a Guide Through the States of Connecticut, Rhode Island, Massachusetts, Vermont, New Hampshire, and Maine* (New York: John Disturnell, 1848). One of the several works by the New Yorker, James Kirke Paulding, *A New Mirror for Travellers, and Guide to the Springs* (New York: G. and C. Carvill, 1828), is a different kind of travel book that dares to lampoon some of the very travelers, including southerners, for whom it was intended.

The problem raised by the Paulding work—of trying to separate fact from fiction—is underscored when one encounters the work of another northerner on southern travelers. Hiram Fuller, owner of the New York *Daily Mirror*, was a close observer of southern visitors in the North. While the pseudonym he assumed of a young southern girl suggests his enjoyment at the expense of his subjects, one should not overlook his *Belle Brittan On a Tour, At Newport and Here and There* (New York: Derby and Jackson, 1858). Even accounts that are clearly fictional are valuable, as long as they are used critically. Perhaps the best work of fiction is the novel by William Alexander Caruthers, *A Kentuckian in New York* (2 vols.; New York: Harper and Brothers, 1834). Another, which deals with a Virginia family in the North is Sarah S. Cohoone, *Visit to Grand-Papa; Or, A Week at Newport* (New York: Taylor and Dodd, 1840).

The most important sources for this study are the manuscript diaries, journals, and letters written by southerners who visited the North. The materials in the Southern Historical Collection of the University of North Carolina and the Manuscripts Collection of Duke University are unusually rich, but there are important collections elsewhere, such as Tulane University, Louisiana State University in Baton Rouge, the South Carolina Archives, and the Moorland-Spingarn Research Center of Howard University.

The following listings are merely examples of the types of materials that were used. The Southern Historical Collection of the University of North Carolina: Joseph Brevard's Diary of a tour from Camden, South Carolina, to New York and Philadelphia in 1791, in the Alexander and Joseph Brevard Papers; the letters of Mrs. Ann Wagner to her children, written while on a journey to Philadelphia, New York, Providence, and Boston, in the Cheves-Wagner Papers; James H. Hammond's letters from New York, telling of making purchases for his house in Columbia, South Carolina, in the James H. Hammond Papers; and James Harrison's letters to his family in Mississippi, describing in great detail his extensive northern tour in 1853, in the James T. Harrison Papers. The Manuscripts Collection of Duke University: Mary Fraser's account books and memoranda kept while on a tour from Charleston to Philadelphia, in the Mary (De Soussure) Fraser Papers; the correspondence of the Ball brothers of South Carolina, some of whom were in northern schools and colleges, in the John Ball, Sr., and John Ball, Jr., Papers; and the letters of the Clement Clays during their numerous visits to the North, in the Clement Comer Clay Papers. There are engaging letters of Andrew Durnford, a slave who was virtually free, in the John McDonogh Papers at the Tulane University Library; and there is the autobiography of James Thomas, free Negro, at the Moorland-Spingarn Research Center at Howard University.

Some of the best accounts of experiences in the North have

been made more available thanks to scholars who have edited and published them. Among them are R. D. W. Connor (ed.), *Autobiography of Asa Briggs, Including a Journal of a Trip from North Carolina to New York in 1832* (Raleigh: Edwards and Broughton, 1915); Arney Robinson Childs (ed.), *The Private Journal of Henry William Ravenel, 1859–1887* (Columbia: University of South Carolina Press, 1947); and J. Harold Easterby, *The South Carolina Rice Plantation As Revealed in the Papers of Robert F. W. Allston* (Chicago: University of Chicago Press, 1945). Nor have the scholars neglected the records that young southerners made of their own travels. See, for example, Barnes F. Lathrop (ed.), "A Southern Girl at Saratoga Springs, 1834," *North Carolina Historical Review*, XV (April, 1938), 159–61; Fitzgerald Flourney, "Hugh Blair Grigsby at Yale," *Virginia Magazine of History and Biography*, XXII (April, 1954), 166–80; and Arthur H. Cole (ed.), *Charleston Goes to Harvard: The Diary of a Harvard Student of 1831* (Cambridge: Harvard University Press, 1940). Among other valuable contemporary writings that have been edited and published are Ada Sterling (ed.), *A Belle of the Fifties: Memoirs of Mrs. Clay of Alabama* (New York: Doubleday, Page and Company, 1905); Helen T. Catterall (ed.), *Judicial Cases Concerning American Slavery and the Negro* (5 vols.; Washington, D.C.: Carnegie Institute, 1926–1937); William R. Hogan and Edwin A. Davis (eds.), *William Johnson's Natchez: The Ante-Bellum Diary of a Free Negro* (Baton Route: Louisiana State University Press, 1951); William Kauffman Scarborough (ed.), *The Diary of Edmund Ruffin* (3 vols. projected; Baton Rouge: Louisiana State University Press, 1972); and Mary C. Simms Oliphant and T. C. Duncan Eaves (eds.), *The Letters of William Gilmore Simms* (5 vols.; Columbia: University of South Carolina Press, 1954).

There are texts or partial texts of many of the speeches that southerners made in the North. Unfortunately, George Fitzhugh did not prepare a manuscript for his New Haven appearance.

The text for William Gilmore Simms's principal address in New York is reprinted in Mary Simms's edition of his *Letters*. Among the texts of other speakers are Elwood Fisher, *Lecture on the North and the South, Delivered before the Young Men's Mercantile Library Association of Cincinnati, Ohio, January 16, 1849* (Charleston: A. J. Burke, 1849); Fred A. Ross, *Slavery Ordained of God* (Philadelphia: Lippincott, 1857); and Robert A. Toombs, *Lecture Delivered in the Tremont Temple, Boston, Massachusetts, on January 24, 1856* (Washington, D.C.: John T. and Lem Towers, 1858). The principal speeches that Henry W. Hilliard delivered in the North are in his *Politics and Pen Pictures at Home and Abroad* (New York: Putnam's, 1892). The speeches of William G. Brownlow are in *Ought American Slavery to be Perpetuated? A Debate between Rev. W. G. Brownlow and Rev. A. Pryne, Held at Philadelphia, September, 1858* (Philadelphia: J. B. Lippincott, 1858). Partial texts of speeches delivered by William L. Yancey on his celebrated tour of the North in 1860 are in John W. DuBose, *The Life and Times of William Lowndes Yancey* (2 vols.; Birmingham: Roberts and Son, 1892).

Three contemporary commentaries are of immense value in understanding the economic and political consequences of extensive southern travel in the North. William Gregg, *Essays on Domestic Industry* (Charleston: Burgess and James, 1845) is based on travel throughout New England and is critical of the South's unnecessary dependence on the North. Hinton Rowan Helper, *The Impending Crisis of the South: How to Meet It* (New York: A. B. Burdick, 1859) is intemperate in its strictures on southern travel and all other contacts with the North that kept the South from developing its own economic and cultural independence. Thomas Prentice Kettell, *Southern Wealth and Northern Profits, As Exhibited in Statistical Facts and Official Figures* (New York: George W. and John A. Wood, 1860) provides some of the most reliable figures on expenditures of southerners visiting the North.

The secondary materials dealing with various aspects of southern life and the North-South relationship are abundant, but they do not require listing here. There are several types of material that deserve mention for their clear relevance to this study. Virtually all of Clement Eaton's works are important in appreciating the southern connection with the North, especially *The Growth of Southern Civilization, 1790–1860* (New York: Harper and Brothers, 1961), and *The Mind of the Old South* (Baton Rouge: Louisiana State University Press, 1964). Robert G. Albion's two major works, *Square Riggers on Schedule: The New York Sailing Packets to England, France, and the Cotton Ports* (Princeton, N.J.: Princeton University Press, 1938), and *The Rise of the New York Port, 1815–1860* (New York: Charles Scribner's Sons, 1939), are most important for understanding the impact of southern travel on the development of transportation and on mercantile business in the North. Also very important along similar lines are Philip S. Foner, *Business and Slavery: The New York Merchants and the Irrepressible Conflict* (Chapel Hill: University of North Carolina Press, 1941), and Harold Woodman, *King Cotton and His Retainers: Financing and Marketing the Cotton Crop of the South, 1800–1925* (Lexington: University of Kentucky Press, 1968).

Of the many works dealing with social, cultural, and recreational life in the South, two of them suggested additional areas of inquiry for this work. They are D. Clayton James, *Antebellum Natchez* (Baton Rouge: Louisiana State University Press, 1968), and Lawrence F. Brewster, *Summer Migrations and Resorts of South Carolina Low-Country Planters* (Durham: Duke University Press, 1947). In a similar fashion two important articles were suggestive: Paul W. Gates, "Southern Investments in Northern Lands Before the Civil War," *Journal of Southern History*, V (May, 1939), and John S. Ezell, "A Southern Education for Southrons," *Journal of Southern History*, XVII (August, 1951). Three works that indicate the problems of Negroes in the North, especially in connection with their contacts with southerners, are Leon Litwack, *North of Slavery: The Negro in the Free States, 1790–1860* (Chicago: University of Chicago Press, 1961), Stanley W. Campbell, *The Slave Catchers: Enforcement of the Fugitive Slave Law, 1850–1860* (Chapel Hill: University of North Carolina Press, 1968), and Thomas D. Morris, *Free Men All: The Personal Liberty Laws of the North, 1780–1861* (Baltimore: Johns Hopkins Press, 1974). Paul H. Buck was the first major historian to study the resumption of North-South contacts after the Civil War in *The Road to Reunion, 1865–1900* (Boston: Little, Brown and Company, 1937).

Index